Cobbler in Congress

Cobbler in Congress

The Life of
Henry Wilson, 1812-1875

Richard H. Abbott

The University Press of Kentucky

E
415.9
. W6A64
/972

ISBN: 0-8131-1249-4

Library of Congress Catalog Card Number: 70-147856

Copyright © 1972 by The University Press of Kentucky

A statewide cooperative publishing agency serving Berea College, Centre
College of Kentucky, Eastern Kentucky University, Kentucky State College,
Morehead State University, Murray State University, University of Kentucky,
University of Louisville, and Western Kentucky University.

Editorial and Sales Offices: Lexington, Kentucky 40506

To my mother,
Anne M. Abbott

Contents

	Preface	xi
1	*Birth of a Political Career*	1
2	*Wilson and the Whig Party*	19
3	*Coalition Politics*	35
4	*From Defeat to Victory*	46
5	*Wilson Finds His Party*	64
6	*Hammering out Republican Policy*	88
7	*From Ballots to Bullets*	104
8	*Raising an Army*	121
9	*The Politics of Abolition*	142
10	*The Spirit of Slavery Still Lives*	158
11	*Reunion Politics*	180
12	*Reconciliation and Civil Rights*	196
13	*The New Departure*	214
14	*A Career Draws to a Close*	226
15	*Wilson's Last Years*	239
16	*Wilson in Retrospect*	260
	Bibliography	267
	Index	281

Illustrations

To be found between pages 124 & 125:

Senator Henry Wilson (ca. 1856)

Colonel Wilson (1861)

Wilson as Vice President

Harriet H. Wilson

Preface

Some years ago, while a graduate student in William B. Hesseltine's seminar at the University of Wisconsin, I became interested in the Radical Republicans of the Civil War and Reconstruction era. That other students of American history shared the same interest is revealed by the number of biographies and group treatments of the Radicals that have appeared in the last decade. Most of these books, written during the peak of the modern civil rights movement, evince a decided sympathy for the Radical cause, which included emancipation and enfranchisement for Southern blacks. They emphasize the Radicals' humanitarianism and dedication to racial equality and thus tend to qualify, if not reverse, the more traditional interpretations that stress their personal ambition, concern for the economic and political needs of the North, and vindictiveness toward the former Confederates. Some of the newer studies, however, have criticized the Radicals for their racial bias and their political and economic conservatism which prevented their seeking a real social revolution in the South and in the nation.

Since I have written about only one of the Radicals, I have not entered the debate over the general strengths and weaknesses of the Radical cause. As for Wilson, I believe he reflects to an uncommon degree the combination of political ambition and practical idealism that typified the Radical movement. Some readers may conclude that his ambition prevailed over his idealism. The men who knew Wilson best, his friends and political associates, were frequently critical of his political opportunism; yet their general assessment of his role in the events of his day was a favorable one. In that judgment I would concur. His moral commitments kept him from becoming a cynical manipulator of the political process for selfish or partisan ends.

My search for an understanding of Henry Wilson was complicated by the lack of any sizable collection of Wilson papers. Librarians and manuscript curators and their staffs from the following institutions were of particular assistance in locating Wilson materials: the Library of Congress, the National Archives, the Houghton Library of Harvard University, the Massachusetts Historical Society, the State Historical Society of Wisconsin, the Morse Institute of Natick, Massachusetts, the Rutherford B. Hayes Library of Fremont, Ohio, the Boston Public Library, and the Historical Society of Pennsylvania. I would also like to thank the Adams Manuscript Trust for permission to quote from the papers of Charles Francis Adams; John T. Hubbell, editor of *Civil War History,* for permission to use material in chapter eight previously published in that journal; Frank O. Gatell, for sharing with me information gained from the John G. Palfrey papers; and Gaynor O'Gorman, of the United Shoe Machinery Corporation of Boston, and Harold Schwartz for helping me locate Wilson materials.

A number of individuals rendered me a great service by reading all or parts of this manuscript: Charles Beveridge, Otto Olsen, Heinz K. Meier, Avery Craven, Richard N. Current, Edward M. Coffman, and Richard and Nancy Goff. I owe a great debt to Ernest Isaacs, who first suggested that I undertake a biography of Wilson, who shared with me his knowledge of the Radicals, and who supplied me with encouragement at crucial moments.

No list of acknowledgments would be complete without reference to my wife Nancy, whose assistance and support contributed in myriad ways to the creation of this book. Finally, I wish to pay my respects to the memory of William B. Hesseltine; although he died several years before I had finished this book, he guided and criticized my earliest explorations of Wilson's career. Only those students who worked with him can truly appreciate the contributions he made to this study. To him I owe the greatest debt.

1

Birth of a Political Career

On February 16, 1812, in a flimsy, snow-covered cottage in southern New Hampshire, Abigail Colbath gave birth to a son. Her poverty-stricken husband, Winthrop, named his first-born after a rich bachelor neighbor, Jeremiah Jones, thereby hoping to gain an inheritance if Jones died without heirs.[1] Jeremiah Jones Colbath would later change his name to Henry Wilson and achieve prominence as a successful politician. Serving as state legislator, then as United States senator, and finally as vice-president of the United States, he would hold public office for almost three decades. During that time he would help guide his nation through four years of civil war and aid in emancipating and enfranchising the Southern slaves.

The Colbaths, if they cared to do so, could trace an undistinguished lineage back to Ireland and Scotland. Scottish forebears, who earlier had migrated to northern Ireland, moved during the 1720s across the ocean to New Hampshire. In 1730 George Colbath bought land just outside Portsmouth, and there he and his wife Mary raised their eight children. The eldest, James, born in 1715, attained some success as a merchant. His progeny, also numbering eight, included a son, Winthrop, born in 1751. At the age of thirty-two Winthrop Colbath married a local girl, followed many of his relatives up the Cocheco River, and settled near Farmington, New Hampshire. There, on April 7, 1787, Henry Wilson's father, Winthrop, Jr., was born.[2]

Winthrop, Jr., grew quickly into a tall, agile, handsome young man; neighbors warmed easily to his likable manner. Unfortunately,

Winthrop was lazy and overly fond of hard cider, and his indolence and intemperance doomed him to remain one of the poorest of the poor men in a poor county. Yet with his ready wit and easy conversation, he captivated Abigail Witham, a neighbor girl with black eyes and thrifty ways. Though her suitor was careless in dress and habits, Abigail could not resist his advances, and on October 14, 1811, she married the indolent charmer.[3]

Just prior to his marriage, Winthrop built his bride a cottage on the banks of the Cocheco River. He brought the lumber from a sawmill down on the water, where he worked as a day laborer when he worked at all. Colbath had presumably done his best, but the faults in the new home were barely offset by the pleasant prospect it commanded of the river and surrounding country. The cottage had two rooms and a loft; the roof was covered with rough-hewn shingles. Light streamed into the building through four windows, two of which on the south side were uncovered. Winthrop Colbath had had little time to prepare the house; quite possibly he found little time to prepare for the marriage either. Four months after he married Abigail, his son was born.[4]

[1] Natick *Bulletin,* Feb. 26, 1892.

[2] Elias Nason, "Biographical Sketch of Henry Wilson," *New England Historical and Genealogical Register,* XXXII (1878), 261; Adelaide C. Waldron, "Reminiscences of Henry Wilson," in Natick *Bulletin,* Feb. 26, 1892; letter signed "W" in Boston *Herald,* quoted in Natick *Bulletin,* Feb. 14, 1902. I also gained genealogical information from clippings in a scrapbook owned by Wilson's grandnephew, Mr. Ernest Colbath, of Natick, Mass. Occasionally, during and after Wilson's life, people maintained he was descended from English gypsies. F. B. Sanborn, in his *Life of Henry David Thoreau* (Boston, 1917), 340, claims Wilson was related to the Leathers family of New Hampshire—and that the Leathers were "gypsies." The Rev. Dr. A. H. Quint, in *Edward Leathers and his Descendants* (reprinted from Dover, N. H., *Enquirer*), denies the allegation that the Leathers were in any way related to gypsies. See another denial of the gypsy rumor published in the New York *Times,* Dec. 15, 1875, by a member of the Colbath family.

[3] "Rochester Church Records," in *The New Hampshire Genealogical Record,* VI (1908), 146. Mrs. Waldron, a citizen of Farmington, compared Winthrop Colbath to Sam Lawson, one of the characters in Harriet Beecher Stowe's *Old Town Folks.* Lawson was the village do-nothing who nevertheless won the hearts of the inhabitants. Natick *Bulletin,* Feb. 26, 1892. See also J. B. Mann, *Life of Henry Wilson* (Boston, 1872), 1-2.

[4] Natick *Bulletin,* Feb. 26, 1892.

Local conditions were not auspicious for the future advancement of Jeremiah Jones Colbath. In 1810 the township of Farmington had only 1,272 people. The village itself, two years later, had only a dozen houses. The nearby Cocheco River, which cut a deep valley through the coarse glacial drift, only emphasized the rough, broken aspect of the countryside. Pine forests, which marched up to the very door of the Colbath cottage, covered a sandy, slaty soil that yielded to cultivation only after heavy labor had subdued it. Yale President Timothy Dwight, traveling through the area a year after Jeremiah's birth, found the land lean and unpromising.[5]

New England's hill country suffered hard times after the War of 1812. In 1813 drought struck hard at southern New Hampshire, and three years later a severe frost killed all the crops in the area. Livestock died for lack of forage; in the following winter food prices soared. Jeremiah, ill-clad against the harsh New Hampshire climate, often had to beg pork or a little meal from nearby farmers. He later vividly recalled that "want sat by my cradle."[6] As soon as he was able, the boy had to go to work to help provide for the growing family, for seven more children were born to Abigail. Three infant girls soon died, but Jeremiah's four brothers all grew to manhood.

The young Jeremiah, raised in such an environment, had little chance to acquire manners or learning. He soon developed into a rude and profane urchin. Abigail, a woman of industrious and serious nature, endeavored to give her growing boy the training and discipline that he needed. Fond of books, she encouraged Jeremiah to learn to read. She first tried to tutor him herself and then sent him off to a neighbor's home for schooling. When he began to read, she borrowed newspapers for him. As her family grew, however, she was able to devote less and less time to her son.[7]

[5] John Farmer and Jacob B. Moore, *Gazetteer of the State of New Hampshire* (Concord, N. H., 1823), 52-53, 134, 273; Timothy Dwight, *Travels in New England and New York* (4 vols.; New Haven, Conn., 1821-1822), IV, 160.

[6] Harold F. Wilson, *The Hill Country of Northern New England* (New York, 1936), 19-24; Natick *Bulletin*, Feb. 26, 1892; Henry Wilson, *Stand by the Republican Colors* (n.p., 1872), 2.

[7] Mann, *Wilson*, 4.

Fortunately for Jeremiah, others took an interest in his education. One day Mrs. Nehemiah Eastman, wife of one of the community's most prominent citizens, found Jeremiah wrestling in the dust with a neighbor boy. Startled by the ferocity of the fight and the profanity of the combatant's language, she separated the two boys and bade them come home with her. Jeremiah followed; his opponent ran away. Mrs. Eastman gave the young lad a book and told him to read it; he finished the assignment in two days. Pleasantly surprised, she allowed the boy to make full use of her husband's library. Jeremiah then sought out another Farmington citizen, Judge George L. Whitehouse, and the dignified, white-haired gentleman willingly lent his young visitor even more books.[8]

The boy's education was short-lived. In August, 1822, when Jeremiah was only ten years old, his father bound him out to a nearby farmer, William Knight. By the terms of the apprenticeship, Jeremiah was to live with Knight and serve him loyally; he was not to waste his master's goods, "haunt or frequent taverns, play houses, or ale houses," marry, or leave the farm without permission. In return, Knight was to feed and house the lad, teach him to farm, and on termination of the contract, give him cattle, sheep, and a new suit of clothes. Jeremiah was bound by these terms until he was twenty-one.[9]

When the Colbaths sent Jeremiah off to work, the tenuous ties uniting parents and son were broken. Squire Knight replaced Winthrop and Abigail as the chief influence upon the young boy's life. From Knight, who worked his apprentice hard, Jeremiah learned discipline and subordination. In the summer, instead of hunting and fishing, he drove cattle and sheep; in the winter, instead of skating and sledding, he cut wood, repaired harness, and shelled corn. He was permitted to attend school one month every year, but only when there was no work to be done. Thus the boy rarely had more than two or three days of school at a time. He had no chance

[8] John Scales, *History of Strafford County, New Hampshire* (Chicago, 1914), 41, 505, 601, 628.

[9] Nason, "Biographical Sketch," 262; a copy of the indenture can be found in the Natick *Bulletin,* March 2, 1912.

to indulge in the usual boyish pranks and escapades at school, and he made no childhood friends he could afterward remember with affection. According to rumor, he became infatuated with one of Knight's daughters, but she scorned him as being beneath her station.[10]

Jeremiah's underprivileged status did not produce defiance or insubordination; rather it prompted him to struggle hard to improve himself. One of Knight's daughters, perhaps the one who spurned his advances, recalled that he "was not much inclined to play with other boys, but was anxious to read every book or paper about the house." He would hasten through his meals in order to have more time for reading. He was ready to scour the country for books, and when he heard that someone in Rochester owned a copy of John Marshall's biography of George Washington, he walked seven miles to get it. By the time he had served out his indenture, the young farm hand had read over seven hundred volumes.[11]

On Saturday, February 16, 1833, Jeremiah Jones Colbath's twenty-first birthday, he became a free man. Already he had reached maturity in a number of ways. The long years of constant work had given him a strong, tough body. Closely resembling his father, he stood almost six feet tall and was lean and muscular. Long black hair hung in disarray around a face roughened and reddened by outdoor work. The young Colbath was not handsome, but a broad forehead and piercing eyes gave him an impressive countenance. His manners were rude and his language unpolished; he knew no trade or profession; he lacked any kind of formal education.[12] Jeremiah Jones Colbath might well have followed the path of his forbears and remained a poor and undistinguished man.

The farmer's apprentice, however, had no desire to fall into his father's indolent and intemperate ways. At the age of nineteen, he had taken a pledge of total abstinence from alcohol.[13] Now, at the

[10] Natick *Bulletin*, Jan. 28, 1876, Nov. 12, 19, 1909.

[11] Mann, *Wilson*, 4-7; Natick *Bulletin*, Feb. 26, 1892.

[12] Mann, *Wilson*, 3; Natick *Citizen*, March 14, 1884.

[13] Elias Nason and Thomas Russell, *Life and Public Services of Henry Wilson* (Boston, 1876), 43.

age of twenty-one and filled with ambition and a craving for recognition and acceptance which his humble beginnings had failed to satisfy, Jeremiah Jones Colbath determined to free himself completely and finally from his past. Without consulting his family, he changed his name to Henry Wilson. He had always resented the name of Jeremiah Jones and decided to be rid of the family name too. His parents regretted his decision, but for Henry, abstinence pledges, book learning, and industrious habits were not sufficient to divorce him from his family's heritage. Only a new name would suffice. Years later, when as a successful politician he returned to Farmington to speak to his former neighbors, he recalled his early poverty but remained silent concerning the family from which he had sprung.[14]

Eager to embark upon a new career, Wilson sold the oxen and sheep Knight gave him at the end of his indenture. He continued to work on neighboring farms until the end of the summer, when he had saved $150. Now he was ready to leave Farmington for good.[15] One of Wilson's few friends, Martin Luther Hayes, had similarly been bound out on indenture, apprenticed not to a farmer but to a shoemaker near Farmington. Hayes quickly learned the trade, and in 1832 he journeyed to Massachusetts to take up shoemaking in the town of Natick. Wilson, learning of Hayes's success, decided to follow him to Natick. But unlike Hayes who took a stage, Wilson walked, even though he made the trip in December, to save the $150 he had earned. After a four-day trip, he reached his destination quite

[14] Natick *Bulletin,* Feb. 14, 1902; New York *Independent,* Dec. 17, 1875. When Wilson died, the editor of the *Army and Navy Journal* commented: "It is an open secret now that the family into which he was born . . . bore a local reputation so discreditable as to render the change of his name by act of Legislature expedient" (Nov. 27, 1875). There are several explanations of why Jeremiah Jones Colbath selected the name Henry Wilson. "W," in the Boston *Herald,* says one of Wilson's brothers claimed Jeremiah had been reading a biography of a Philadelphia school teacher named Henry Wilson (quoted in Natick *Bulletin,* Feb. 14, 1902). Mrs. Waldron of Farmington states she learned from Jeremiah Jones's daughter that the young Colbath greatly admired General James Wilson of Keene, N. H., and also was fond of a portrait of the Rev. Henry Wilson in a book on English clergymen (Natick *Bulletin,* Feb. 26, 1892).

pleased at having spent only one dollar and five cents in traveling the one hundred miles.[16]

A town of only a thousand people, situated seventeen miles southwest of Boston, Natick lay near the blue waters of Lake Cochituate, surrounded by timbered hills and gentle valleys. Wilson had no time to enjoy the scenery; he was intent on establishing himself in the shoe business. He had refused to stop at New Durham, in his home state, because artisans there wanted him to serve a two-year apprenticeship. Instead, he found a master shoemaker in Natick who agreed to teach him to make brogans in return for signing for a five-month apprenticeship. Eager to begin his own work, Wilson bought out his contract at the end of three weeks, believing he was quite prepared to make shoes by himself.[17]

In 1834 the art of making shoes was not highly developed. The business had barely begun in Natick, which only slowly changed from an agricultural to a manufacturing center. About 1830, a few enterprising citizens began to make extra shoes to sell in Southern and Western markets, carrying on the trade principally by bartering with Boston dealers. The market for shoes was good; Southern planters wanted cheap brogans for their slaves, and Natick soon began to specialize in this branch of the industry. Business remained sluggish, however, until 1835, when the Boston and Worcester railroad entered the town. Stimulated by the new transportation, shoe production boomed.[18]

Thus Wilson joined the trade at an opportune time. Since demand was brisk, quality was not important, and standards for shoemaking were not high. Wilson could afford to start making shoes after only three weeks of preparation. Rather than attempt to improve the quality of his work, he sought to increase the quantity. He worked

[15] Natick *Bulletin,* June 17, 1881; Wilson, *Stand by the Republican Colors,* 4.

[16] Hamilton D. Hurd, *History of Rockingham and Strafford Counties, New Hampshire* (Philadelphia, 1882), 635; Nason and Russell, *Wilson,* 22-23.

[17] Natick *Citizen,* Jan. 31, 1879; Mann, *Wilson,* 8.

[18] Blanche E. Hazard, *The Organization of the Boot and Shoe Industry in Massachusetts before 1875* (Cambridge, Mass., 1921), 42-44, 53-54.

fifteen hours a day; once he collapsed while trying to make fifty pairs of shoes without stopping. As he worked through the winter, his clothes smelled of the acrid odor of burning leather, for he cast bits and pieces of old stock into the stove to help heat his tiny workshop. His landlord complained about the sound of his hammer, which often continued far into the night.[19]

Wilson's industry revealed his ambition. He continually sought to improve himself. He brought to Massachusetts his intense craving for books and education and, as in Farmington, he sought out prominent citizens in Natick who could help him. One such man was the Reverend Erasmus D. Moore of the Natick Congregational Church, who Wilson discovered held "a position of influence and power." Later, recalling that Moore was a "friend at a time when I had neither friends nor power in the town or state," Wilson tried to reward him with a political appointment. Although he did not become a communicant in Moore's church, he attended services and consequently met many other citizens, men like Edward Walcott, a genial round-faced soul of honesty and integrity. Walcott was one of the founders of Natick's shoe industry and owned several homes and shops. He became one of Wilson's closest friends. Wilson also became acquainted with another influential Congregationalist, Deacon Coolidge. A patriarchal old Yankee, Coolidge looked approvingly on the aspirations of young men like Wilson and offered him the use of his library, the largest in town. Wilson gladly accepted, and soon, upon Coolidge's suggestion, he moved his shoe shop to the Deacon's barn and boarded with the family. Coolidge played an active and influential role in the community, and through his extensive connections he was able to assist his young boarder with his entry into Natick's social and political life.[20]

Wilson quickly became acquainted with other young men his own

[19] Natick *Citizen,* Jan. 31, 1879; Nason and Russell, *Wilson,* 25-26; undated newspaper clipping on early nineteenth century shoemaking, in scrapbook of Mr. Ernest Colbath, Natick, Mass.

[20] Oliver N. Bacon, *History of Natick* (Boston, 1856), 146-47; Nason and Russell, *Wilson,* 24, 28-29; Natick *Citizen,* Jan. 31, 1879; New York *Times,* Nov. 23, 1875; Henry Wilson to William Claflin, Feb. 1, 1858, William Claflin MSS, Rutherford B. Hayes Library, Fremont, Ohio.

age who were likewise active, ambitious, and eager to better themselves. Early in 1835 he met Alexander Thayer, who had a passion
for history similar to his own. Often the two friends, after closing
their shops, would retire to Coolidge's to talk of history and politics.
Wilson revealed to Thayer his desire to form a debating club, and in
June, 1835, the two men and eleven others established the Natick
Debating Society. Wilson used the society to develop his speaking
power, test his ideas, and improve his limited literary ability.[21]

Reading books and arguing in the debating club, however, did not
satisfy his desire for learning. He continued to work hard at his
cobbling, hoping to earn enough money to finance a year or two of
formal schooling. Unfortunately, Wilson, who never learned how to
relax, worked himself into bad health. By the spring of 1836 he had
managed to save $700, but the money came at the cost of a lung
hemorrhage. A doctor recommended that he vacation in a warmer
climate. Hence Wilson left Natick in May and journeyed as far south
as Washington, D. C., where he remained several weeks. There he
witnessed social and political scenes that influenced his career.[22]

At the end of June, Wilson returned to his home state of New
Hampshire and during the following year studied at academies in
Strafford, Wolfeborough, and Concord. In the fall of 1837 he returned to Natick with only twelve dollars in his pocket. He had
completed less than a year of school in the academies, but that was
sufficient to permit him to teach in Natick until the winter was
over.[23] Wilson then returned to his cobbler's shop but was unable to
keep his mind on his work. He was mulling over new ideas and
contemplating a different career.

The decade of the 1830s, particularly in New England, was a time
of a great ferment of ideas. A number of reformers hoped to improve man's environment and increase his opportunity for advancement. In Boston Horace Mann was experimenting with progressive
education; temperance advocates were forming the Massachusetts

[21] Reminiscences of Thayer in Natick *Bulletin,* May 5, 1876; Bacon,
Natick, 163; Natick *Bulletin,* Sept. 18, 1903.

[22] Nason and Russell, *Wilson,* 29.

[23] Bacon, *Natick,* 144; Natick *Bulletin,* March 11, 1892.

Temperance Union; and organizers for the American Anti-Slavery Society were finding in the state a rich harvest of new members. In 1836 the society had 163 members in Natick and almost a thousand in Middlesex County, where Natick was situated. In Wilson's adopted home town, one of his earliest benefactors and closest advisors, Edward Walcott, ran a station on the underground railroad.[24]

Henry Wilson's early experiences made him receptive to various reform movements. His own life bore ample illustration of the evils of liquor. He later recalled that "when my eyes first saw light, and when I came to recognize anything, I saw and felt liquor's effects on my kith and kin." His struggle for education also had convinced him of the merits of learning, and he later proved eager to extend opportunities for schooling to all children of whatever race or class. In the debating club at Natick, Wilson found a chance to expound and develop his views on reform. Other debaters noted that Wilson hesitated to defend a position he did not favor. He advocated increased educational opportunities, abolition of capital punishment, and restrictions on corporations. He was most interested, however, in attacking license laws that permitted the sale of liquor and in opposing slavery in all its forms.[25]

Although Wilson maintained a deep interest in the temperance crusade, abolitionism quickly assumed priority among the causes he supported. When abolitionist Lydia Maria Child visited her father in Natick, Wilson and other club members avidly discussed the question of slavery with her.[26] From his own life of poverty and hard labor, when for over a decade he could not call his life his own, Henry

[24] *Fifth Annual Report* of the Executive Committee of the American Anti-Slavery Society (New York, 1839), 133-37; Wilbur H. Siebert, "The Underground Railroad in Massachusetts," *Proceedings of the American Antiquarian Society,* n.s. XLV (1935), 48.

[25] Natick *Times,* April 20, 1867; Natick *Citizen,* March 16, 1883; Minutes of the Natick Debating Society, *passim,* in the Morse Institute, Natick, Mass.

[26] J. B. Mann claims Lydia Maria Child was quite important in shaping young Wilson's thoughts on slavery. Mann, *Wilson,* 12. See also Alexander Thayer's reminiscences in Natick *Bulletin,* May 5, 1876. Wilson later told Mrs. Child's husband that her writings had a great influence on his thinking. Lydia Maria Child to Charles Sumner, July 7, 1856, Charles Sumner MSS, Houghton Library, Harvard University, Cambridge, Mass.

Wilson had gained a sympathy for the downtrodden and underprivileged. He had worked for a demanding and unbending master; he sympathized intuitively with others in the same condition, though they might be of another race and work as slaves rather than as indentured servants. In 1872, when Wilson spoke before his former neighbors in Farmington, he recalled that "I became an anti-slavery man thirty-six years ago, because the poor bondsman was the lowest, most degraded, and helpless type of manhood." After Wilson's death the New York *Times* remarked that he had "continually spoken from a class which hated an aristocratic institution founded on the compulsory labors of a race."[27]

Wilson's trip to the nation's capital had brought him in contact with slave pens and auction blocks, and while traveling through Maryland he had observed crews of blacks working tobacco fields under the watchful eye of an overseer. When he returned north to attend Strafford Academy, he had seized his first opportunity for public speaking to advocate the abolition of slavery in the District of Columbia. Twenty-five years later, he introduced legislation in Congress to effect the very reform he had demanded as a student.[28]

While attending schools in New Hampshire, Wilson found further encouragement for his advocating the eradication of slavery. At Wolfeborough he met evangelist Thomas P. Beach, who was then an instructor at the academy. Beach, a dedicated abolitionist, never hesitated to speak his mind. Five years after Wilson left, local authorities jailed Beach for disrupting a Newburyport church service. Though Wilson was critical of Beach's methods, he sympathized with his views. When the young student moved over to Concord Academy, he joined the local abolitionist society. The society's members selected him as their delegate to a state antislavery convention; there he delivered a strong speech in behalf of freedom.[29]

[27] Wilson, *Stand by the Republican Colors*; New York *Times,* Nov. 26, 1875.

[28] Nason and Russell, *Wilson,* 30-31; Natick *Bulletin,* March 11, 1892.

[29] Boston *Mercantile Journal,* Nov. 4, 1842; Henry Wilson, *History of the Rise and Fall of the Slave Power in America* (3 vols.; Boston, 1872-1877), I, 565; Nason and Russell, *Wilson,* 34; *Herald of Freedom* (Concord, N. H.), Aug. 26, 1837.

By 1838, Wilson's reform proclivities had begun to take shape. He was indeed eager to battle the evils that kept men from rising as he hoped to rise. Unfortunately, a cobbler could do little to ameliorate the lot of mankind, except by giving his fellows shoes to protect their feet. Shoemaking brought Wilson a living, but throughout his life he sought recognition rather than wealth. He was able to maintain the somewhat paradoxical position of selling shoes to slave-owners while demanding freedom for the slave because he regarded the occupation as merely a bridge to a more rewarding career.

Wilson had little doubt about the career he would choose. He lacked education, wealth, family background, and social standing, any of which would have eased his entry into some field of business, law, teaching, or medicine. Politicians, however, did not need such qualifications. A political career was suited to Wilson's nature; he had inherited his father's geniality and essential good humor, and he preferred to deal with people rather than with books or machinery. Also, a political career might offer him a chance to make his mark in the world. Most of the men Wilson had read about and admired, including the Founding Fathers and Daniel Webster, had made their imprint upon the page of history through careers in government.

Political activity offered Wilson more than a chance to obtain the recognition he would have been denied as a cobbler or farmer. Through legislative action he could generate the reforms he had already begun to champion. In Massachusetts, temperance advocates had repudiated the technique of moral suasion and had begun a campaign for legislation to further their cause. In 1838 abolitionists in Wilson's county of Middlesex, also eager to take their crusade into politics, withheld their votes from the Whig congressional candidate in their district, preventing anyone from winning a clear majority.[30]

Throughout the rest of Wilson's life, political and humanitarian concerns struggled for priority in his mind. In deciding that by winning elections he could strike effective blows at slavery and its concomitant evils, he was able to reconcile his personal ambition with his reform principles. During his visit to Washington he had

[30] Wilson, *Slave Power,* I, 546.

observed how effectively Southerners used political power to protect their property. Sitting in the Senate gallery he had watched as South Carolina's John C. Calhoun pressed a bill to stop circulation of abolitionist tracts in the South. Concurrently in the House of Representatives other Southerners forced through a gag rule to limit discussion of antislavery petitions.[31] Wilson soon concluded that the political power of slavery could only be smashed by mobilizing the political power of freedom.

From the time Wilson had helped to organize the Natick Debating Society, his antislavery opinions had taken on a political cast. Alexander Thayer recalled that the debaters became antislavery "not so much because of sympathy for the slave—which, to be sure, was not wanting—as because of the influence of slavery on politics." Some years later, after he had entered the United States Senate, one of his colleagues commented that although Wilson seemed aware of the moral evil of slavery, he was animated more "by opposition to the political encroachments of the Slave Power."[32]

Administering political defeat to slaveholders would also provide Wilson with an opportunity "to rebuke . . . aristocratic intolerance and exclusiveness." His own class consciousness was the source of his ambivalent attitude toward men of higher status and place. He could respect friends and associates like Whitehouse and Eastman, and defer to their superior learning and social position. Yet a friend observed that Wilson was also "in all respects a democrat" who harbored some resentment at class distinctions and sneered at snobbery and aristocratic pretension. He was especially angered at the mannerisms and demeanor of Southern slaveholders.[33] Throughout his political career, he constantly warned that the same spirit of privilege that oppressed and degraded blacks of the South would depress the white workers of the North. Wilson was quite aware of

[31] Nason and Russell, *Wilson,* 30.

[32] Natick *Bulletin,* Jan. 28, May 5, 1876; Salmon P. Chase to Charles Sumner, July 16, 1858, in "Diary and Correspondence of Salmon P. Chase," *Annual Report* of the American Historical Association, 1902 (2 vols.; Washington, D. C., 1903), II, 278.

[33] Natick *Bulletin,* Jan. 28, May 5, 1876; Mrs. W. S. Robinson, ed., *Warrington Pen-Portraits* (Boston, 1877), 544-45.

the political appeal of such statements, but he uttered them because they expressed his own deep convictions.

Wilson faced some personal problems that handicapped his efforts to prepare for a political career. The struggling cobbler, whom a friend recalled as a very bashful "backwoods curiosity," needed to acquire some polish and urbanity. He also had to overcome his barbarous grammar and a speech impediment. At first Wilson sought to compensate for these handicaps by using coarse and indignant language, for he had inherited his father's impulsive nature. Such a technique proved more a hindrance than a help. He practiced oratory in empty barns, but truly to improve his speech and thought, he needed an audience and criticism. He hoped to gain this from the Natick Debating Society. Wilson insisted that the club members debate rather then spout memorized speeches. When his better-educated colleagues laughed at his language, he withstood the ridicule and sought to benefit from the corrections. His speeches still bore evidence of his passionate nature, but he gradually learned to control his impetuosity and reply to his opponents with argument rather than invective. He overcame the speech impediment and conquered the trembling in his voice.[34]

By the summer of 1839 Wilson was ready to try his newly acquired political skills. The previous year the state legislature had forbidden the purchase of drinks over the bar. In 1839 the state political campaign turned on the liquor law. Wilson, who was quite interested in the issue, let his friends present his name as a temperance candidate for the state legislature. In the election, however, no candidate won a majority, and the town went without representation the following year. Wilson was forced to remain at home and make shoes.[35]

During 1839 and 1840 Wilson worked hard to enlarge his business. A severe depression had struck hard at all industry, and in shoe

[34] Natick *Bulletin,* May 5, 1876; March 11, 1892; Natick *Citizen,* March 14, 1884.

[35] Bacon, *Natick,* 145; Arthur B. Darling, *Political Changes in Massachusetts, 1824-1848* (New Haven, Conn., 1925), 239-42; Nason and Russell, *Wilson,* 43-44.

manufacturing, only men with small trade and smaller risks were able to hold on. Wilson was one of the few who survived, and he moved quickly to take advantage of the failure of many of his bigger competitors. He began making use of banks for discounts and loans. He also consigned boots and shoes to local laborers for fitting and sewing. In 1838, he employed eighteen men and with them produced 18,000 pairs of shoes; two years later, with thirty-four hands, he more than doubled his production.[36]

The cobbler was now twenty-eight years old. With his business thriving, he was ready to take a wife. In the winter of 1837, when he was teaching school in Natick, he had noticed in his class a slight, unassuming girl whose long black hair curled down to her neck, accentuating her thin face and high cheekbones. Her name was Harriet Malvina Howe, and in November, 1840, Wilson took her hand in marriage. She was only sixteen years old. Her family could offer Wilson nothing in the way of social prestige, influence, or wealth. Harriet's steady habits, Christian upbringing, unostentatious manner, and gentle dispostion, however, provided her husband with a happy domestic life until her death.[37]

Despite Wilson's defeat in the 1839 election, his ambition for office blossomed. He confided in only a few men, one of them Jonathan B. Mann, his future biographer. He and Mann often held lengthy political discussions, and late one night Mann listened in utter astonishment as Wilson declared that, before he died, he wished to be a member of the Massachusetts Senate. This in itself was not an unusually high goal, but, as Mann noted, Wilson was not yet prepared to be a town clerk. Mann suspected that his friend held even higher aspirations, but for the moment Wilson planned to run again for the General Court. The year 1840 promised to be a good one; the recent economic downturn had aroused a good deal of public interest in elections and legislation. [38]

[36] Hazard, *Shoe Industry,* 64-71; Bacon, *Natick,* 152-53.

[37] Natick *Bulletin,* April 15, 1892; Nason and Russell, *Wilson,* 42; Thomas W. Baldwin, comp., *Vital Records of Natick, Massachusetts to the Year 1850* (Boston, 1910), 197.

[38] Natick *Bulletin,* Feb. 14, 1902.

In such a time of political ferment, Wilson might have found it hard to choose a party. His early benefactors, Whitehouse and Eastman, had been active Democrats. In Massachusetts the Democratic party had put forward a platform which appealed to the small businessman, worker, and farmer. Most of the reforms submitted by the Democrats, however, were economic in nature, and throughout his life Wilson remained rather indifferent to any proposals that did not affect slavery or liquor. What disturbed him about the Democratic party was its apparent opposition to temperance legislation on the state level and its support of slavery in national politics. He still remembered his visit to Washington, when he had witnessed Democrats legislate in behalf of slaveholders.[39]

If Wilson's affinity for temperance and antislavery had not been enough to guide him into Whig councils, certainly the political atmosphere of 1840 would have sufficed to lead him there. Reaction against the Van Buren administration was running strong, and Democrats were forced to bear responsibility for the economic depression. On the state level, the Whigs, noting the Democratic governor's failure to realize any of his legislative proposals and the wide popularity of their own candidate, John Davis, were confident of victory. As Wilson recalled a year later, "everything told in language not to be misunderstood that defeat and disaster awaited [the Democratic] party." The antislavery Liberty party also took part in the state elections, but its political weakness ruled it out of Wilson's consideration. Thus, expediency, hope of some action on temperance and slavery, and an eye for his own political advancement guided Wilson to the Whigs.[40]

The campaign of 1840 provided the fledgling office-seeker with a perfect opportunity to project himself into the thick of state as well as local politics. Utilizing the distress caused by the depression, early in the year he began condemning the Van Buren administration for

[39] Darling, *Political Changes,* 252-59, 277-78; Nason and Russell, *Wilson,* 30.

[40] Darling, *Political Changes,* 268-73; Wilson to William Schouler, Aug. 5, 1841, William Schouler MSS, Massachusetts Historical Society, Boston, Mass.

its economic program. He managed to rile local Democrats into challenging him to a debate, which he easily won. Angered at their humiliation before the village shoemaker, the Democrats promised another challenger and went off to neighboring Framingham to find one. Somewhat unnerved at this development, Wilson hastily sought out his friend Mann and took him to Deacon Coolidge's parlor, where for a week the two worked to prepare insurmountable arguments. On the day of the debate, in the local Methodist church, Wilson and Mann arrived early and loaded down the front table with an ostentatious pile of books. The Democrat, arriving late, was disconcerted by the sight of so much preparation. Wilson appeared calm as he stroked his long black locks, "thus displaying his ample forehead to the admiring crowd with great advantage," but he was actually nervous. When he found that his opponent was unprepared for his own flood of documentary matter, however, he gained confidence and delivered a powerful oration. The crowd unanimously acclaimed him victor. Chagrined, the Democrats sought to ridicule the triumphant debater by labeling him the "Natick Cobbler." Wilson turned the intended slur to his own advantage, taking a stance as a friend of the working class.[41]

The Whigs were delighted to find a speaker who could counter the party's reputation as an aristocratic organization, and they urged Wilson to plunge into the political campaign. The cobbler needed little encouragement, and by mid-June he was in full swing around the state. He spoke in at least sixty towns in Massachusetts and New Hampshire, enabling him to spread his name beyond the bounds of Natick and Middlesex County. With great enthusiasm, he delivered a speech he had prepared on tariffs and banks. He was still so slim that he appeared even taller than he actually was. When speaking, he bent low over his desk, as if seeking complete contact with his audience. He bombarded his listeners with a hail of facts and quotations gleaned from his histories. Massachusetts farmers warmed to his determined and enthusiastic manner. One listener later recalled

[41] Mann's article in Natick *Citizen,* March 16, 1883; Boston semiweekly *Atlas,* March 28, April 11, 18, May 13, 1840.

Wilson as "an earnest man" who preferred to present "the cold facts of a case" rather than attempt flamboyant oratory.[42]

Wilson served the Whig cause well in the summer and fall of 1840. The fall elections gave the Whigs a resounding victory in both state and national elections, and in the landslide Wilson won a seat in the General Court.

[42] Charles T. Congdon, *Reminiscences of a Journalist* (Boston, 1880), 70; Robinson, ed., *Warrington,* 20; Natick *Bulletin,* June 12, 1896; Boston *Journal,* Jan. 27, 1870; Boston semiweekly *Atlas,* June 20, 1840.

2

Wilson and the Whig Party

In January, 1841, Henry Wilson, still full of the excitement of the previous fall's campaign, took his seat in the lower house of the Massachusetts legislature. From that moment on, as a political associate later recalled, the Natick cobbler "devoted himself to the occupation [of politics], sacrificing everything else to it." Harriet Wilson had already found that her husband stood prepared to abandon even her to politics; on their wedding night only inclement weather prevented him from giving a speech in Gloucester. Wilson disclaimed any political ambitions; yet in 1842 he successfully ran for reelection to the legislature, and in 1843 he tried and failed to win a seat in the state Senate. The following year he attained the post, and eight times in the years from 1841 to 1852 he served in either the upper or lower house.[1]

When Wilson took his seat in the legislative halls in Boston, he was still unable to write a resolution in his own hand. A political associate later recalled that he saw papers in Wilson's handwriting "in which the rule requiring a sentence to commence with a capital letter was disregarded uniformly." The twenty-eight-year-old legislator was determined, however, to make up in earnestness and effort what he lacked in rhetorical and literary skills. When he entered the Massachusetts House he found he had been assigned a seat in the back of the chamber. Desiring to be nearer the center of activity, he bought a seat closer to the speaker's chair. The move reflected his desire to succeed; for the rest of his life he would constantly be seeking the center of political action.[2]

Wilson was prepared to remain a loyal Whig as long as the organization promised to serve both his principles and his own ambitions. Such an assignment called for a good deal of political juggling, for not all of Wilson's constituents approved the policies of his party. Middlesex County's economy was largely agricultural, but its rising industrial towns challenged the farmer's dominance and created a varied pattern of economic interests. Wilson had to look beyond Middlesex to Boston, however, for his party's politics were controlled in the Massachusetts capital. Wealthy urban merchants, financiers, and industrialists, men like Abbott Lawrence and Nathan Appleton, dominated the party. In conjunction with their political representatives—Daniel Webster, Levi Lincoln, Edward Everett, and John Davis—the coterie formulated policies and selected candidates for the more important state and national offices. Ties of religion and marriage further strengthened the economic and political bonds uniting the small and exclusive group. Under the guidance of their leading men, the Whigs of Massachusetts upheld their party's banking institutions and distribution of the national revenue, while in Massachusetts they passed special incorporation acts and pledged the state's credit to internal improvements.[3]

The state's Democrats mounted a rather ineffective challenge to the Whig program. They advocated general incorporation laws, individual liability for stockholders, abolition of property qualifications for voting, the secret ballot, abolition of imprisonment for debt, elimination of state aid for railroads, and reduction of crimes punishable by death. Although the party was weak in the state,

[1] Charles Francis Adams Diary, Nov. 22, 1875, microfilm copy in manuscripts division of the State Historical Society of Wisconsin, Madison, Wis.; Boston *Commonwealth,* Nov. 4, 1865; Wilson to William S. Robinson, July 15, 1841, in Natick Historical Society Museum, South Natick, Mass.; Wilson to William Schouler, July 5, Aug. 5, 1841, June 2, 1842, William Schouler MSS.

[2] Nason and Russell, *Wilson,* 46; Boston *Morning Journal,* Nov. 29, 1875; Congdon, *Reminiscences,* 70; George S. Boutwell, *Reminiscences of Sixty Years in Public Affairs* (2 vols.; New York, 1902), I, 79; Robinson, ed., *Warrington,* 401.

[3] Kinley J. Brauer, *Cotton Versus Conscience: Massachusetts Whig Politics and Southwestern Expansionism, 1843–1848* (Lexington, Ky., 1967), 7-18.

many Democratic proposals found favor in Middlesex, and during the 1840s the county's allegiance swayed back and forth between the two parties. Henry Wilson had to tread carefully between his constituents and the Boston oligarchy, and he often had to perform intellectual gymnastics to prove that his views were in the interest "of the poor man with whom I have been reared, and with whom I now stand."[4]

On matters of corporations, creditor legislation, and railroad bills, Wilson showed little initiative or enthusiasm and perfunctorily voted for his party's position.[5] He lacked interest in economic questions and displayed a growing irritation with his party's concern with property rather than human rights. Many years later, as a Republican senator, he scornfully referred to "the old Whig party, that never professed to have an idea on earth, a party that simply advocated tariffs and banks and moneyed measures." In 1842, when he drew up a committee report favoring a protective tariff, he seized the opportunity to remind his colleagues that "labor is bone, sinew, and intellect; whereas property is dead, and incapable of feeling." This conviction led him to break Whig lines to vote for abolishing imprisonment for debt and for giving laborers a lien on property to secure their wages. He supported Democratic proposals to reduce the poll tax and introduced a bill to end the death penalty in the state.[6]

Wilson also sought the passage of stronger temperance laws, but his reforming zeal was drawn increasingly toward championing equal rights for Massachusetts Negroes. Wilson was uncertain about the equality of the black man. Alexander Thayer recalled that although the members of the Natick debating club were opposed to slavery,

[4] Darling, *Political Changes,* 252-59, 277-78, 293-95; Boston semiweekly *Atlas,* Jan. 26, Feb. 3, 19, 1841.

[5] Boston *Post,* Feb. 3, 1845; Boston *Daily Atlas,* Jan. 18, Feb. 2, 1842, Jan. 25, Feb. 2, 5, 1844; Massachusetts House Journal, 1841, appendix 11; *ibid.,* 1842, appendices 1, 3, 4, 5, 12, 14.

[6] U.S., Congress, Senate, *Congressional Globe,* 39th Cong., 1st sess., 1865, p. 341; Massachusetts House *Legislative Documents, 1842,* Document 22; Boston *Mercantile Journal,* March 15, 1845; Boston semiweekly *Atlas,* Feb. 16, 1841; Massachusetts House Journal, 1841, appendices 1, 5, 6, 7; Massachusetts House *Legislative Documents, 1841,* House Report 15.

only one, a man named Fiske, was a "negrophilist." In 1836 Wilson argued before the club that Negroes were mentally inferior to whites.[7] Whatever his opinions on racial equality, however, the young legislator insisted that the free Negro population have equal rights under the law. Having come from a poor family, he was opposed to legal discriminations based on status, education, or property. In 1838, Massachusetts abolitionist societies began a campaign to repeal a law forbidding racial intermarriage. In one of Wilson's first acts as a legislator, he voted for the repeal. The move failed; Wilson, declaring the law was founded on "wrong principles," continued to fight for its elimination, and the law's opponents finally won in 1843. The next year, Wilson sought to amend state militia laws to remove racial distinctions.

In 1845 Wilson threw his support behind legislation to integrate public schools in Massachusetts, a crusade that did not succeed for another ten years. In speaking in behalf of the proposal, the Natick cobbler revealed his deep indignation at social discrimination. The recommended legislation, he said, was the most important of the session. It did not involve the interests of some of the large corporate institutions "whose interests and rights were so eagerly watched here." Rather it concerned the feelings and rights of "a large but humble portion of our people." who, unlike the corporation lobbyists, "have not thronged our halls looking for favors." Wilson reminded his colleagues that the common-school system of Massachusetts was the pride of the state and demanded that "the sons of rich and poor, learned and ignorant" all should be able to enjoy its benefits. The former farmer's apprentice sounded his favorite theme when he warned that the same spirit of caste and prejudice that would exclude colored children from the public schools would also discriminate against "the children of laboring men and mechanics." Looking to the future, Wilson proclaimed that "the tide of advancing civilization and Christianity is setting against all those factitious and arbitrary distinctions that have so long enabled the few to

[7] Minutes of the Natick Debating Society, April 14, 1836, Morse Institute; Natick *Bulletin*, May 5, 1876.

oppress the many." The Natick legislator's rhetoric was stirring enough to catch the attention of abolitionist William Lloyd Garrison, who praised his "honorable . . . and manly speech."[8]

While Wilson battled for the rights of free Negroes in Massachusetts, he was even more eager to strike at the political power of those who held the Negro in bondage in the South. As early as 1841 Wilson and the Natick debating club, along with prominent shoemakers Edward Walcott and George M. Herring, agreed to join with Whigs of similar sentiments in other Middlesex towns to attempt to send antislavery Whigs to party conventions. In 1842, Wilson, perturbed because some Massachusetts newspapers sought to recommend Henry Clay of Kentucky as the Whig nominee for president in 1844, supported John McLean of Ohio, who he thought was more opposed to slavery than Clay. He wanted to publish letters on the subject in the Boston papers, but, admitting that "I do not write but very little and to tell the truth I do not like it," he sought the help of his minister friend, Samuel Hunt, who had recently replaced Moore in the Natick Congregational Church. With his assistance, Wilson published several letters urging the Whigs to take antislavery ground, drop Clay in favor of McLean, and "sweep the North."[9]

Thus, as early as 1842, Wilson had decided on a method for ending the political power of the Southern slaveholder and thereby easing the path to emancipation. He would turn the Whig party into a Northern antislavery organization, win control of the national government, and deprive Southerners of the federal power they depended upon to preserve and strengthen the institution of slavery. In order to achieve this purpose, Wilson needed a popular issue that would stimulate party realignment on a sectional basis. He would also need the support of other Whigs who shared his views.

[8] Massachusetts House Journal, 1841, appendix 3; Boston *Mercantile Journal*, Feb. 15, 1842, Jan. 24, 1844; *Liberator* (Boston), Feb. 25, 1842, March 7, 1845; Wilson, *Slave Power*, I, 496-97; Boston *Post*, Feb. 21, 1845. And see Louis Ruchames, "Race, Marriage, and Abolition in Massachusetts," *Journal of Negro History*, XL (1955), 250-74.

[9] Natick *Bulletin*, May 5, 1876, Feb. 2, 1877; Mann, *Wilson*, 25; Bacon, *Natick*, 147; Wilson to Schouler, June 2, 1842, William Schouler MSS.

In 1843 President John Tyler provided the issue Wilson sought when he revived an earlier proposal to annex the slaveholding Republic of Texas to the United States. Wilson found allies for his cause among younger members of the Massachusetts Whig party who chafed under the dominance of the Boston industrialists. Wilson and his associates endeavored to use Texas as a symbol of Southern desires to expand and perpetuate human bondage. Massachusetts Whigs as a group despised slavery, but the party's leaders did not wish to push the Texas question to the point of disrupting their economic and political ties with the South. Consequently, the young Whigs, or Conscience Whigs as they became known, represented an anti-Boston as well as an antislavery wing of their party. Several of their leading spokesmen came from other parts of the state. S. C. Phillips, a Salem merchant who had been mayor of his town, was a proven advocate of the rights of Negroes. Worcester supplied two antislavery lawyers, Charles Allen and E. R. Hoar. Three important members of the group, Charles Francis Adams, Charles Sumner, and John G. Palfrey, came from Boston or its environs; but they shared with the others a sense of alienation from the sources of political, economic, and social power within the city. This alienation made it easier for the group to challenge the party regulars and criticize their policy toward Southern slaveholders.[10]

Wilson's estrangement from the conservative or "Cotton" Whigs was deeper than that of his young Whig allies. He had been uncomfortable in a party whose members demonstrated a contempt for democracy and the lower social and economic classes. Many of the Conscience Whigs shared the same aristocratic disdain for their social

[10] For the most recent treatment of the rise of Conscience Whiggery in Massachusetts, see Brauer, *Cotton Versus Conscience,* esp. 1-6, 23-29. See also Frank Otto Gatell, "Conscience and Judgment: The Bolt of the Massachusetts Conscience Whigs," *The Historian,* XXI (1958), 18-45. Several recent biographies of leading Massachusetts Conscience Whigs and Free-Soilers have been of great assistance in tracing political movements of the 1840s and 1850s: David Donald, *Charles Sumner and the Coming of the Civil War* (New York, 1960); Frank O. Gatell, *John Gorham Palfrey* (Cambridge, Mass., 1963); Martin Duberman, *Charles Francis Adams, 1807-1886* (Boston, 1961); Harold Schwartz, *Samuel Gridley Howe* (Cambridge, Mass., 1956); Samuel Shapiro, *Richard Henry Dana, Jr.* (East Lansing, Mich., 1961).

inferiors, but Wilson could nevertheless cooperate with them because they shared his opposition to slavery.[11] Yet as his involvement in the agitation against Texas and related issues deepened, he proved more willing than his party colleagues to associate with abolitionists and to advocate independent political action.

Throughout 1844 and 1845, both in the legislature and at a series of meetings around the state, Wilson condemned the scheme of the Southern planters, whom he identified as the "Slave Power," to annex Texas and expand slavery. He was so vehement that even the Democratic Boston *Post* took note of his "unappeasable hatred of Texas." Whig party leaders, who were likewise opposed to the annexation of the slaveholding republic, withdrew from further agitation after Congress passed a joint resolution to add the territory to the Union.[12] Refusing to follow his party chiefs, Wilson strayed further from the Whig organization. Appealing to all, "regardless of party," to support the anti-Texas meetings, he sat on platforms with large numbers of Garrisonian abolitionists. Among the Conscience Whigs only Wilson asserted his outright sympathy for the abolitionist cause. He admired the Garrisonians for their boldness and insistence on principle. A few years later, he would complain that their dogmatism endangered the success of the political abolitionists, but during the Texas struggle he preferred their position over that of Massachusetts Whigs who tended to sacrifice principle to economic and political considerations. He maintained his membership in an abolitionist society, frequently attended their meetings, and read Garrison's *Liberator*. Garrison, who noted that Wilson's speech-making was "frowned upon by the time-serving leaders of his party," praised the Natick politician for "his manly and unfaltering course on the subject of slavery."[13]

[11] Brauer, *Cotton Versus Conscience*, 1-2.

[12] Boston *Daily Atlas*, Feb. 21, March 8, 12, 1844; Boston *Courier*, Feb. 24, April 24, 1844; Wilson to Schouler, April 16, 1844, William Schouler MSS; Boston *Post* quoted in Lowell *Daily Courier*, Oct. 2, 1845; Brauer, *Cotton Versus Conscience*, 114-25; *Liberator* (Boston), May 16, 1845; Massachusetts Senate Journal, 1845, March 4, 7, 18; Boston *Mercantile Journal*, March 19, 1845.

[13] C. F. Adams Diary, Oct. 1, 21, 22, 1845; *Liberator*, (Boston), May 16,

Late in September, 1845, Wilson joined with other antislavery politicians and abolitionists to organize an anti-Texas committee to begin a weekly paper, circulate petitions, and draw up an address to the people of the state. By November the committee had collected tens of thousands of signatures for a petition against the admission of Texas as a slave state, and Wilson took the document to Washington to present to John Quincy Adams, then serving Massachusetts in the House of Representatives. Upon his return to Boston, Wilson was shocked and dismayed to learn that his associates had decided to disband the committee. Interest in the Texas issue was fading rapidly. Wishing the agitation to continue in some form, Wilson argued vehemently but fruitlessly against such a step. He was fast losing his crusade.[14]

In December, 1845, Congress admitted Texas as a slave state, thus stifling any further protest from Massachusetts. Wilson, however, launched a one-man campaign in the state legislature against slavery. On February 3 he introduced a preamble and resolution in the House to condemn the aggressions of the Slave Power and demand that Massachusetts do all that was constitutional to accomplish the "overthrow and entire extinction" of slavery. Wilson spoke for an hour and a half in support of his proposal; it was the greatest performance of his short career as legislator and antislavery politician. Garrison found it "unquestionably the best antislavery speech that has ever been delivered in any legislative assembly in the country" and considered it a long step in advance of both party and public sentiment.[15]

In the speech Wilson utilized all the arguments against slavery that abolitionists and Liberty party men had long been propounding. He began by dissociating himself from the latter group, but he stated that he was "proud of the name of abolitionist." Then he launched

---

Oct. 31, 1845, Feb. 13, 1846; Boston *Mercantile Journal,* Jan. 20, 1842; clipping in Wilson to E. A. Stansbury, Jan. 31, 1851, in Henry Wilson MSS, Library of Congress, Washington, D. C.; Boston *Journal,* Sept. 25, 1845, Feb. 27, 1846; Lowell *Daily Courier,* Aug. 4, Oct. 22, 1845.

[14] Wilson, *Slave Power,* I, 641-44; C. F. Adams Diary, Nov. 4, 28, 29, Dec. 2, 30, 1845.

[15] *Liberator* (Boston) Feb. 3, 1846.

into a long tirade against the Slave Power, which he found standing with one foot "upon the crushed, bruised and palpitating hearts of three millions of men, and with the other, upon the broken, violated and bleeding Constitution." According to Wilson, slavery undermined the moral, social, and intellectual condition of both slave and slaveholder. It had corrupted and destroyed empires and now threatened the death of democracy. "Freedom and slavery are now arrayed against each other," he warned; "we must destroy slavery, or it will destroy liberty."

Wilson then told his colleagues that such an irrepressible conflict could be resolved by wresting the control of the federal government from the South and using its powers for freedom rather than slavery. The government could ban slavery from the territories and the District of Columbia and deny slaveowners the right to chase their fugitive slaves into the North. He asserted that the agitation of such subjects would not rend the nation; yet he impulsively declared that he preferred "liberty without union [to] union without liberty."

Wilson, noting that the Whigs had lost the confidence of the South by resisting Texan annexation, urged the party to abandon that section to the Democrats and pledge itself to an emancipation policy. Within five years, he predicted, the Whigs could sweep the North and win control of the federal government. If the Whig machinery proved resistant to his ideas, Wilson warned, he would act with others, be they "Democrat, Abolitionist, Christian, or Infidel," who would join him in the cause of emancipation.[16]

Unfortunately, in early 1846 Wilson was standing alone; Charles Francis Adams congratulated him on his speech but admitted he was pessimistic about accomplishing anything. Most of his friends agreed.[17] It remained for President Polk, on May 11, to deliver Wilson's associates from their lethargy with a message to Congress demanding war with Mexico. For the Conscience Whigs, this was striking proof that the Slave Power dictated national policies and was even ready to begin a war to extend the slave system. Since Robert Winthrop, the leading Massachusetts Whig in the House of

[16] Wilson, *Slave Power*, II, 115-17.
[17] C. F. Adams Diary, April 18, 1846.

Representatives, voted money for the war, the Conscience Whigs seized the opportunity to condemn not only the slaveocracy but its Northern Whig allies.

The war was not popular among Massachusetts Whig leaders. The party press in the state was generally critical of it, and in Congress, all Massachusetts Whigs save Webster and Winthrop voted against a resolution stating that war existed by act of Mexico. Yet the tone of party opposition was moderate. The Conscience men, hoping to prove that they, not Boston's cotton aristocrats, represented Whig sentiment in the state, bought control of a Boston newspaper and used its columns to berate the war and its supporters.[18] In an unsigned letter published July 31, Henry Wilson provided a clear statement of the convictions of the Conscience men. He complained that manufacturers had gained a monopoly of the Whig party and had used it to serve their own selfish interests. The time had come, he declared, for the Conscience Whigs to win control of the party and "give it nobler views and a nobler aim."[19] While Wilson called upon the Whigs to forswear the "worship of mammon," Palfrey, Sumner, and Adams charged Abbott Lawrence, Winthrop, and Nathan Appleton with muting antislavery agitation in order to conserve profits made from milling Southern cotton.

In September, at the state Whig convention, the Conscience men made their first organized effort to gain control of the party. They hoped to get the delegates to adopt their own set of antislavery resolutions, but the proposals of the regular Whigs were accepted instead. Although a small group of Conscience Whigs in Boston ran an independent congressional candidate against Robert Winthrop, most of Wilson's associates accepted their defeat. Even Wilson agreed to support the Whig gubernatorial candidate.[20]

After the Conscience Whigs' failure in the 1846 convention, Henry Wilson took temporary leave of public affairs. For seven years

[18] Brauer, *Cotton Versus Conscience,* 164-66.

[19] Part of the letter is quoted in *ibid.,* 167-68. Brauer has suggested that Wilson wrote the letter. I am convinced he did; the phrasing is very similar to that of his earlier speeches.

[20] Ibid., 168-69, 185-94; Wilson to Schouler, Nov. 26, 1846, William Schouler MSS.

he had given all his free time to politics, and now domestic concerns demanded his full attention. He had managed to raise his shoe production from 38,000 pairs in 1840 to 62,000 pairs in 1844; by the later date he was employing fifty-nine men to work his leather on consignment. Two years after his marriage he could afford to build a comfortable, two-story yellow frame house on Central Street, a few blocks from the town's business center. Compared to the drafty, rough-hewn, rude cottage Winthrop Colbath had built for Abigail, Henry's house was truly a mansion. In 1846, besides the house, Wilson had a shop, a lot, large stocks of raw materials, and a carriage. He was doing a $23,000 business in shoes, but he had several notes due at the bank. After deducting all his liabilities, Wilson netted over $5,000 for the year's efforts.[21]

Despite his prosperity, Wilson's shoe production had fallen off to 47,000 pairs in 1846. In any other year this decline in production would not have disturbed him but now his wife was pregnant. The baby was due in November, and Harriet, who had frequently been in bad heath, was completely incapacitated. Consequently, the aspiring legislator decided to interrupt his political junketing; in view of his lack of political success, it was not hard for him to return to his cobbling shop and his ailing wife.[22]

On November 11 Harriet gave birth to a son. A very proud father named the boy Henry Hamilton and announced to a friend that the new addition to the family was a "first rate little fellow, fat and hearty." Though his wife was still sick, she was improving, and Wilson confessed that he felt "quite large." Determined that his son would have a better start in life than he himself had had, Henry Wilson turned to hammering out brogans at a great rate. By the end of the next year his production had soared to 122,000 pairs and he employed slightly over one hundred hands.[23]

[21] Bacon, *Natick,* 153; Nason and Russell, *Wilson,* 42; Wilson to Schouler, June 2, 1842, William Schouler MSS; Wilson's manuscript ledger for 1846, Natick Historical Society Museum.

[22] Wilson to Schouler, Oct. 31, Nov. 26, 1846, William Schouler MSS; Bacon, *Natick,* 153; Lowell *Daily Courier,* Oct. 7, 1846.

[23] Wilson to Schouler, Nov. 26, 1846, William Schouler MSS; Bacon, *Natick,* 153.

Although Wilson had few moments to spare, he made what contributions he could to Natick's civic and cultural life. He served as
secretary of the town lyceum and planned programs for its meetings,
helped organize a "Citizen's Library," and actively promoted
temperance organizations in Natick.[24] Busy as he was, Wilson also
found time to take an active role in the local militia. Admittedly it
provided him with new friendships helpful to his political aspirations, but he had a great personal interest in joining the military
organization. As a wide-eyed youth he had read of military campaigns, and in Farmington he had wandered to the militia training
field to watch the older men march. There one of the officers gave
Jeremiah Colbath one of the few thrills of his childhood when he
awarded the boy an honorary commission.[25]

Wilson came to Natick after the state had created an active volunteer organization to add to the enrolled but passive militia. He
immediately joined the volunteer militia and by 1843 was a major in
a brigade commanded by his friend William Schouler. Quickly, he
moved from this rank to colonel, and in 1846 he became a brigadier
general. From that time on, political associates frequently called him
"General Wilson," an appellation which pleased him immensely. In
the state legislature, he served as chairman of the joint standing
committee on militia. As the militia's advocate and defender, he
worked hard to revive enthusiasm, promote enlistment, improve the
drill and efficiency of the volunteer companies, and make sure the
whole system was put on a permanent basis. As a result of this
experience in Massachusetts, when Wilson advanced to the Senate he
became chairman of the Senate committee on military affairs, a post
he held when the Civil War began.[26]

Despite Wilson's concern with his family, the shoe business, the

[24] Wilson to Schouler, Aug. 5, 1841, William Schouler MSS; Lowell *Daily
Courier,* Aug. 15, 1844; Boston *Journal,* Sept. 1, 1845; J. W. Bacon, "Natick
Public Libraries and Their Origin," *Historical Collections of Historical, Natural
History and Library Society* (Natick), II (1910), 42.

[25] Mann, *Wilson,* 6; Nason and Russell, *Wilson,* 51-52.

[26] Thomas F. Edmand, "The Massachusetts Militia," *New England
Magazine,* XI (Feb., 1895), 770-84; Mann, *Wilson,* 23; Boston *Daily Atlas,*
Feb. 15, 1844.

militia, and other local affairs, he could not ignore the call of politics. Some Boston Whigs, led by Abbott Lawrence, were busily promoting Zachary Taylor, a general who had made his reputation in the Mexican War, as their presidential candidate in 1848. Conscience Whigs found the textile manufacturer's support of the slaveholding Taylor but another instance of the alliance between the "lords of the lash and the lords of the loom." Wilson was particularly upset at this new example of Whig perfidy. Conscience men were neither certain of what steps to take to head off Taylor nor agreed on what to do if Taylor did receive the nomination. Wilson had no doubts about the proper course, however. As early as February 6, 1847, he adamantly told Joshua Reed Giddings of Ohio that if the general got the nomination, antislavery Whigs should bolt the party and name their own candidate.[27] He was the only one of the Conscience Whigs who at that time seriously considered leaving the party. In September his associates tried and failed to win over the party's state convention to their opposition to any presidential candidate not pledged against slavery expansion. It was increasingly clear that they had little influence in Whig councils.[28]

Just at the time the Conscience men were beginning to agree with Wilson that they might have to abandon the Whigs, the Natick cobbler proved reluctant to oppose his parent political organization. In March, 1848, Whigs in his congressional district were to select a successor to John Quincy Adams, who had just died. Wilson was eager for the honor of succeeding the ex-president in Congress. Although he was ready to destroy the Whig party if it selected Taylor in June, until then he would seek Whig support for higher office. Personal ambition was blurring his determination to form an antislavery party.[29] On March 15, when the balloting took place, Wilson finished far behind the winner, Horace Mann, the renowned

[27] C. F. Adams Diary, April 7, 1847; Wilson to Giddings, Feb. 6, 1847, Joshua Giddings MSS, Ohio Historical Society, Columbus, Ohio.

[28] Donald, *Sumner,* 156-59.

[29] C. F. Adams Diary, March 9, 1848; Palfrey to Charles Sumner, Feb. 28, March 2, 4, 1848, John G. Palfrey MSS, Houghton Library, Harvard University; H. B. Stanton to Sumner, Feb. 25, 1848, Sumner MSS.

educational reformer. To compensate Wilson the district voters chose him as their representative in the coming national convention.[30]

Wilson was full of suggestions about what measures to take before and after the Whigs met at Philadelphia. He thought the antislavery men should support Daniel Webster at the convention, in the hope that when the Whigs chose Taylor, angry Websterites might support them. When the Conscience Whigs debated the advisability of organizing an opposition candidacy if Taylor should be selected, Wilson supported the idea "warmly and earnestly." Most of his associates agreed, and the group proceeded to draw up plans for their own convention after the one in Philadelphia. Wilson made no secret of his intentions. J. N. Brewer, editor of the Whig Boston *Atlas,* became alarmed at the rumors and asked William Schouler to advise Wilson "not to act silly." Brewer, valuing Wilson's services, wanted to keep him in the party.[31]

At Philadelphia, both Wilson and his associate, Charles Allen, voted fruitlessly for Webster, but the Whigs turned instead to Taylor. When the general was nominated, Allen leaped to his feet, shouted over the roar of the crowd that the Whig party was "this day dissolved," and stamped out of the gathering, but Wilson waited until nominations for vice-president began. Then, before Abbott Lawrence's name could be offered, he sought the floor to assert amid hisses and boos that Taylor's managers had used the second spot on the ticket to bribe Massachusetts and the North. Shouting to make himself heard over the chorus of catcalls that greeted his announcement, Wilson indignantly announced that his state "spurned the

[30] Boston *Atlas,* March 17, 1848; Wilson to Mann, March 17, 1848, Horace Mann MSS, Massachusetts Historical Society.

[31] C. F. Adams Diary, April 21, May 27, June 1, 1848; Wilson to Horace Greeley, March 25, 1848, in New York *Daily Tribune,* April 1, 1848; *Emancipator* (Boston), May 24, 1848; Duberman, *Adams,* 136-38; Wilson to C. F. Adams, New York, June 3, 1848, Adams MSS; Wilson to Joshua Giddings, April 10, 1847, Giddings MSS; J. N. Brewer to Schouler, May, 1848, William Schouler MSS; Wilson to Daniel Webster, May 31, 1848, Daniel Webster MSS, Dartmouth College, Hanover, N. H.; Edward L. Pierce, *Memoir and Letters of Charles Sumner* (4 vols.; Boston, 1877-1894), III, 164; J. B. Mann, *Reunion of Free Soilers in 1877* (Boston, 1877).

bribe." After adding that he planned to do all in his power to defeat Taylor, he marched out after Allen. Another delegate later told Amos A. Lawrence that Wilson, who had "behaved very impudently," cost Abbott Lawrence the nomination. Nathan Appleton blamed Lawrence's defeat on a "real conspiracy." Furious, he charged Allen and Wilson with "the most disgraceful piece of political swindling which has ever fallen within my ken." Such criticism from Whig capitalists did not harm Wilson, whereas his action at Philadelphia won him a good deal of public attention. The party bolter became a favorite target of the Whig press, which unintentionally helped to spread his name.[32]

The evening after Taylor's nomination, Wilson and fourteen other delegates from five states met in the emptied convention hall. Wilson, who had called the meeting, wanted to plan a national convention in August to organize a new Free Soil party. The others quickly agreed to his proposal and then left to go to their respective states to make preparations.[33] Wilson returned to Boston, where he was to embark upon an eight-year search for a new political party. No longer would he find a haven in a national political organization; he had willingly left the Whigs to seek the companionship of men who shared his opposition to "the contemptible oligarchy of the South" that controlled both Whigs and Democrats.[34]

Back in Massachusetts, Conscience Whigs began to meet with a few antislavery Democrats dissatisfied with their party's presidential nominee, Lewis Cass, in order to consolidate a third-party movement in the state. They issued a call for a state convention to meet in Worcester in June and watched with eager anticipation as similar conventions were held in New York and Ohio. At Worcester, the

[32]*Liberator* (Boston), June 16, 1848; H. E. Eastman to A. A. Lawrence, June 14, 1848, Amos A. Lawrence MSS, Massachusetts Historical Society; Nathan Appleton to Charles Sumner, Sept. 4, 1848, Sumner MSS; Boston *Atlas,* June 8, 10, 20, 21, 1848. Wilson wrote a letter to his constituents explaining his course at the convention; it was published in Boston *Atlas,* June 22, 1848. See *Atlas's* reply, June 22, and following issues, esp. June 29, July 24, Aug. 29, 1848.

[33]Pierce, *Sumner,* III, 165; Wilson, *Slave Power,* II, 142-44.

[34]Wilson's letter to constituents, Boston *Atlas,* June 22, 1848.

Massachusetts antislaveryites appointed a committee to coordinate a state campaign and selected delegates for a national convention of opponents of slavery extension. The national convention, which met at Buffalo in August, launched the Free Soil party and nominated Martin Van Buren of New York for president of the United States. The Conscience Whig leader from Massachusetts, Charles Francis Adams, was selected to run on the ticket with Van Buren.[35]

Massachusetts Free-Soilers selected S. C. Phillips as their gubernatorial candidate in the state campaign. In November the new party obtained about 30 percent of the state's vote and finished ahead of the Democrats, but the Whigs carried the state and national elections. Although a majority of the new party's leaders were former Whigs, much of the Free Soil vote came from Democrats who left their fast-sinking party. The 1848 campaign thus completed the ruin of the already divided Democratic party in Massachusetts, but it did not demonstrate the viability of the new political organization. The next two years would be important in determining whether the Massachusetts Free Soil party would maintain its independence and increase its power, or go the way of the Democrats.[36]

[35] Brauer, *Cotton Versus Conscience,* 239-43.

[36] Duberman, *Adams,* 157; Darling, *Political Changes,* 353-59.

3

Coalition Politics

Henry Wilson would play a key role in determining the future of the Free Soil party in Massachusetts. Its emergence marked a great personal victory for the man who had struggled since his entry into politics to create a party opposed to the Slave Power and its allies. Also, for the first time in his political career he could apply his developing political craftsmanship with some hope for personal success. His political intimate, J. B. Mann, admitted his friend was "intensely ambitious." For Wilson, the Free Soil party was the vanguard in the army of freedom; he wanted to be one of its highest officers. In 1849, his fellow Free-Soilers, respecting his talent for political management, elected him chairman of the state organization.[1]

The new position, which he held until 1853, gave Wilson great influence in party affairs. For the next four years, he traveled about the state patching and building the Free Soil organization, meeting party leaders, and familiarizing himself with local political conditions. He tried to supply what Palfrey and Adams failed to realize a new party needed: grass-roots organization, statewide political machinery, and shrewd management.[2] Unlike his rivals for leadership in the new political amalgam, the Natick cobbler was prepared to devote his every waking moment to politics. Palfrey was too timid and too afraid of controversy; Adams refused to subordinate himself to party discipline; Sumner lacked the willingness to give constant and careful attention to details of party organization; the Hoars and Allen were too busy with their legal careers. On the other hand, Wilson rebelled at the sight of his cobbler's bench. His shoe production, which had reached a high in 1847, fell off 50 percent during

the following election year. In the later summer of 1848, he decided
to take off his apron for good and devote his full attention to ballots
rather than brogans.[3]

Wilson's decision was a major step in his career. After 1848,
income from political office would be his sole source of livelihood.
The fact that his family's welfare depended on his political success
helps explain how for the next six years, until he won a seat in the
United States Senate, Wilson often appeared to place his personal
success ahead of party considerations. In abandoning the shoe business, Wilson also revealed his confidence in his own political abilities.
One of his former associates in the Whig party sneeringly remarked
that if Wilson "had as much modesty as he has of assurance and
brass, it would have much better comport with his standing and
talents."[4]

Wilson sought to turn his lack of social standing to political use.
Unlike his Boston associates, he had no compunction about mingling
with men from all walks of life. In his trips about the state he visited
factories, restaurants, and even saloons.[5] Soon he had formed a
corps of lieutenants of background and interest similar to his own.
Many of Wilson's new associates were journalists; so sensitive was he
to the power of the press, that he soon acquired his own paper. In
August, 1848, he and two Boston publishers assumed control of the
Boston *Whig*, which they renamed the *Republican*. The former cobbler hoped the paper would prove a money-making venture as well as
a political mouthpiece. Although it was primarily an antislavery Free
Soil organ, he included a variety of news topics and strove to increase its circulation. He edited the *Republican* until 1851. The new
enterprise kept him in Boston almost constantly; he saw even less of

[1] J. B. Mann, *Reunion of Free Soilers, 1877* (Boston, 1877); Sumner to
Palfrey, June 21, 1848, Palfrey MSS; Chester Adams to Mann, June 14, 1848,
Mann MSS; Nason and Russell, *Wilson*, 91.

[2] Donald, *Sumner*, 168; J. B. Mann in Natick *Bulletin*, Feb. 7, 1902.

[3] Bacon, *Natick*, 153; C. F. Adams Diary, Aug. 24, 1848.

[4] Chester Adams to Mann, June 14, 1848, Mann MSS.

[5] George F. Hoar, *Autobiography of Seventy Years* (2 vols.; New York,
1903), I, 218; Boutwell, *Reminiscences*, I, 79; Palfrey manuscript autobiography, p. 221, Palfrey MSS.

his family and friends in Natick. On the other hand his operations as editor of a metropolitan newspaper allowed him to meet hundreds of people both inside the state and out.[6]

The new editor wasted little time in announcing his proposals concerning the future course of the Free Soil party. Impatient for immediate success, he refused to wait while the new organization gathered enough adherents to challenge successfully the Massachusetts Whigs. Knowing Democrats as well as Free-Soilers shared a common enmity toward Boston and the state's "money power," he hoped that in the 1849 elections the two parties between them could gain enough votes to control the state legislature, keep the Whigs from gaining a popular majority, and then cooperate to fill the state offices. Former Democrat Amasa Walker encouraged his fellow Free-Soilers to enlarge their state platform to include Democratic proposals to regulate corporations more effectively, and Wilson heartily agreed. He had never been devoted to the interest of chartered groups. To ease the dismay of some Free-Soilers of Whig antecedents, who rebelled at Democratic proposals to reexamine and reform the whole corporate system in Massachusetts, Wilson insisted that the Bay State Democrats were moving toward a Free Soil position.[7]

As the state Free Soil convention of 1849 approached, the coalition movement gathered strength. The Democrats made a decided gesture toward fusion by passing antislavery resolutions. Massachusetts politicians found that similar coalitions had been effected in other states; talk of bargain and alliance filled the air. Wilson continued to load his paper with criticisms of "wealthy corporation influence" and called on Free-Soilers to support the "Free Democracy" and crush forever the "selfish, conservative, and corrupt money power." At the party convention, Wilson worked on the floor while Sumner presented a set of resolutions incorporating many Demo-

[6] The paper changed its name several times. *Emancipator and Republican,* Nov. 17, 1848, Feb. 6, 1849, Dec. 26, 1850.

[7] *Ibid.,* Dec. 12, 1848, Jan. 12, May 3, June 28, July 26, 1849; C. F. Adams Diary, Feb. 19, 23, 1849; Francis Bowen to Palfrey, Nov. 26, 1849, Palfrey MSS; Donald, *Sumner,* 178-79.

cratic proposals. The convention agreed to the resolutions but refused to recommend uniting with the Democrats. Undaunted, Wilson organized fusion nominations in Middlesex County to serve as an example for similar local coalitions across the state. He then took advantage of Democratic support to run successfully for the lower house of the state legislature.[8]

During 1850, from his position in the House, Wilson redoubled his efforts to form a full-scale coalition with the Democrats. Local alliances had returned 13 senators and 130 representatives to the state legislature. Wilson saw clearly that with better organization the Free-Soilers and Democrats could control both houses. In pursuing his plans, Wilson found two capable Democratic allies in the newly elected legislature. One of them, George Boutwell, Wilson already knew well; they had served together in the state legislature since 1842. The other, Nathaniel Banks, was new to Wilson, but the two men were similar enough in temperament and outlook to make cooperation easy. Banks and Boutwell shared with Wilson some degree of antislavery sentiment, although their position, more than his, smacked of political opportunism. Being practical politicians each was suspicious of the other—Banks once referred to Wilson as "the enemy of every man"—but they agreeably entered into a partnership benefiting them all.[9]

In the legislature the three men formulated a program on which to base a Free Soil-Democratic coalition. Wilson sought legislative approval of measures regulating corporation stock issues and railroad capitalization; he also revived his own proposal to abolish the death penalty for all crimes but murder, backed a mechanic's lien law, and joined Boutwell to press Democratic demands for increased popular control of Whiggish Harvard College. Wilson referred to the latter as the most important measure of the session and threatened to "cut

[8] *Emancipator and Republican,* Aug. 2, 23, 1849; Donald, *Sumner,* 182; Sumner to Palfrey, Sept. 13, 1849, Estes Howe to Palfrey, Sept. 13, 1849, Palfrey MSS; and letters from party members to Sumner, July through Aug., 1849, Sumner MSS.

[9] Pierce, *Sumner,* III, 188; Fred Harvey Harrington, *Fighting Politician: Major General N. P. Banks* (Philadelphia, 1948), 9.

the college adrift" if the bill failed. In addition, he supported a new temperance law restricting the sale of liquor and advocated legislation limiting hours of labor.[10]

Practically none of the measures Wilson introduced or advocated were passed by the Whig legislature, but the Natick politician had given the coalition a solid platform for the 1850 elections, and he could bitterly condemn the Whigs for resisting reform. He had satisfied the Democrats; now he needed the support of wavering Free-Soilers. As chairman of the Free Soil party, he tried hard to be friendly to all factions. Yet no matter what Wilson did, he managed to antagonize, either separately or as a group, Adams, Palfrey, S. C. Phillips, and the Hoars of Worcester.

The Adams-Palfrey clique centered their criticisms on Wilson's advocacy of a coalition with Democrats, which they were sure would lead to the destruction of the Free Soil party and its antislavery platform. Bitterly they condemned Wilson's attempt to get up "another truck and dicker." In 1849, however, Adams and Palfrey accepted coalition support in their bids for office. Unfortunately, Adams failed to gain a seat in the state Senate, while Palfrey proved unable to win a hotly contested congressional election. Both tended to blame Wilson and the coalition for their failure. Palfrey, who only a year before had praised Wilson as "a man of great courage . . . of superior mind, and uncommon powers of speech and action," now condemned him as an excessively ambitious "jobber and intriguer." In the legislature Wilson further antagonized the Free-Soilers of Whig antecedents by advocating greater public control of Harvard College as well as of business corporations.[11]

[10] *Emancipator and Republican,* Jan. 24, 31, Feb. 14, 21, 28, March 7, 14, 30, April 23, May 2, 1850; Massachusetts House Journal, 1850, appendices 2 and 16; Massachusetts House *Legislative Documents, 1850,* no. 34.

[11] C. F. Adams Diary, June 7, Oct. 4, Nov. 3, 10, 15, 1849; Sumner to Giddings, Oct. 19, 1849, Giddings MSS; Anson Burlingame to Robert Winthrop, Sept. 19, 1850, in Robert C. Winthrop, Jr., *A Memoir of Robert C. Winthrop* (Boston, 1897), 141; Hoar, *Autobiography,* I, 28-29, 217; Congdon, *Reminiscences,* 132; Richard Henry Dana, Jr., manuscript journal, Oct. 1849, Richard Henry Dana, Jr., MSS, Massachusetts Historical Society; Palfrey to Sumner, Feb. 28, March 4, 1848, and Palfrey manuscript autobiography, pp. 228, 284, Palfrey MSS. Palfrey was wrong about Wilson's coolness toward his

In January, 1850, when the Whig governor of Massachusetts attacked the expansion of slavery and supported abolition of the interstate slave trade and of slavery in the District of Columbia, Wilson was hard-pressed to convince his Free Soil critics that the coalition was the best vehicle for antislavery sentiment in the state. In February Wilson introduced his own antislavery resolutions, but they were referred to a committee, which kept them over a month.[12] In the meantime, on March 7, Wilson received unexpected assistance from Daniel Webster. On that day the Massachusetts senator called for support for a series of compromise proposals that would settle several issues relating to slavery then before the Congress. Webster's speech aroused and angered antislavery men throughout the state who were opposed to any accommodation to the interests of slaveholders. Wilson, realizing that Webster came up for reelection in 1851, now saw that he had an issue that would rally the faint-hearted Free-Soilers. He could use Webster to prove that the Whigs were not sufficiently antislavery and call for the coalition to control the next legislature and replace Webster with a man "true to the principles and sentiments of the commonwealth." When Webster resigned his Senate seat to become secretary of state and Robert Winthrop replaced him, Wilson did not cease agitating. Instead, ignoring the fact that Winthrop was no friend of the compromise, he insisted the move proved anew that nothing could be hoped for from the Whigs.[13]

Although in the fall Palfrey, Adams, and Richard Henry Dana, Jr., the latter a scion of one of Massachusetts' leading families, once again prevented the Free Soil party from endorsing the coalition, Wilson did obtain an agreement whereby individual members of the

---

candidacy. See *Emancipator and Republican,* Feb. 15, 1849; Sumner to Giddings, Aug. 20, 1849, Giddings-Julian MSS, Library of Congress; Wilson to E. A. Stansbury, May 8, 1851, Norcross MSS, Massachusetts Historical Society.

[12] Massachusetts House Journal, 1850, Jan. 11, 21, Feb. 4, 12, March 14, 19, 21; House *Legislative Documents, 1850,* Nos. 33, 87; J. Daniel Loubert, "The Orientation of Henry Wilson, 1812-1856" (Ph.D. dissertation, Boston University, 1956), 84-86.

[13] *Emancipator and Republican,* March 21, April 4, 18, June 20, Aug. 1, 1850; Pierce, *Sumner,* III, 221.

party could form local coalitions around the state.[14] Once again he received joint support for a Senate seat in the coming legislature. The resulting election revealed a clear-cut victory for the Free Soil-Democratic alliance. The coalition sent twenty-two senators to the upper house, whereas the Whigs elected only eight; there were ten vacancies which the coalitionists later filled. In the House, the coalition won a safe majority. Charles Francis Adams, noting that no congressional candidates won except those endorsed by Free-Soilers, could not restrain himself from approving the victory of the political arrangement he had so resisted: "The domination of Daniel Webster has been demolished." Wilson had done his work well. Instead of relaxing, however, he and the other coalitionists began planning for a division of state offices. Democrats were promised the posts of governor, speaker of the house, and short-term United States senator. Free-Soilers were to receive the six-year Senate post. When the Whig gubernatorial candidate realized the coalitionists would unite to displace him and bitterly attacked the "trading and swapping of oxen," Wilson simply replied "so long as the people were satisfied with the trade, it did not become the oxen to complain."[15]

In January, 1851, coalitionists in the Senate easily elected Wilson to the president's chair. When the Natick cobbler banged the gavel to convene the first session of the upper house, the noise awakened Massachusetts to the arrival of a new political order. Wilson, a former farm laborer and shoemaker, held a position formerly filled by scions of the best families of the state. He succeeded men like Josiah Quincy, Leverett Saltonstall, Harrison Gray Otis, and Levi Lincoln, who had classical educations, high social standing, and proper political associations. Massachusetts aristocrats watched with dismay as Wilson's coadjutants, Banks and Boutwell, likewise of obscure origin, accepted their rewards from the fusion movement; Boutwell became governor and Banks speaker of the house. When the coalitionists made Amasa Walker secretary of the Common-

[14]C. F. Adams Diary, Sept. 5, 10, 1850; Dana to R. H. Dana, Sr., Sept. 11, 1850, Dana MSS.
[15]Richard Henry Dana, Jr., to Ned, Nov. 12, 1850, Dana MSS; Hoar, *Autobiography*, I, 179; C. F. Adams Diary, Nov. 12, 1850.

wealth and former cobbler John Alley a member of the governor's council, Caleb Cushing, a former Whig turned ardent Democrat, caustically inquired if "the state was to be shoemakerized or not."[16]

Wilson wasted no time in putting the coalition agreement on office distribution into effect. He did not expect the senatorship, for Charles Sumner had the support of most Free-Soilers for the post. Once again conflicting ambitions plagued Wilson's plans. Adams considered running for the Senate with Whig support; S. C. Phillips, three-time Free Soil gubernatorial candidate, bitterly objected to being sacrificed while Sumner got the coveted nomination. Palfrey, feeling neglected in his continuing battle for a congressional seat, wrote an open letter to the Free Soil legislators disavowing the existence of any agreement to divide the state and national offices. The breach in the Free Soil party was growing wider.[17]

Wilson's main problem in electing Sumner did not lie with Free-Soilers. His party promptly fulfilled its half of the bargain by voting for Democratic candidates for state office and the post of short-term senator. Then the Democrats revolted. A small group of recalcitrants led by Caleb Cushing and encouraged by former governor Marcus Morton refused to vote for Sumner. Wilson was outraged, but he suppressed his anger in order to avoid alienating other Democrats. Quickly he formed a committee, which he headed, to devote every effort to securing Sumner's election. As balloting and debate dragged on through February, March, and into April, Wilson refused to allow the Free-Soilers to become discouraged. He visited members of both parties at their daily meetings and sought out legislators at their homes and in the state house lobbies. When Sumner gave Wilson a letter authorizing his withdrawal from the race, he refused to print it.[18]

---

[16] Boutwell, *Reminiscences,* I, 120; Boston *Commonwealth,* Jan. 2, 1850.

[17] C. F. Adams Diary, Oct. 15, 16, Dec. 20, 1850; S. C. Phillips to Sumner, Jan. 9, 1851, Sumner MSS; Marcus Morton to John B. Alley, March 21, 1851, Marcus Morton MSS, Massachusetts Historical Society. See also Richard Henry Dana, Jr., to Ned, March 2, 1851, Dana MSS; Samuel Gridley Howe to Horace Mann, Dec. 29, 1850, Samuel Gridley Howe MSS, Houghton Library, Harvard University. Even Marcus Morton agreed Free-Soilers were entitled to the United States senatorship.

Several Democrats offered to elect Wilson as a compromise candidate, but he ignored their overtures. He knew the Free-Soilers who opposed the coalition were not strongly opposed to Sumner, but they would revolt completely if he became the candidate. The Free Soil manager placed carefully phrased letters and editorials in the *Commonwealth,* praising Democrats who voted for Sumner and criticizing Morton and those who opposed the Free Soil candidate.[19] Still the handful of Democrats refused to move. When Wilson rejected suggestions that the Free-Soilers coerce the Democrats by opposing their reform measures, party members like Stephen Higginson attacked his "whining system" of seeking Democratic votes. He complained that the party's "strongest men" sat outside its councils, leaving in control "the same drivers who have run our good Free Soil coach plump into the mire."[20]

On April 24, the state legislature silenced Wilson's critics by finally making Charles Sumner a United States senator. That evening a great crowd gathered on Beacon Street and moved on to the Old State House, where Wilson and a few other Free Soil leaders spoke to them. The coalitionist leader insisted that he bore no grudges; he praised the "mass of the Democracy" for standing by Sumner and pleaded with Free-Soilers to "let bygones be bygones." Wilson was never one to let anger and personal frustration interfere with his political schemes. But when a few voices in the crowd sent up a cheer for Daniel Webster, Wilson grew stern. He stopped the scattered applause with the observation that from March 7, 1850, the day Webster repudiated the sentiments of Massachusetts, "the Whig party has been prostrated and iron heels are upon it."[21]

For a time Wilson basked in Sumner's reflected glory, as Free-Soilers praised his energy, skill, and perseverance in obtaining

---

[18] C. F. Adams Diary, Dec. 27, 1850; Boston *Commonwealth,* March 18, April 26, 1851; Wilson to E. A. Stansbury, Jan. 31, 1851, Wilson MSS, Library of Congress.

[19] Pierce, *Sumner,* III, 242. Wilson gave a detailed history of the negotiations over the coalition, in letters to the Boston *Commonwealth,* Jan. 30 and Feb. 18, 1851.

[20] Stephen Higginson to Sumner, Jan. 17, 1851, Sumner MSS.

[21] Boston *Commonwealth,* April 25, 1851.

Sumner's election. When Sumner told Wilson "you must take the responsibility of having placed me in the Senate of the United States," he gladly accepted the charge. He knew the new senator owed him a debt that might deter him from challenging Wilson's future schemes.[22]

The success of the coalition raised Wilson's hopes. For a moment he had been worried; at the beginning of the year he had been forced to admit his newspaper was a failure, and he had closed it down. The venture cost him $7,000, yet the newspaper had served its purpose. With its aid Wilson had circulated his plans for a coalition, met new people, and solidified his control over party machinery. If the coalition's disparate elements could be held together he might have several more years of political office. In the summer of 1851 he was renominated for the state Senate; but he now had his eye on a higher post, that of governor of the state.[23]

To strengthen his candidacy, Wilson worked quietly to soothe wounded feelings and heal over old breaches within Free Soil ranks. His friendly, benign disposition aided his political calculations. Even bitter Charles Francis Adams weakened somewhat in the face of Wilson's "naturally good temperament" as Wilson paid him compliments and sought his advice.[24] Yet Wilson's efforts went for naught. At the party convention in September he overplayed his hand, trying "by the force of mere authority" to get the convention to adopt a set of resolutions he introduced, and then by spreading rumors against John Palfrey, who seemed to have the most support to replace Phillips as the standard-bearer. Too many delegates proved unwilling to nominate the scheming cobbler. Quickly sizing up the situation, Wilson withdrew his own feelers and instead sought to gain

[22] *Ibid.*, May 3, 15, 1851; Sumner to Wilson, April 25, 1851, quoted in Pierce, *Sumner*, III, 249; Wilson to Sumner, Dec. 15, 1851, Sept. 5, 1852, Feb. 26, July 2, 1854, Sumner MSS.

[23] Mann, *Wilson*, 91; Boston *Commonwealth*, Oct. 2, 1851; C. F. Adams Diary, July 21, 1851.

[24] Wilson to Mann, Oct. 16, 1851 (two letters), Mann MSS; Wilson to Palfrey, May 19, 1851, Palfrey MSS; Wilson to G. F. Hoar, Oct. 13, 1851, Hoar Family MSS, Massachusetts Historical Society; C. F. Adams to Wilson, Oct. 31, 1851, Boston Public Library; C. F. Adams Diary, Nov. 21, 1851.

credit for the ultimate nomination of Palfrey. The Boston ex-clergy-man, who had been so bitterly critical of the coalition, readily accepted the proffered candidacy.[25]

In the November elections, the coalition worked well again. Democrats in Middlesex chose not to run a candidate for the state Senate against Wilson, who defeated his Whig opponent easily. Once more voters gave the coalition a majority of the legislature; again the Democrat, Boutwell, became governor rather than the Free Soil candidate, while Wilson resumed the presidency of the Senate. He looked forward with eagerness and anticipation to the new legislative year.[26]

[25] C. F. Adams Diary, Sept. 15, 22, 1851; Boston *Commonwealth,* Sept. 17, 1851; T. W. Higginson to Mother, Oct. 30, 1851, Thomas W. Higginson MSS, Houghton Library, Harvard University.

[26] Boston *Commonwealth,* Nov. 12, 17, 1851.

4

From Defeat to Victory

By November, 1851, Henry Wilson had achieved a good deal of success in advancing both himself and the antislavery cause. He had left the Whigs to help create a Free Soil party opposed to Southern interests, and he had formed a coalition that sent a dedicated opponent of slavery to the United States Senate. Already president of the state Senate, Wilson could hope to become governor the following year or perhaps even go to Washington. His old friend, the Reverend Samuel Hunt, was amazed at the Natick politician's self-assurance; he seemed to feel he was far more qualified to sit in Congress than many of the men who were there.[1] Unfortunately for Wilson, the events of the next two years would bring him one defeat after another, erase his confidence, and leave him with his political ambitions all but destroyed.

The presidential campaign and election in 1852 provided Wilson with his first warning of political disaster. The Free Soil party had already lost strength in the North in local elections, and now Free Soil Democrats, anticipating a Democratic victory in the fall, showed signs of rejecting coalition tactics in order to rejoin their old party comrades. The country seemed tired of antislavery agitation, and Wilson began to look elsewhere for issues upon which to erect a strong Northern political party.[2]

In the first years of the 1850s, such issues abounded. Americans were especially interested in the revolutions which had burst out in Europe in 1848 and were quite excited when Louis Kossuth, leader of the Hungarian battle for national independence, came to the

United States in 1851 to seek assistance for his cause. Wilson, who was quite impressionable and easily swayed by popular currents or emotional issues, responded enthusiastically when Kossuth visited Massachusetts. Yet his impetuous nature, which he clearly revealed in the case of Kossuth, rarely led him into paths which he could not turn to practical account. He was convinced that support for American intervention in the European revolutions would be strong enough to provide the basis of a new political party, which could later be used in the cause of freedom at home. So confident was Wilson that Northern Democrats would join Free-Soilers in such a party that he utterly astonished his friends by suggesting that they support Michigan Democrat Lewis Cass for president. Cass had strenuously avoided the slavery issue, but he had spoken strongly in favor of American aid to Hungary.[3]

Enthusiasm for the Hungarian cause quickly dwindled, however, and Cass soon softened his own belligerent stand on the question. Discouraged in his hopes of merging the Free Soil movement into a larger organization dedicated to freedom, Wilson went off to Pittsburgh to attend the party's national convention. He was delighted that the Free-Soilers had decided to meet in the Western city. He wanted to win the support of the West for the antislavery cause and had been advising Sumner in the Senate "to adopt a liberal line of policy toward that section." In August he made his first trip across the mountains to visit the Pennsylvania city. There delegates chose him president of the convention. Once organized, the party nominated Senator John P. Hale of New Hampshire for president.[4]

[1] John G. Palfrey manuscript journal, Sept. 6, 1852, Palfrey MSS; Hunt's reminiscences in Natick *Bulletin*, Jan. 28, 1876.

[2] Wilson to Sumner, Feb. 3, 17, March 9, 1852, Sumner MSS.

[3] [Lajos Kossuth], *Kossuth in New England* (Boston, 1852); Boston *Commonwealth*, Feb. 17, May 5, 1852; Pierce, *Sumner*, III, 269; Wilson to Sumner, Dec. 15, 1851, Jan. 5, 10, Feb. 17, May 4, Aug. 3, 1852, James W. Stone to Sumner, Dec. 16, 1851, July 3, 1852, C. F. Adams to Sumner, Jan. 1, 1852, E. L. Pierce to Sumner, Jan. 17, 1852, Sumner MSS.

[4] Wilson to Sumner, Feb. 3, 1852, Sumner MSS; Boston *Commonwealth*, Aug. 12, 13, 1852. In the Massachusetts Senate Wilson also advocated a liberal land policy for the West. See Boston *Commonwealth*, March 24, 25, 1852.

Returning to Massachusetts, Wilson worked to save the coalition for another state election. In 1852 the biggest danger to the alliance was the handsome egotist in the United States Senate, Charles Sumner. By working hard to get Sumner into the Senate, Wilson had managed to overcome fears that the coalition would destroy antislavery agitation. Unfortunately, much to the anguish of Wilson and his fellow Free-Soilers, the great voice of Free-Soilism, instead of bursting forth with denunciations of the Slave Power, had chosen to remain silent. Sumner's lack of activity seemed to justify the Free-Soiler who wailed that "the *morale* of our party is *chloroformed.*"[5]

Only a speech from Sumner would save the party from asphyxiation. At first Wilson merely told the senator he hoped Sumner would speak on slavery before the session closed. As late as May, he advised the senator to consult his own "sense of duty" in choosing the right moment for a speech. The next month, however, he visited Sumner in Washington to ask him to speak out. The Whigs had begun to taunt coalitionists and Free-Soilers about their senator's silence, and the sarcasm stung Wilson. In August, dropping his none-too-subtle hints to Sumner, he excitedly pleaded with the senator: "Do not for Heaven's sake fail to speak, cost what it may of effort or trouble . . . our people are in a state of disappointment and almost of despair."[6]

As Wilson struggled with Sumner over antislavery speeches, Free-Soilers in Massachusetts prepared to select their gubernatorial nominee. Although Wilson publicly denied his ambition for the honor, privately he sounded out Free-Soilers about his possible nomination. At the convention, his supporters were overconfident and failed to speak to several important delegations. The anti-Wilsonites, however, who were eager to defeat the ambitions of the man whom Charles Francis Adams regarded as a "third rate man, with the arts of a first rate demagogue," were quite active in behalf of Horace Mann, and to

[5] Donald, *Sumner,* 222-27; Samuel Downer to Charles Sumner, May 7, 1852, Sumner MSS.

[6] Wilson to Sumner, March 9, June 29, July 7, Aug. 3, 1852; J. W. Stone to Sumner, June 9, 1852 (two letters), Sumner MSS; Boston *Traveller,* June 8, 1852.

the surprise of all, Mann won the gubernatorial candidacy.[7] Wilson
was furious, but he soon stemmed his anger. Mann was retiring from
Congress, and again Wilson sought to fill the opening. On October 12
the Free Soil district convention chose him, and he immediately
sought to insure his election by getting the Democratic nominee,
bulky Benjamin F. Butler of Lowell, to agree to control the vote and
allow Wilson to defeat the Whig candidate. Butler refused to withdraw in favor of Wilson, however, and once more the Natick cobbler
failed in his bid for office.[8]

The fall of 1852 brought nothing but defeat and disappointment
for Henry Wilson. Not only had he lost his bid for the governorship
and the House of Representatives, but the coalition was disintegrat-
ing. Enough Free Soil and coalition Democrats returned to their
former allegiance to allow the Whigs to carry the state for the first
time since 1848. On the national scene, the Democratic party,
instead of collapsing, won the election and installed its own candidate in the White House. Wilson was crushed. Dismally observing to
Sumner that "these are dark days for us and for our cause," he
decided to "hope on and labor for a better day."[9]

The 1852 election had left Wilson with one hopeful result. The
citizenry of Massachusetts, while throwing the coalition out of
office, had accepted the alliance's demand for a constitutional
convention. Through the operations of the convention, which was to
meet in May, 1853, Wilson and other coalitionist leaders hoped to
revive their near-dead political fortunes and deal the state Whig party
a fatal blow. Their chief aim was to increase the legislative representation of the smaller cities and towns at the expense of the large

[7]C. F. Adams Diary, Sept. 3, 6, 9, 11, 13, 14, 15, 18, 1852; R. M. Devens
to Wilson, Aug. 12, 1852 (copy), Mann MSS; R. H. Dana, Jr., manuscript
journal, Sept. 15, 1852, Dana, Jr., to R. H. Dana, Sr., Sept. 14, 17, 1852, R.
H. Dana, Sr., to Dana, Jr., Sept. 18, 1852, Dana MSS; T. W. Higginson to
Palfrey, Sept. 16, 1852, Palfrey MSS; Boston *Commonwealth*, Sept. 8, 14, 16,
17, 1852.

[8]C. F. Adams Diary, Sept. 15, 18, 1852; Boston *Commonwealth*, Oct. 13,
22, Nov. 10, 24, Dec. 6, 17, 1852; Pierce, *Sumner*, III, 318; Robinson, ed.,
Warrington, 401.

[9]Wilson to Sumner, Dec. 21, 1852, Sumner MSS.

Whig-dominated eastern cities. In particular, Wilson and his friends
hoped to reduce Boston's delegation in the legislature and substitute
ward elections for the general ticket system in the city. Use of the
general ticket allowed the Whigs to send a solid delegation of forty-
-four party members to the General Court. Coalitionists also wanted
to institute the secret ballot and thereby weaken Whig industrialists'
control over their workers' votes. The Democrats, and some of their
Free Soil allies, also planned on expanding public control over
Harvard, increasing elective offices, limiting judicial tenures, removing property qualifications for voting and office-holding, and insert-
ing a general incorporation law in the constitution.[10]

As the coalitionists busied themselves with preparations for the
convention, Wilson grew more optimistic. He was certain the voters
of Massachusetts would approve a new body of organic law and
simultaneously propel the Free Soil-Democratic alliance into power
again. And, as "the leading spirit" of the coalition, Wilson was sure
he could gain the elusive gubernatorial nomination.[11] The coalitionist leader planned his moves carefully. By taking advantage of
the fact that candidates for the convention could run from towns
where they did not reside, Wilson could load the convention with
dedicated coalitionists. He did offer to assist Palfrey, Mann, and
Phillips in elections for delegate seats, but they refused to enter their
names. Adams and Dana chose to run, but only the latter was victorious. Wilson created rotten boroughs for Boutwell, Sumner, and
several other coalitionists and insured his own election by running in
Berlin as well as Natick.[12]

[10] For a general discussion of the coalitionists and the constitutional
convention, see Samuel Shapiro, "The Conservative Dilemma: The Massachusetts Constitutional Convention of 1853," *New England Quarterly,*
XXXIII (June, 1960), 207-24; Carol Jean Kenney, "An Analysis of Political
Alignments in Massachusetts as Revealed in the Constitutional Convention of
1853" (M.A. thesis, Smith College, 1951), *passim.*

[11] Samuel Downer to Horace Mann, Feb. 16, 1853, Mann MSS; Samuel
Gridley Howe to Sumner, Jan. 16, 1853, quoted in Laura E. Richards, ed.,
Letters and Journals of Samuel Gridley Howe (2 vols.; Boston, 1906-1909), II,
391; C. F. Adams Diary, Feb. 12, March 26, 1853.

[12] C. F. Adams Diary, Feb. 10, 12, March 3, 5, 9, 16, 1853; Wilson to
Gentlemen of the State Committee, Feb. 26, 1853, Houghton Library, Har-

Wilson's earnest efforts resulted in utter defeat for the Whigs,
who won only about one-third of the convention seats. He also
managed to lay the groundwork for his own plans to dominate the
convention. One of the Free-Soilers estimated that at least 100 of
the 420 delegates were ready to follow Wilson's lead. Most of the
prominent coalitionists attended, while the Whigs sent a galaxy of
ex-governors, newspaper editors, and lawyers. Despite the number of
famous names that filled the list of delegates, Wilson and George
Boutwell shaped proceedings more than any other convention
members. The former secured several important committee chair-
manships and carefully shepherded his flock of followers; the latter
became president of the convention and deftly guided its proceedings.[13]

During the seventy-two day session, which lasted until August 1,
Wilson was constantly on the convention floor. He did not miss an
hour of the proceedings. In the middle of July, when Boutwell
became ill, he served about a week as president *pro tem* of the
convention; Dana found him "clumsy and forgetful and undecided"
in the chair. He talked with representatives of all parties and appeared good natured and well disposed toward all attending.[14]

Wilson's speeches, though lacking the eloquence of Sumner's and
the brilliance of Dana's, were frequent and effective. He knew that
the coalition's large majority in the convention represented only a
slim majority of the state's population. He also realized that the
coalition was threatened by divisions between Democrats and Free-
Soilers, city and rural Democrats, and Free-Soilers of Whig and

---

vard University; Robinson, ed., *Warrington*, 402-3; Richard Henry Dana, Jr.,
manuscript journal, Feb. 23, 1853, Dana MSS; Boston *Commonwealth*, March
8, 1853; Wilson to Sumner, March 5, 10, 1853, Sumner MSS; Donald, *Sumner*,
244-46.

[13] Kenney, "Constitution," 29, 32-33; Boutwell, *Reminiscences*, I, 228;
James Schouler, "Massachusetts Convention of 1853," Massachusetts Histor-
ical Society *Proceedings*, 2nd ser. XVIII (1903-1904), 30-48; Pierce, *Sumner*,
III, 328.

[14] *Official Report of the Debates and Proceedings in the State Convention
Assembled May 4, 1853, to Revise and Amend the Constitution of the
Commonwealth of Massachusetts* (2 vols.; Boston, 1853), I, 148; II, 257;
Richard H. Dana, Jr., manuscript journal, Aug. 2, 1853, Dana MSS.

Democratic antecedents. Therefore he constantly and openly introduced compromises on a variety of controversial issues, until delegates began to wonder if he would bargain away every major reform
the coalitionists hoped to effect. One of the convention members
observed that Wilson played a leading role "as a manager and con-
triver of expedients, and a feeler of the public pulse." The delegate
from Natick put his political philosophy that "half a loaf is better
than no bread" to good use.[15]

Although Wilson proved willing to compromise most issues
confronting the convention, he attacked various forms of legal privilege with conviction and determination. Arraigning the Boston
aristocracy for dictating "to those more intelligent but less wealthy
than themselves," he condemned tax paying qualifications for office
and voting and demanded the secret ballot to protect workers from
oppression by their wealthy employers. Reflecting on his own childhood, he observed that "poverty is bitter enough to be borne without the degradation of disfranchisement." Enthusiastically pressing
the coalition's plan to increase popular control over Harvard, he
condemned the class of Boston men who thought they were born to
"guard, guide, govern, direct, and control" the school and protect it
from "outside barbarians." He also continued his battle of the previous decade to gain equal rights for Massachusetts Negroes. He
condemned discrimination in the state militia, demanded equality
for all before the law, and made sure that blacks were eligible for the
governorship.[16]

Wilson and the coalitionists did their work well. If the people
accepted the constitution in the fall elections Whig political power
would be greatly weakened. Quickly Wilson went to work to secure
ratification of the constitution and also the Free Soil nomination for
governor. He defended the new organic law before his local constituents, reminding "ardent reformers" who were not satisfied with the

[15] Kenney, "Constitution," 36-38, 49-50, 74-75; *Official Report of
Debates,* I, 160-62, 214, 215, 369; II, 7-10, 25-27, 36-38, 49-50, 228, 238-40;
Richard Henry Dana, Jr., manuscript journal, Aug. 2, 1853, Dana MSS.

[16] *Official Report of Debates,* I, 63, 66-67, 74, 99, 174, 180, 247-48, 301,
348, 407, 555-58; II, 348, 376, 436, 441-45.

constitution that Massachusetts was an old state, with ancient traditions. Her people "shrank from untried experiments [and] . . . radical measures." The editors of the *Commonwealth* accurately predicted that Wilson would receive the Free Soil gubernatorial nomination. When the party convention met on September 16, he met no resistance. Gladly Wilson accepted the proffered honor.[17]

At last Henry Wilson had achieved an important victory. Although he was optimistic about the election, he expected a sharp fight and demanded that the *Commonwealth* editors put more sting into their editorials and cease being "respectable." He ranted to Sumner that "I for one don't want the endorsement of 'the best society' in Boston until I am dead—then all of us are sure of it—for it endorses everything that is dead." The Whigs were blistering Wilson with editorials, and in return he wanted a paper that would "fling bricks!" The Free Soil gubernatorial candidate expected to bombard Whigs, however, not his own party members. Unfortunately it became increasingly clear that the Adams group intended to destroy his political ambitions.[18]

At first, Free Soil opposition to Wilson and the constitution remained private rather than public. Adams, who viewed Wilson "as a mere demagogue, untrue, flexible, needy and ambitious," decided not to vote for him, but he hesitated to come out publicly against the constitution. Richard Henry Dana, who had little use for Wilson, or any "men who eat, and drink, and breathe politics . . . [who have] ousted men like myself . . . who stay at home, and have but few hours to devote to the subject," still decided to support the party and the constitution. Adams was sure the young aristocrat had been softened "by Wilson's deferential manners, and . . . by the serpent's whisper of the Attorney Generalship." Fearing the constitution would endanger an independent judiciary, E. R. Hoar called a meeting of those opposed to the document and demanded public declarations against it. In October, just three weeks before the elec-

[17]George S. Boutwell, *Address . . . to the People of Berlin, Upon the Provisions of the New Constitution* (Boston, 1853), 1-16; Boston *Commonwealth,* Sept. 7, 16, 1853; Wilson, *Address to Constituents* (Boston, 1853).

[18]Wilson to Sumner, Sept. 1, 1853, Sumner MSS.

tion, Palfrey published an open letter condemning the constitution. Adams then joined Palfrey and the Hoars in public denunciation of the document.[19]

With the first election returns, Wilson realized the voters were demolishing his hopes for a revival of the coalition and his own political fortunes. He was badly beaten in the gubernatorial race. The constitution fared better, but a heavy voter turnout defeated the document by a narrow margin. Wilson was both bitter and humiliated. For the first time Whig ridicule penetrated his defenses. A Free-Soiler pityingly noted that "the Whigs are taunting, sneering, and levelling all their envenomed shafts at him."[20]

A variety of factors had combined to give victory to the Whigs. Large towns, fearing loss of representation, voted against the constitution; Irish Catholics, critical of a clause withdrawing public money for parochial schools, voted solidly for the Whigs; Caleb Cushing, now in President Pierce's administration, condemned the coalition and instructed Democrats to withdraw from it; large numbers of western Whigs refused to bolt their party in order to increase their representation. Wilson, however, blamed Free Soil opposition to his schemes. He sent a caustic letter to Gamaliel Bailey of the Washington *National Era,* in which he criticized Adams and Palfrey; the editor refused to print the attack.[21]

Bitter attacks on the enemies of the constitution could not assuage Wilson's disappointment. The disintegration of the coalition left him without office, with a shattered party, and few dependable friends. Also, his plans for creating a Northern political organization to take possession of the national government had dissolved with the

[19] C. F. Adams Diary, Sept. 16, 19, 29, Oct. 28, 1853; E. R. Hoar to Palfrey, Oct. 7, 1853, Palfrey MSS; Richard H. Dana, Jr., manuscript journal, Sept. 29, 1853, Dana MSS; Shapiro, "Conservative Dilemma," 216, 223.

[20] Pierce, *Sumner,* III, 342.

[21] Shapiro, "Conservative Dilemma," 220-24; Pierce, *Sumner,* III, 339-40; Kenney, "Constitution," 85-90; *Commonwealth,* Nov. 15, 24, 1853; E. L. Pierce to Charles Sumner, Jan. 23, 1854, Sumner MSS; *National Era* (Washington), Dec. 15, 1853; Robinson, ed., *Warrington,* 204. One Free-Soiler thought the division in the party stemmed from Adams's and Palfrey's jealousy "of the favor shown by the masses to Wilson." A. G. Browne to Charles Sumner, Feb. 22, 1854, Sumner MSS.

decline of antislavery agitation and the demonstrated strength of the
national Democratic party. Wilson, dependent on political success to
provide him with an income, had to return to Natick to begin
making brogans once more.[22]

In January, 1854, the despondent cobbler was working in his
shop on Central Street in Natick when he first received word that
Senator Stephen A. Douglas had asked Congress to repeal the ban
against slavery in the territories of Kansas and Nebraska. As the
congressional debate on the proposed legislation grew more embittered, and as public criticism of Douglas and his bill grew more
vociferous, Wilson became greatly excited. Exultantly he told
Sumner that "whatever the results of the bill . . . one good has come
of it. The seals are broken and all will now discuss the question of
slavery." For the first time, the North seemed ready to unite in the
face of renewed aggressions of the Slave Power. With a proper
amount of agitation and activity, Wilson and his antislavery friends
might be able to parlay Northern anger into a new political movement.[23]

His political instincts aroused, Wilson joined with others in Massachusetts in attacking Sumner's colleague in the Senate, Edward Everett, for not condemning Douglas's actions. According to Wilson,
Everett was "down among the dead men"; he hoped the old Whig
would resign.[24] On May 17, Everett bowed before the pressure and
stepped from his Senate seat. The state's governor made an interim
appointment, but the legislature to be elected in the fall would have
to make a permanent choice. Wilson, eager to make sure the legislature would be antislavery, asked his party members to "relinquish all
party considerations" and seek a fusion of state voters opposed to
"the Nebraska iniquity." Full of jubilation, he and his friends drew

[22] Wilson to Sumner, Jan. 5, 1854, Sumner MSS; Pierce, *Sumner,* III, 342;
C. F. Adams Diary, Feb. 23, 1853. In 1854 Wilson made 23,000 pairs of shoes
and employed twenty-eight hands. Natick *Bulletin,* Oct. 29, 1870.

[23] Wilson to Sumner, Jan. 18, Feb. 26, 1854, Sumner MSS; Samuel Gridley
Howe to Sumner, Jan. 29, 1854, Howe MSS, Houghton Library, Harvard
University.

[24] For Wilson's denunciations of Everett's course, see Wilson to Sumner,
Feb. ?, 26, March 15, 16, 22, 1854, Sumner MSS.

up a call for a fusion meeting at Worcester and urged representatives of all parties to attend.[25]

The convention, which met on July 20, unfortunately contained few Whigs and Democrats. Adams and his friends also shunned the gathering, leaving the Natick cobbler and his associates to run the meeting. Urging the delegates to forget their differences, Wilson asked them to "create an organization that will place antislavery men in Congress." Conventioners proclaimed the organization of a "Republican party" and set a date for a meeting to nominate candidates for state office. When the second convention met in September, delegates immediately made Wilson the Republican gubernatorial candidate.[26]

Thus Wilson's frantic anti-Nebraska activity bore quick fruit. His plans, however, were not very successful. He had counted on large accessions of Massachusetts Whigs to bolster the new party's vote, but they preferred to carry on their own opposition to Douglas's territorial bill. Many of the old Free-Soilers also refused to follow Wilson into the new Republican movement; they stayed on the sidelines with Adams and his friends. Wilson's agitation against Nebraska and his willingness to forgo past differences in an effort to create a new antislavery party had won him the respect of many who had criticized his coalition schemes, but some of his former adherents, like Frank Bird, viewed Wilson's gubernatorial nomination with foreboding. Bird and Adams thought that the Republican party was just a move to save old coalitionists, and Bird feared Wilson would use his nomination to bargain with yet another newly formed political organization, the Know-Nothing party.[27]

Political disintegration swept Massachusetts in 1854. The emergence of the mysterious Know-Nothing organization only emphasized the utter unpredictability of state political develop-

[25] John B. Alley to Sumner, June 5, 1854, Wilson to Sumner, July 2, 1854, Sumner MSS; Boston *Commonwealth,* June 1, 19, 29, 1854.

[26] Boston *Commonwealth,* July 21, 27, Aug. 5, Sept. 8, 1854; George S. Merriam, *Life and Times of Samuel Bowles* (2 vols.; New York, 1885), I, 121-23; Duberman, *Adams,* 192; Donald, *Sumner,* 267.

[27] F. A. Bird to Charles Sumner, April 16, 1854, Sumner MSS; Bird to C. F. Adams, Sept. 7, 1854, C. F. Adams Diary, July 22, Sept. 7, 19, 1854.

ments. The new order first appeared in Massachusetts in the winter of 1853-1854, when inhabitants of towns across the state began to notice heart-shaped bits of white paper scattered in the streets. Inquirers learned that the papers announced the gatherings of unnamed members of an unknown fraternal group in undesignated rooms in order to discuss limiting the political power of immigrants and Catholics. Such clandestine activities seemed harmless, until voters in city elections saw well-known Whig and Democratic nominees completely overwhelmed by an avalanche of votes cast for mystery candidates. The secret organization had moved into politics. In March Know-Nothings seized control of a dozen cities and towns in eastern Massachusetts. Few had any idea of what the new order might accomplish in statewide elections.

The new political party drew its power from a variety of sources. From 1850 to 1855, to the alarm of natives anxious to maintain control over jobs and politics, immigration into the state had rapidly increased. The new immigrants were mostly Irish Catholics, and they tended to vote as a group. In Massachusetts, from 1845 to 1855, a single party was rarely able to gain a popular majority in elections. Therefore the Irish block vote became an important force in determining election results. The Irish almost always supported the Democrats, but in 1853 they voted solidly against the proposed constitution. They also resisted the passage of an 1852 prohibition law. Free-Soilers were alarmed when many Irishmen supported the fugitive slave law, aided the rendition of a fugitive slave, Anthony Burns, and defended the Kansas-Nebraska Act. Convinced that the Irish would have to be eliminated from politics before reform could take place, coalitionists flocked by the hundreds into the Know-Nothing party. Nathaniel Banks and Anson Burlingame led the movement. They were joined by thousands of Massachusetts citizens who were tired of "rum and Niggers" and who hoped to concentrate on new issues.[28]

[28] Edward Everett to Mrs. Charles Eames, Oct. 9, 1854, Edward Everett MSS, Massachusetts Historical Society; James W. Stone to Sumner, March 15, 1854, Sumner MSS; Oscar Handlin, *Boston's Immigrants* (rev. ed.; Cambridge, Mass., 1959), 191-98; George H. Haynes, "Causes of Know Nothing Success in

The large Free Soil coalitionist element in the Know-Nothing party gave it a fairly strong antislavery bent. Since many of Wilson's friends were Know-Nothings, members of the budding Republican party wondered what their standard-bearer might do; some were afraid that Bird's fears might be justified. Few had any idea of the actual strength of the new political organization. In the bewildering array of parties—Free Soil, Republican, Democratic, Whig, and now Know-Nothing—only the most incautious were ready to hazard a guess as to the outcome of the fall elections. Wilson, who through his wide net of local connections had always been excellently informed about state politics, had no doubt of the nativists' political power. Early in 1854, before the formation of the Republican party, he had furtively joined the new order.[29]

The new Know-Nothing convert had no strong personal views on nativism. In 1845 he had joined the Whig party in demanding revision of naturalization laws, but in 1853 in the constitutional convention he had defended the rights of "men of every race, clime and country." His views depended on the pressures of politics. In 1845 he sought the votes of nativists; in 1853 he wanted the support of Irish Catholics. Now, in 1854, he was ready to take advantage of the renewal of a powerful nativist sentiment in Massachusetts. He made no public statements on nativism, but in accepting the Republican gubernatorial nomination, he had praised "the descendants of that sturdy Puritan race, which from the beginning of our history has ever been prompt and resolute in defense of liberty." By late September most people in the state accepted the rumor that Wilson

---

Massachusetts," *American Historical Review,* III (1897), 77-82; Godfrey T. Anderson, "The Slavery Issue in Massachusetts Politics from the Compromise of 1850 to the Outbreak of the Civil War" (Ph.D. dissertation, University of Chicago, 1944), 121, 146. Bean's helpful study of Massachusetts politics in the 1850s indicates the Know-Nothing legislature was a revival of the coalition. See W. G. Bean, "Puritan versus Celt, 1850-1860," *New England Quarterly,* VII (1934), 70-89.

[29] Edward Everett to Mrs. Charles Eames, Sept. 30, 1854, Everett MSS; Wilson to Sumner, July 2, 1854, Seth Webb to Sumner, July 14, 1854, Sumner MSS; Samuel Gridley Howe to Theodore Parker [Sept. 1854], Howe MSS, Houghton Library, Harvard University; Nason and Russell, *Wilson,* 119; Boston *Commonwealth,* Sept. 12, 16, 1854.

had indeed joined the new party. Robert Winthrop believed that if the order had enlisted Wilson, "they are not unlikely to become a power. He is far too shrewd to allow himself to be made a cats-paw."[30]

When the state Know-Nothing convention met on October 18, Wilson attended, but he declined to seek the party's nomination for governor. Samuel Bowles, editor of the *Springfield Republican,* charged Wilson with conniving with Anson Burlingame and Henry Gardner, a Boston wool merchant and former Whig, in order to get Gardner the gubernatorial nomination. In return, Burlingame was to go to the House and Wilson to the Senate. Whatever the agreement, Gardner did become the Know-Nothing candidate for governor.[31]

Republican party leaders were aghast at Wilson's actions. No one yet knew what he would do about the gubernatorial nomination the party had given him, but many feared he would not run against Gardner. Old Free-Soiler Charles Allen attended a Republican meeting in order to attack Wilson and the Know-Nothings. He felt Wilson's intrigues were "beyond conception" and wished Sumner would use his influence against the conniver. Sumner, however, said nothing; he would not attack the man who had engineered his election to the Senate. Wilson continued to attend Republican meetings, defended the Republican platform, which had an explicit disclaimer of all regard for any distinctions of birth or color, and permitted no one to divine his intentions. Finally, only a few days before the election, he notified the Republican state committee that he declined his nomination. The committee, after long discussion, agreed not to accept Wilson's withdrawal, but the publication of his letter presaged the complete collapse of the Republican fusion organization.[32]

[30] Massachusetts Senate Journal, Feb. 6, 1845; Massachusetts Senate *Legislative Documents, 1845,* Document No. 44; *Official Report of the Debates,* I, 99, 166-67; Winthrop, *Memoir,* 168; C. F. Adams Diary, Aug. 30, 1854; Boston *Evening Telegraph,* Oct. 3, 1854.

[31] Boston *Evening Telegraph,* Oct. 17, 20, 1854; Merriam, *Bowles,* I, 125.

[32] Boston *Evening Telegraph,* Oct. 27, Nov. 1, 2, 4, 1854; C. F. Adams Diary, Oct. 25, 1854.

No one then expected the Republicans to make any showing in the fall elections; few, however, foresaw the shattering blow that the Know-Nothings were to deal all three of their party rivals. Gardner received 80,102 votes, giving him a majority of 35,000 over the Republican, Democratic, and Whig nominees. Wilson's total of 13,416 placed him third, behind Gardner and the Whig candidate. Massachusetts citizens found the Know-Nothing sweep of legislative seats even more incredible; the party seized control of every Senate seat and left only two places in the House for its rivals. The new organization could claim the most thorough victory of any political party in the history of the state.[33]

Anson Burlingame, the Free-Soiler who had joined Wilson in moving into the Know-Nothing party, won election to Congress. If the hitherto unknown Burlingame could achieve such instant success, many thought that Wilson would easily win the Senate post he coveted. Wilson vehemently denied the existence of any kind of bargain with Know-Nothing leaders, but he did not hesitate to strengthen his connections with the party. When the election results were in, he went to Gardner's house to congratulate him on his victory. During the rest of the month of November, he attended Know-Nothing gatherings.[34]

At a Know-Nothing dinner held in late November, Wilson sought to define his view of nativist principles. While he hoped the party would eliminate bloc voting and make Irish and Germans into Americans, he did not want Know-Nothings to use their power "to the prejudice of foreigners, simply because they are foreigners." He declared his sympathy for every man, "wherever he was born, and whatever might be the complexion the Almighty had impressed upon him." After this clear reference to Negroes, Wilson added his personal wish that the Know-Nothings would stand for liberty. Despite such evidence that Wilson had not forgotten the antislavery

[33] Boston *Evening Telegraph,* Nov. 14, 1854.

[34] Samuel Gridley Howe to Theodore Parker, [Sept., 1854], Howe to Horace Mann, Nov. 14, 1854, Howe MSS, Houghton Library, Harvard University; Robinson, ed., *Warrington,* 428; Edward Everett to Mrs. Charles Eames, Nov. 4, 13, 1854, Everett MSS.

crusade, Free-Soilers and Republicans disdainful of his methods sought to revive and reorganize the Free Soil party without him. Many were bitter enough with Wilson to hope that he would lose his bid for the senatorship, so that his Free Soil associates in the Know-Nothing party would leave the new organization to rejoin their old associates.[35]

As the Know-Nothing legislature met in January to choose a new senator, Wilson faced considerable opposition. Ardent nativists wanted someone more dedicated to the new party's principles. They also feared that selecting a radical Free-Soiler would outrage Southerners and endanger the party's growing national organization.[36] Wilson's opponents in the legislature managed to defeat a proposal that both houses caucus together to nominate a senatorial candidate. Free-Soilers could control the House for their leader, but they were not sure of winning a majority in the Senate. On January 12 a House caucus nominated Wilson without much ado, but four days later the Senate deferred the election of a senator until January 31. Wilson's opponents thus gained an additional two weeks in their drive to choose someone more loyal to nativist principles. The legislative battle began to draw extensive newspaper comment. Three New York papers, the *Evening Post, Tribune,* and *Times,* hoped Wilson would be elected; the editors found him to possess "superior abilities" and "acknowledged talent." Boston's voice of nativism, the *Know-Nothing and American Crusader,* damned "the scheming, fraud, humbug, and injustice" involved in selecting a senator and urged the party to choose someone other than Wilson. The Boston *Chronicle* pronounced him the "Talleyrand of Massachusetts politi-

[35] Boston *Evening Telegraph,* Nov. 25, 29, 1854; Samuel Gridley Howe to Horace Mann, Nov. 14, 1854, Howe MSS, Houghton Library, Harvard University; C. F. Adams Diary, Nov. 15, 19, Dec. 27, 1854; J. W. Stone to Sumner, Dec. 22, 29, 1854, S. C. Phillips to Sumner, Nov. 15, 1854, S. P. Chase to Sumner, Oct. 30, 1854, Sumner MSS.

[36] Edward Everett to Mrs. Charles Eames, Nov. 14, 16, 22, 1854, Everett MSS; Amos Lawrence to William Appleton, Jan. 4, 1855, Lawrence to M. L. Williams, Jan. 20, March 2, 1855, Lawrence MSS; George H. Haynes, "A Know Nothing Legislature," *Annual Report* of the American Historical Association, 1896, (2 vols.; Washington, D.C., 1897), I, 181; Congdon, *Reminiscenses,* 146.

cians" and derided his shoemaking background. The city's leading Whig and Democratic newspapers, the *Atlas* and *Post,* united in condemning Wilson's candidacy. Whigs sought to revenge themselves on the former coalitionist leader, and Democrats attacked his antislavery views.[37]

Although Wilson had capable managers in both the House and the Senate, he personally promoted his candidacy by scurrying around Boston to bolster his followers and deny the charges against him. When one legislator questioned Wilson's antinativist statements in the constitutional convention, Wilson wrote an open letter to the Boston newspapers, qualifying the stand he had taken in 1853. He insisted that the American movement did not deny anyone the equal protection of the laws; rather, it sought to protect the United States from the adverse influences of thousands of immigrants reared under differing social, religious, and political institutions. Making his gesture to the rampant anti-Catholic sentiment that furnished strength to Know-Nothingism, he condemned "the insidious and malign tendencies of that sectarian power that instinctively sympathizes with oppression in the Old World and the New." Wilson's letter only angered his Free Soil supporters and gave further fuel to opposition newspapers who were busily emphasizing his contradictory statements on nativism.[38]

On January 23 the House elected Wilson without a contest, but his supporters feared he might lose in the Senate. As legislative caucuses continued, his opponents charged that Wilson was not a nativist, that he was too dangerously antislavery, or that he was too ambitious to be loyal to any party or organization. Some insisted he had purchased votes by promising offices to his supporters; others complained that Governor Gardner was holding up the distribution of state patronage until the Senate had made a choice. On January

[37] Boston *Evening Telegraph,* Jan. 9, 13, 16, 1855, and the various Boston and New York newspapers cited in *ibid.,* Jan. 15, 18, 22, 24, 27, 30, 1855; James W. Stone to Sumner, Jan. 20, 1855, Sumner MSS; Edward Everett to Mrs. Charles Eames, Jan. 13, 1855, Everett MSS.

[38] Boston *Evening Telegraph,* Jan. 18, 20, 23, 1855; James W. Stone to Sumner, Jan. 29, 1855, Sumner MSS.

30, the day before the Senate balloted, Amos Lawrence thought that Wilson, "humanly speaking," could not win; but he regretfully added that "the free-soil politicians are super-human in managing for office" and that Wilson therefore would be elected.[39]

Henry Wilson waited anxiously as the Senate met on January 31. Personal ambition, compounded by some economic distress, had driven him from the coalition to the Republicans and thence to the Know-Nothings. Along the way he had abused the confidence which people had placed in him, and he had alienated many important supporters. Most of his critics thought he had sacrificed all his principles in his frantic quest for office. If he should lose his bid for a Senate seat, he would never have a chance to prove them wrong. Now his whole career, his whole future, rested on the decision of the state's forty senators. In the galleries of the upper house, a huge crowd watched as the voting began. Wilson needed twenty-one of the forty votes of the Senate to obtain his coveted post. The crowd waited breathlessly as the president counted the ballots. Then he intoned the verdict: E. M. Wright, Wilson's chief opponent, had obtained fifteen votes; Wilson, the required twenty-one. Cannon boomed to announce the choice of a new senator. The Boston *Atlas* fumed that Wilson had won his office "by intrigue, by duplicity, by bargain and sale of his party, by denying his own language, and ignoring his own sentiments." Wilson would have four years in which to redeem himself from such well-directed charges.[40]

[39] Boston *Evening Telegraph,* Jan. 17, 18, 19, 20, 1855; Boston semiweekly *Atlas,* Jan. 20, 31, 1855; Amos Lawrence to Sally Lawrence, Jan. 30, 1855, Lawrence MSS; Edward Everett to Mrs. Charles Eames, Jan. 27, 1855, Everett MSS.

[40] Boston *Evening Telegraph,* Jan. 23, 31, 1855; Boston semiweekly *Atlas,* Feb. 3, 1855; Edward Everett to Mrs. Charles Eames, Feb. 18, 1855, Everett MSS.

5

Wilson
Finds His Party

When the people of Natick heard that Wilson had won a seat in the United States Senate, they held a celebration. The honored guest sat with his family and listened as one orator after another praised him. At one point a speaker referred to Wilson's "humble origins," and Winthrop Colbath burst out, "—— him, what does he mean? I've a good mind to get up and kick his ——."[1] The uproar and laughter following those remarks interrupted Wilson's thoughts; he was already pondering his new legislative role. Quickly he accepted congratulations, made his preparations to leave for the capital, said goodbye to friends, and boarded a train for Washington. Since the last session of the Thirty-third Congress had about ended, he left Harriet at home with their young son. Traveling alone, he had time to take stock of his political career.

In his progress from the shoe shop in Natick to a Senate seat in Washington, Henry Wilson had demonstrated quite clearly the characteristics that would accompany him throughout the rest of his life. Even his political opponents testified to his political abilities. Edward Everett, the man Wilson replaced in the Senate, complained that his successor was propelled "principally by audacity" but acknowledged him to be a man "of a good deal of native power." Amos Lawrence grudgingly admitted that "he has risen from the cow yard to the Senate, and therefore he *may* rise to great respectability by the use of his varied talents." Another Whig adversary, Robert C. Winthrop, pronounced Wilson shrewd and able. Yet the new Massachusetts senator had not won his place of power through a strong, forceful personality. Most associates found him unassuming and modest in his dealings with others. Even his critics testified to his simple living and frugal habits. His dress was plain and unostentatious, his tastes and habits inexpensive. Such qualities, however laudatory, kept him from making a strong personal impression upon those around him. One of his Natick neighbors later recalled that "I never seemed to see Henry Wilson, only his cause."[2]

Such a comment was not surprising, for Henry Wilson sought personal advancement and recognition through his attempts to advance the antislavery cause that he championed. His strongly impulsive nature made him an able antislavery advocate. As one of his friends commented, "[Wilson] has no strength except when he speaks frankly his own convictions." And his convictions were, as an acquaintance observed, "to serve humanity, to lift up the lowly, to champion the cause of the poor and him who was weak and had no helper."[3]

Everyone who came into contact with Wilson emphasized both his personal ambition and his dedication to principle, yet they all complained about the methods he used to advance both himself and his cause in politics. A Massachusetts journalist, a contemporary of Wilson, found that "the vice of his political constitution was that he could see no wrong in bargains, coalitions, agreements, alliances ... [that were] unnatural, unnecessary, and based on personal ambitions and chronic hunger for office." George F. Hoar saw the validity of this complaint, but he later wryly suggested that "the man in public life who has not sinned cast the first stone at him." Although it is true that Wilson's own livelihood had come to depend upon his ability to gain public office, he found great enjoyment in arranging political deals and alliances, and he found nothing wrong

[1] New York *Times,* Nov. 26, 1875.

[2] Edward Everett to John Wise, Feb. 23, 1855, Everett MSS; Amos Lawrence to Mrs. Lawrence, Feb. 1, 1855, Lawrence MSS; Winthrop, *Memoir,* 168; Reminiscences of R.E. Farwell, in Natick *Bulletin,* June 12, 1896.

[3] Amasa Walker to Sumner, March 14, 1855, Sumner MSS; Robinson, ed., *Warrington,* 544-45.

with them if, in the process of advancing his cause, they advanced him too.[4]

His compatriots in the Massachusetts Free Soil party were variously repelled, fascinated, and attracted to Wilson's intrigues with the Democrats in setting up the coalition. Adams, Palfrey, Dana, and the Hoars professed to disdain such political machinations, but others defended him. Stephen Higginson said he had seen enough of Wilson to have confidence in his "essential honesty" and in "the general soundness of his views as a politician." E. L. Pierce, another active Free-Soiler, contended that Wilson was "a noble man. The current of his aspirations is right." During the constitutional convention even Dana admitted that Wilson was "considered by his political opponents a more honest man than they were disposed to regard him."[5]

Many more of Wilson's political colleagues were aghast at his membership in the Know-Nothing order. Charles Francis Adams, who was already quite critical of Wilson, was now convinced that "a man who will cheat as he has done in the last campaign, can never be expected to do otherwise, provided the temptation is sufficient." That being the case, Samuel Gridley Howe hoped that Wilson might "never be tempted again; for he cannot withstand it, when in hope of high office." Pierce moaned in anguish that "when the freedom of an empire is at issue, Wilson runs off to chase a paddy" and another Free-Soiler found that the former coalition leader's Know-Nothing affiliations "made him something a little less than a *man*."[6]

Yet even Wilson's machinations with the Know-Nothings could not destroy the faith that most of those who knew him well had in his dedication to principle. Charles Sumner assured his friends in

[4] Congdon, *Reminiscences,* 132; Hoar reminiscences in Natick *Bulletin,* April 17, 1896; Pierce, *Sumner,* III, 342.

[5] Stephen Higginson to Sumner, Jan. 17, 1851, E. L. Pierce to Sumner, Dec. 6, 1852 and Jan. 23, 1854, Sumner MSS; Richard H. Dana, Jr., manuscript journal, Aug. 2, 1853, Dana MSS.

[6] C. F. Adams Diary, March 24, 1855; Samuel Gridley Howe to Sumner, Feb. 9, 1855, Amasa Walker to Sumner, March 14, 1855, in Sumner MSS; E. L. Pierce to Horace Mann, Jan. 18, 1855, Mann MSS.

Washington that he and his colleague shared the same views on the question of slavery. Richard Henry Dana, Jr., likewise admitted that the former cobbler's election "secured the voice of Massachusetts in the Senate for antislavery," and E. L. Pierce also testified to the soundness of Wilson's views on liberty. Those in Massachusetts who knew Wilson only through his reputation repeated similar sentiments. A Boston minister told Sumner that "I encouraged our representatives to vote for Wilson because I thought he best represented the antislavery sentiment of the state." A scholar hidden behind the ivied walls in Cambridge criticized the new senator's lack of qualification for the office yet confessed that "he has a stiff backbone as regards slavery." The editor of the Democratic Boston *Post* sought to criticize Wilson by insisting that no one would go further than he "in pushing on the antislavery cause."[7]

Theodore Parker, the virulent and outspoken Unitarian minister and abolitionist, who had formed a rather close acquaintance with Wilson, most clearly summarized the perplexity shared by most of the new senator's friends when they contemplated his rise to power. Parker informed Wilson that although he felt a strong personal friendship for him, he would have preferred Adams or S. C. Phillips in the Senate, since they had been free of Wilson's intense ambition. He reminded the former cobbler that "*you have been seeking for office with all your might.*" Parker went on to thank Wilson for doing more than any man in New England "to liberalize and harmonize the actions of political parties," for organizing the Free Soil party, for "the revolution of fogyism at Harvard," for the constitutional convention, and for the election of Sumner. Parker admitted his pleasure at seeing "a shoemaker get right up off his bench

[7] Richard H. Dana, Jr., manuscript journal, Feb. 9, 1855, Dana MSS; E.L. Pierce to Sumner, Jan. 23, 1854, A. G. Browne to Sumner, Jan. 2, 1855, Sumner to Samuel Gridley Howe, Feb. 1, 1855, W. C. Whitcomb to Sumner, Jan. 16, 1855, all in Sumner MSS; Charles Eliot Norton to A. H. Clough, Feb. 8, 1855, in Sara Norton and M. A. DeWolfe Howe, eds., *Letters of Charles Eliot Norton* (2 vols.; Boston, 1913), I, 120; Natick *Bulletin,* April 17, 1896; Boston *Post,* Jan. 25, 1855. Some newspapers carried rumors, subsequently denied, that Sumner was not pleased with his new colleague. Boston *Evening Telegraph,* Feb. 9, 13, 1855.

and go to the Senate." He was sure that Wilson sympathized with mankind—and he hoped therefore he would be faithful in the fight against slavery.[8]

Wilson could convince himself that in joining the nativists he had not abandoned the antislavery cause, for in Massachusetts the Know-Nothing party was strongly flavored with Free-Soilism. To him the nativist organization had performed a great service by smashing old state parties. In the previous October, when he declined the Republican nomination for governor, he had asserted that in the chaotic condition of parties he could discern elements of a new party pledged to freedom. After his election to the Senate, he attended an antislavery lecture given by Anson Burlingame in Boston, where he endorsed the speaker's strictures against slavery and said he would be unrelenting in his hostility to the institution. Certainly antislavery men in Washington eagerly awaited his arrival. William Henry Seward, leader of the antislavery Whigs in the Senate, was certain that "the cause of Political justice will have a worthy and noble supporter" in the new Massachusetts senator. Salmon P. Chase of Ohio, former Liberty party member and leading Free-Soiler, regarded Wilson as "hot shot from abolition cannon" and saw his election as "a decided triumph of the Antislavery element in the Know Nothing organization."[9]

When Wilson arrived at the nation's capital, he stopped to take stock of his new surroundings. Washington was growing rapidly; in 1855 the capital city, as well as the nation, stood as if poised between past and future. Only partially did the new brick and stone buildings replace the many dilapidated, shambling, wooden structures scattered about the city. Pennsylvania Avenue was in need of repair. Near one end of the street the Washington Monument was under construction; at the opposite end of the avenue, scaffolding

[8] Parker to Wilson, Feb. 15, 1855, Wilson MSS, Library of Congress.

[9] Boston *Evening Telegraph,* Nov. 4, 1854, Feb. 2, 5, 1855; William Henry Seward to Charles Sumner, Sept. 22, 1853, Sumner MSS; Salmon P. Chase to E. S. Hamlin, Jan. 22, Feb. 9, 1855, and to A.M.G., Feb. 15, 1855, in Chase, "Diary and Correspondence," II, 268, 270, 272.

surrounded the likewise unfinished new dome of the Capitol. Two
and one half inches of snow covered the whole scene, for Washington was in the middle of one of its coldest snaps in years. Tem-
perature hovered around twenty degrees above zero.[10]

Such a raw, unpolished, even rustic environment seemed to suit
Wilson well. He was still rather crude in manner; his writing was still
ungrammatical and his spelling poor. To be sure, Washington society
was quite sophisticated, but since it centered around the White
House, which was filled with Democrats, he did not expect to
attend. Southerners did most of the entertaining in the city, and the
former farmer and cobbler felt ill at ease amid Paris gowns, lace,
punch, wines, diamonds, and women with bared throats and plung-
ing necklines. Nor did he wish to enjoy the many gambling houses
on the north side of Pennsylvania Avenue. Rather, he sought out
some of his Massachusetts friends who lived in a rooming house near
the Capitol and took up quarters with them. He was interested in
politics, not parties, high society, cards, or liquor.[11]

Wilson came into the Senate at a time when little business was
being transacted. As a newspaperman noted, "it is dead low water at
Washington. The foaming political currents of the last session have
subsided." The Kansas-Nebraska Act filled the remaining waste
"with the stranded wrecks of numberless politicians." One such
politician had been Edward Everett; his successor was careful to test
out the new ground. When Wilson first entered the floor of the
Senate, "Whig Know-Nothings" and Free-Soilers each tried to seat
him near them; he compromised by taking a seat on the aisle near
the back, thus classifying himself, according to one observer, as an
"Anti-Nebraska-Know-Nothing." The freshman senator was reluctant to antagonize the American party men, for they had achieved
what he had been trying to do for years: unite enough Free-Soilers,
Whigs, and Democrats to challenge effectively the two major parties.

[10] New York *Daily Tribune,* Feb. 8, 1855.
[11] Descriptions of Washington are in Allan Nevins, *Ordeal of the Union* (2
vols.; New York, 1947), II, 51-58.

He was not prepared to seek the destruction of the organization and sacrifice its power unless it refused to oppose slavery.[12]

For the moment, Wilson chose not to force the issue on the party. When Vespasian Ellis, editor of a Know-Nothing paper in Washington, asked the senator for his views on the party's platform, Wilson replied that the organization "did not embrace the question of slavery among those for the regulation of which it was formed."[13] He prepared his first major Senate speech with care, for he knew his remarks would attract close attention from men of all opinions. He asked E. L. Pierce to read the text and anxiously asked him if he thought it would endanger his connections with the Know-Nothings. When Wilson spoke to the Senate, he did not mask his antislavery principles, but he insisted he bore no malice toward the South. He assured his Southern colleagues that he recognized "the Democratic doctrine of State rights in its application to slavery as well as to other local affairs." The government, he hoped, would withdraw from its connections with slavery; if it should do so the "angry debates" on slavery could be banished from Congress, and the Southerners would abolish slavery in their own states "at no distant day."

In an effort to prove himself friendly and amenable, Wilson agreed to answer questions from curious Southern congressmen when his speech was ended. He implied that if the 1850 fugitive slave law were repealed, Massachusetts would still seek to return fleeing bondsmen. He refused to defend the Negro as a racial equal but insisted that "if the African race is inferior" its members should be educated, elevated, and accorded equal rights. After the debate the Washington correspondent of the New York *Evening Post* concluded that the Massachusetts senator had managed to satisfy both Free-Soilers and Know-Nothings. The journalist praised him for

[12] New York *Daily Tribune*, Feb. 3, 1855; Boston *Evening Transcript*, Feb. 12, 1855; Chase to A.M.G., Feb. 15, 1855, in Chase, "Diary and Correspondence," II, 272.

[13] Boston *Evening Telegraph*, Feb. 21, 1855; Boston semiweekly *Atlas*, Feb. 21, 24, 1855.

quickly learning "to cloak his sentiments under national and approved phraseology."[14]

Due to the nature of his election, Wilson's constituents closely observed his actions. Edward Everett, who had resigned his seat because of complaints that he hesitated to condemn the Slave Power, noted that his successor had been somewhat successful "in intriguing at Washington to conciliate the favor of the Southern Know-Nothings." Charles Sumner, who had listened for so long to Wilson's demands that he speak out against slavery, was quite irritated at his colleague's "sinuosities," and many of Wilson's constituents agreed. Now Wilson, not Sumner, was condemned for not speaking out against slavery.[15]

Wilson, stung by the criticism, sought to defend himself. He assured his friends that his reply to Ellis had been drawn up with the approval of Sumner and Chase. As for his Senate speech, he insisted he had not said that Massachusetts would send a fugitive slave back to captivity. Neither had he been "fool enough to say in the Senate of the United States that Massachusetts would not do so." When Theodore Parker and others charged that he had "dodged" a vote on receiving antislavery petitions, Wilson claimed that he had misunderstood the hour the Senate met the day the vote was taken. He assured Parker that he would give no vote in the Senate "which will infringe upon the rights of any man, black or white, native or foreign."[16]

The pressure from Massachusetts had its effect upon the fledgling senator. As he told Parker, "the approbation of men like yourself

[14] Pierce, *Sumner,* III, 412; *Congressional Globe,* 33rd Cong., 2nd sess., 1855, appendix, pp. 237-38; New York *Post* quoted in Boston *Evening Telegraph,* Feb. 27, 1855.

[15] C. F. Adams Diary, March 11, 1855; Edward Everett to President Fillmore, April 4, 1855, Everett MSS; New York *Herald,* March 10, 1855.

[16] Wilson to Robert Carter, Feb. 20, 28, 1855, Houghton Library, Harvard University; Theodore Parker to Charles Sumner, Feb. 15, 1855, Wilson to Parker, Feb. 28, 1855, Theodore Parker MSS, Massachusetts Historical Society; Wilson to Gilbert Pillsbury, March 10, 1855, published in Boston *Evening Telegraph,* March 13, 1855; *ibid.,* March 7, 28, 1855.

whose lives are devoted to the rights of human nature cannot but be dear to me." He added that men in public life must be true to their own consciences, and certainly Wilson's bothered him. He held no real feelings of bigotry or intolerance and could work up no enthusiasm for nativist principles. He was so ashamed of his membership in the Know-Nothing order that he tried to avoid being seen entering Know-Nothing lodges. He was sensitive to the friendships he had lost when he became a nativist, and to the end of his life he regretted ever having joined the order.[17]

Consequently Wilson decided it was time to press the issue of slavery on the Know-Nothings. After the congressional session came to an end, he set out upon a five-month speaking tour through thirteen states to urge American party members to abandon their neutrality and take a stand against slavery. He also called upon the party to drop its secret meetings and its "narrow, bigoted, intolerant spirit that would make war on foreign citizens." Speaking to an audience in New York City, he declared that if any party, Whig, Democratic, or American, avoided the slavery question, it deserved to die, "and by the blessing of God I shall do what little I can to make it die."[18]

These were not idle threats, coming as they did from a man who had led the Conscience Whigs from the Whig party and had helped organize the Free Soil party and the Massachusetts coalition. In June, 1855, when the American party's national council met in Philadelphia, Wilson was prepared to bring his campaign to a climax. He went to the convention at the head of a strong antislavery delegation from Massachusetts. On the other hand, nativists from Virginia, convinced that Wilson's antislavery sentiments had had an important

[17] Hoar, *Autobiography,* I, 216-17; Robinson, ed., *Warrington,* 544-45; Haynes, "Know Nothing Legislature," 180; *Francis William Bird: A Biographical Sketch* [By his children] (Boston, 1897), 39, 47; Wilson to Parker, July 23, 1855, Parker MSS.

[18] Wilson to Salmon P. Chase, April 16, 1855, Salmon P. Chase MSS, Historical Society of Pennsylvania, Philadelphia, Pa.; C. F. Adams Diary, March 24, 1855; Edward Everett to Millard Fillmore, April 4, 1855, Everett MSS; Boston *Evening Telegraph,* March 24, May 15, 17, June 1, 1855; New York *Tribune,* June 2, 1855.

effect in defeating their candidate for governor in a May election, came to Philadelphia prepared to demand that the party ignore the slavery issue.[19]

When the national council convened on June 5 the Virginians refused to allow the Masschusetts delegation to be seated. After Governor Gardner and the rest of the delegation refused to join the assemblage if Wilson were not allowed to come with them, the convention voted to let them in. Wilson was no sooner on the floor than a Virginian delegate denounced him. The Massachusetts senator quickly learned that he would either have to retreat or push his views to the point of disrupting the convention. He did not hesitate about what course to take; he had spent three months telling thousands of people he would destroy the American party if it did not oppose slavery.[20]

Wilson laid his plans carefully. The council's meetings were held in secret; once Wilson had decided to disrupt the proceedings, he had to find a way to make his operations public. He sought out Samuel Bowles, the editor of the *Springfield Republican* who was in Philadelphia to cover the convention for his own newspaper, the Boston *Atlas,* and the New York *Tribune.* Bowles was thirsty for news, and Wilson offered to supply him information on the convention proceedings. Bowles's dispatches, which contained detailed descriptions of activities behind the closed doors of the convention, were then reprinted by newspapers across the North.[21]

By leaking details of his own activities to the journalist, Wilson was able to portray himself as the key figure of the convention. Every Bowles dispatch carefully described the speeches and actions of the sturdy former cobbler. Convention members, loose for a week

[19] Boston *Evening Telegraph,* May 2, 3, 4, 1855; James P. Hambleton, *A Biographical Sketch of Henry A. Wise, With a History of the Political Campaign in Virginia in 1855* (Richmond, Va., 1856), 234-44.

[20] New York *Daily Tribune,* June 7, 1855.

[21] Some of the dispatches read as if they might have been written by Wilson himself. On Wilson and Bowles, see Merriam, *Bowles,* I, 137-39, 196; Jeter A. Isely, *Horace Greeley and the Republican Party, 1853-1861* (Princeton, N.J., 1947), 115-22; Wilson to Bowles, June 23, 1855, Samuel Bowles MSS, Yale University Library, New Haven, Conn.

in the big city, were often drunk and rowdy, enabling Wilson to play up the "gross intoxication" of the Southern delegates. As viewed through Bowles's releases, Wilson bravely defied vulgar, coarse, and drunken Southerners, who belabored him with insults and shook their fists in his face. Wilson himself spoke soberly and with "admirable coolness and bold frankness"; he refused to shrink from his opinions or submit to threats. According to Bowles, Wilson's first speech "cleared the air" and left him and his fellow delegates with the respect of many of the attending nativists.[22]

Know-Nothings, writhing in anger and frustration as they read the columns of the *Tribune,* sought to ferret out the secret informant but could discover nothing. When some accused Wilson, he calmly suggested that if delegates would drink less liquor and talk less freely the leaks would stop. In the meantime, he helped defeat a resolution stating that the question of slavery did not belong in the Know-Nothing platform. Then the majority of the platform committee recommended that the party abide by the existing laws on slavery as a final settlement of the question. They also denied that Congress could exclude a slave state from admission to the Union, and they maintained that Congress should not legislate on slavery in the territories or in the District of Columbia. Angrily, Wilson took the floor to condemn the report as committing the party unconditionally "to the iron domination of the Black Power." He warned that he would "trample with disdain" upon the platform and would not support any man that stood upon it.[23]

After several days of bitter wrangling, the convention agreed to accept the committee report. Wilson had expected the result, and after the convention hall emptied, he gathered with antislavery delegates from twelve Northern states to consider a plan of action. The Massachusetts senator, who presided over the meeting, had consulted previously with Samuel Bowles to draw up a public appeal. The statement was moderate in tone and aimed at providing antislavery

[22] New York *Daily Tribune,* June 7, 9, 10, 1855.

[23] Boston *Bee,* June 27, 1855; New York *Daily Tribune,* June 12, 13, 14, 1855; Boston *Telegraph,* June 15, 1855; W. Darrell Overdyke, *The Know Nothing Party in the South* (Baton Rouge, La., 1950), 128-33.

men and nativists with a basis for political union. It proposed the usual resolutions aimed at freeing the federal government from connection with slavery and added a few mild criticisms of naturalization laws to satisfy insistent nativists. Then Wilson demanded restoration of the Missouri Compromise and admission of Kansas and Nebraska as free states, but he did not ask that Congress ban slavery in all territories. His address was accepted by the gathering, and the delegates returned to their homes to convince their state organizations to adopt it.[24]

Wilson's campaign to force the Know-Nothings to an antislavery position won back some individuals and groups whom he had previously alienated. Bowles, who had once called Wilson a "political harlot," now praised him as "a man worthy of Massachusetts, and worthy to lead the new movement of the people of that state." Abolitionists William Lloyd Garrison and Wendell Phillips lauded Wilson's course. Amasa Walker told him that, by his actions at Philadelphia, he had placed himself "at *the head* of the political antislavery movement—the North looks to you." Congratulations also came from Theodore Parker, who praised Wilson for standing up "most *manfully,* and *heroically,* to do battle for the right."[25]

The senator hurried home to capitalize on the sentiment he had built up in his favor. He told Bowles: "I have labored for seven years in the hope that we should have a great, united party composed of men who agreed in principle and policy. It seems to me that the hour is at hand for such a party." He had high hopes of organizing a new antislavery fusion movement in Massachusetts in time for the 1855 elections. The state Know-Nothing legislature had revealed its antislavery bias by passing a law to impede the capture of fugitive

[24] New York *Daily Tribune,* June 15, 1855; Edward Everett to Mrs. Charles Eames, June 18, 1855, Everett MSS; Wilson, *Slave Power,* II, 426-31.

[25] New York *Daily Tribune,* June 15, 1855; Boston *Bee,* June 23, Oct. 1, 1855; James Ford Rhodes, *History of the United States, 1850-1877* (9 vols.; New York, 1920-1928), II, 96; Theodore Parker to Wilson, July 7, 1855, Wilson MSS, Library of Congress; D. G. Kilgore to Charles Sumner, Aug. 6, 1855, Sumner MSS; Amasa Walker to Wilson, June 22, 1855, quoted in Nason and Russell, *Wilson,* 140-41; D. L. Child to Wilson, June 26, 1855, Boston Public Library, Boston, Mass.; Lorenzo Sears, *Wendell Phillips* (New York, 1909), 166; C. F. Adams Diary, March 24, 1855.

slaves, urging removal of a judge who had enforced the fugitive slave law, and strongly condemning the Kansas-Nebraska Act. Also, the state Know-Nothing council repudiated the national party's platform, broke its connection with the national council, abandoned secret meetings, and invited the cooperation of men of all parties to promote the principles Wilson had enunciated in Philadelphia.[26]

To Wilson's dismay, however, Massachusetts Know-Nothings were not prepared to abandon their nativist principles. On the last day of the session the legislature proposed amending the state constitution to deny immigrants the right to hold office or vote until they had been naturalized citizens for twenty-one years. Wilson condemned the proposals and warned the state party council that bigotry would alienate large masses of immigrants in the Northwest, whose votes were necessary to the success of a Northern fusion movement. Despite his efforts, the state Know-Nothings adopted a platform discriminating against immigrants and settled on a weak proposal to keep slavery only out of territories in the Louisiana Purchase.[27]

Wilson also was disappointed in his efforts to attract prominent Whigs like Ezra Lincoln and Robert Winthrop into a fusion organization. Many Free-Soilers and Republicans were likewise reluctant to commit themselves to a political movement which they feared Know-Nothings would dominate. Wilson, who was well aware of the strength of the nativists, was prepared to let them manage the fusion movement and nominate their own men, as long as they took a strong antislavery stance. Reluctantly, he agreed to let Charles Francis Adams and others who felt antislavery sentiment was stronger than ties of party try to control the state fusion convention called for September in Worcester. He was too controversial to take a leading role himself. The day before the convention, he did appear to appeal to the delegates to make the compromises necessary for success.[28]

[26] Wilson to Bowles, June 23, 1855, Bowles MSS; Handlin, *Boston's Immigrants,* 202; Boston *Bee,* June 29, 1855.

[27] Haynes, "A Know Nothing Legislature," 182; Wilson to Schouler, April 16, 1855, William Schouler MSS; Boston *Bee,* Aug. 8, 9, 16, 1855.

[28] On dealings with Lincoln and Winthrop, see Merriam, *Bowles,* I, 138-39;

Wilson's estimation of the Know-Nothings' loyalty to their party was correct. They were determined to nominate their chieftain, Henry Gardner, for governor again. Free-Soilers, led by Richard Henry Dana, challenged the nativists' loyalty to antislavery principles and urged the convention to nominate an ex-Whig, Julius Rockwell, who was "free from all distracting questions." Some delegates called for Wilson to speak in defense of Gardner, but the Natick politician remained safely out of sight. The debate grew more embittered and the convention more chaotic. Finally the chairman stopped the commotion and ordered a final vote; Rockwell narrowly defeated Gardner to get the nomination of the renewed Republican party.[29]

Wilson endorsed the result of the convention, but Know-Nothings angrily withdrew from the fusion movement to nominate Gardner on a separate ticket. Bitterly they condemned "the chameleon General Wilson" and accused him of betraying the party that had conferred office upon him. The senator replied by promising to "blow the whole party to hell and damnation" and by working energetically for Rockwell. When the election returns came in, Wilson was badly disappointed. Massachusetts voters again swept Gardner and his party into office. Wilson blamed the Republican defeat on inflated optimism and inadequate campaigning.[30]

Although Henry Wilson was disappointed with the 1855 election,

Winthrop, *Memoir,* 172-81; Boutwell, *Reminiscences,* I, 118; Congdon, *Reminiscences,* 87-88. On Free-Soil and Republican negotiations, see Richard H. Dana, Jr., manuscript journal, Aug. 16, 1855, Dana MSS; C. F. Adams Diary, Aug. 21, 22, 27, 1855; C. F. Adams to Gamaliel Bailey, Sept. 2, 1855, C. F. Adams MSS; H. Kreisman to Sumner, Sept. 18, 1855, Sumner MSS; Wilson to Salmon P. Chase, Nov. 17, 1855, Chase MSS, Historical Society of Pennsylvania; Boston *Bee,* Aug. 8, 17, 30, 1855.

[29] Boston *Bee,* Sept. 21, 1855.

[30] Boston *Bee,* Sept. 26, Oct. 4, 6, 8, 9, 1855; Robinson, ed., *Warrington,* 542-44; George H. Haynes, "A Chapter in the Local History of Know Nothingism," *New England Magazine,* XV (Sept. 1896), 90; Henry Gardner to George B. Morton, Nov. 17, 1855, Rutherford B. Hayes Library; Seth Webb, Jr., to Samuel Bowles, Oct. 10, 1855, Henry L. Dawes MSS, Library of Congress; Edward Everett to Caleb Cushing, Oct. 11, 1855, Everett MSS; Joshua Giddings to daughter, Nov. 7, 1855, Giddings-Julian MSS; Wilson to Salmon P. Chase, Nov. 17, 1855, Chase MSS, Historical Society of Pennsylvania.

he was not discouraged. The next year would bring a presidential election; if he could not organize a satisfactory fusion movement on the state level, perhaps he could solidify the young Republican movement both in Massachusetts and across the North by urging a union for national offices. He told Salmon P. Chase that he hoped during the coming session of Congress "something could be done at Washington to help us out of the position we are now in." Issues aplenty existed in Kansas alone, where free- and slave-state adherents had organized rival territorial governments and were nervously eyeing each other over fortified hotel balconies. By agitating such matters, Wilson also hoped to continue to rebuild his reputation in the eyes of associates disillusioned with his connections with the Know-Nothings, and prove himself a worthy opponent of the Slave Power.[31]

Henry Wilson returned to the Senate tired from his extensive fall campaigning. Fortunately for him, for two months Congress transacted little business while the House wrangled over the selection of a speaker. In February, after President Pierce sent Congress a message upholding the proslavery government in Kansas, Wilson moved into action. Insisting that Pierce had ignored many facts, the Massachusetts senator, in a speech lasting two days, sought to supply the correct information on the Kansas imbroglio. Quoting from a variety of dispatches, telegrams, and newspaper reports, he viciously attacked the proslavery territorial government. He roundly condemned Southerners who would banish from the territories the "educated, self-dependent free laboring men of the North" to make room for their slaves. Republican members of the House were so pleased with his remarks that they subscribed money to print ten thousand copies of his speech to spread across the North. According to his Massachusetts colleague, "Wilson has earned his senatorship—it was the great event of his life."[32]

[31] Wilson to Chase, Nov. 17, 1855, Chase MSS, Historical Society of Pennsylvania; Wilson to Theodore Parker, July 23, 1855, Parker MSS.

[32] *Congressional Globe,* 34th Cong., 1st sess., 1855-1856, appendix, pp. 89-95; Boston *Evening Telegraph,* Feb. 25, 1856; Rhodes, *History,* II, 130; Sumner to William Jay, Feb. 22, 1856, and Sumner to Theodore Parker, Feb. 25, 1855, quoted in Pierce, *Sumner,* III, 432.

Sumner also noted that "the slavemongers are very angry with Wilson . . . . It shows he has done his work." With the exception of a few short trips to Washington, Henry Wilson had never come into prolonged contact with Southerners. His impressions of slaveholders as haughty, pretentious, and overbearing aristocrats had been formed from afar, but now his experiences at the Philadelphia Know-Nothing convention in 1855 and his Senate service in 1855 and early 1856 seemed to confirm his previously formed judgments. The bitterness his speeches had stirred up among the Southern delegates to the nativist gathering affected him deeply. He told Parker later in the summer that "for eight days I met the armed, drunken bullies of the Black Power without shrinking," and he was prepared to experience the same treatment in Washington. He even forecast the possibility of "violence and bloodshed . . . on the floors of Congress."[33]

Wilson was not the only Northern senator sensitive to the belligerency of his Southern colleagues. Lyman Trumbull, arriving in Washington in December, 1855, to begin his term as an anti-Nebraska senator from Illinois, found that "it was a time of high party excitement. The majority were domineering and often offensive to the members of the minority. . . . It was not uncommon for the members of the dominant party to go out of their way to seek controversies with and assail certain Senators in the minority." Charles Sumner contended that in Washington, "Seward, Wilson and myself are the special marks of [Southern] disfavor." The senior senator from Massachusetts, known for his imperious attitude, promised that "God willing, something more shall be done to deserve this distinction."[34]

The arrival of May brought hot and humid weather to Washington. The oppressive climate did not slow the bitter flow of words and violent language that filled the Senate and House. Wilson's earlier forecast of "violence and bloodshed" began to take on an ominous significance. In the middle of the month Sumner took the

[33] Pierce, *Sumner,* III, 432; Wilson to Theodore Parker, July 23, 1855, Parker MSS.

[34] Trumbull is quoted in Mark M. Krug, *Lyman Trumbull* (New York, 1965), 111; Sumner to Theodore Parker, Dec. 14, 1855, Parker MSS.

floor of the Senate for two days to denounce "the crime against Kansas" and indulge in personal attacks on Douglas and Senator Andrew Butler of South Carolina. Wilson regretted his colleague's language, but when he heard rumors of threats against Sumner's safety, he did not deem them dangerous enough to report to anyone.[35]

On May 21, the day after Sumner had finished his tirade, both Massachusetts senators remained at their desks after the Senate adjourned. Wilson soon withdrew, leaving his colleague behind with a few other dilatory senators. On his way out, he nodded to Preston Brooks, a representative from South Carolina, who had entered the upper house and was sitting in a vacant seat. He then left the Capitol and was walking down a street outside when a breathless Senate clerk caught up with him and gasped that Brooks had just broken a cane on Sumner's head. Greatly shocked, Wilson ran back to the Senate and burst into the Senate anteroom, where he found his colleague stretched out on a couch, his head bathed in blood. Anxiously he helped dress Sumner's wounds and assisted him to his quarters.[36]

The impetuous Wilson was affected profoundly by the sight of his blood-spattered colleague. That evening he went over to Seward's house to consult with fellow Republican senators about the proper course for them to adopt. On the way to the meeting he ran into a friend from Natick, who was shocked by Wilson's strong language and bitter exasperation. Joshua Giddings of Ohio helped to calm his belligerence, and the senators agreed that on the morrow Wilson should call the Senate's attention to the attack upon his colleague. The Massachusetts senator was urged to make his remarks short and simple. In the Senate the next day, the stocky former cobbler described Brooks's assault, his colleague's defenselessness, and the gravity of the deed. He then asked his fellow senators to "redress the wrongs of a member of this body, and vindicate the honor and

[35] Wilson to Theodore Parker, July 23, 1855, Sumner to Parker, Feb. 25, 1856, Parker MSS; Donald, *Sumner,* 286-88; U.S., Congress, *House Report No. 182,* 34th Cong., 1st sess., 1856, I, 42-43.

[36] *House Report No. 182,* I, 42-43.

dignity of the Senate." When no Democrat made a move to suggest a way of fulfilling the request, Republican Lyman Trumbull of Illinois rose to recommend an investigatory committee.[37]

The cautious approach adopted by the Republican senators met criticism in the free states. As Sumner's colleague, Wilson particularly felt himself under public scrutiny. Four days after his original remarks on the Brooks attack, he again gained the Senate floor to assert that Sumner was struck down "by a brutal, murderous, and cowardly assault." Brooks's uncle, Senator Butler, impulsively retorted, "you are a liar!" The president of the Senate quickly called both men to order; but the sparks showed that the conflagration started by Brooks's attack on Sumner still flared.[38]

Sumner's empty Senate seat spoke with as much eloquence as the man who had filled it. Republicans portrayed him as a martyr to Southern violence; as John Alley told Wilson, "it is the greatest thing for him that ever happened." Wilson was greatly overwrought by the tragedy. He grieved that he had not been by his friend's side when he was assailed. When he helped Sumner to his bed and when he washed the stains of blood from his hands he felt in his "inmost soul" the determination to do his "whole duty, even at a bloody cost." He was convinced that "the bold, insolent, aggressive men here from the South" were ready to do violence to him. "I often hear their curses," he told Parker, "and see their looks of bitter hatred as I pass along the streets." In his excited state of mind he found threatening slaveholders hiding behind every Senate pillar. According to newspaper reports, the Massachusetts senator was carrying several sets of Colt revolvers and a rifle disguised as a walking cane. Hurriedly he dashed off notes to friends at home, requesting that they befriend his family if he should be struck down. John Alley replied: "I cannot feel as you do, that there is any such danger as you apprehend." He calmed Wilson, however, by assuring him that "should

[37] Mary Thomas in Natick *Citizen*, March 14, 1879; Joshua Giddings to Sumner, July 24, 1856, Sumner MSS; Pierce, *Sumner*, III, 476; *Congressional Globe*, 34th Cong., 1st sess., 1856, p. 1279.

[38] Pierce, *Sumner*, III, 477; *Congressional Globe*, 34th Cong., 1st sess., 1856, p. 1306; Wilson to Theodore Parker, May 25, 1856, Parker MSS.

you fall a martyr in this contest for liberty, have no fear for your little son; he shall be as one of my own."[39]

Wilson refused to agree that he was free from personal harm. On May 28, when he caught a train for Trenton, New Jersey, to help Republicans there get their party organized, he brought a bodyguard of friends whose belts bulged with pistols and bowie knives. In Trenton, his speech flowed red; he reminded his listeners that "the same power that spilled the blood of the freemen in Kansas, had used the bludgeon against Senator Sumner." Returning to Washington he found renewed rumors that his own life was in danger. When a friend expressed his fear that Wilson might be murdered, the senator produced his glistening Colt revolvers, laughed, and promised that "then two will be killed; I am a pretty strong man."[40]

If Preston Brooks had contained his anger at Wilson, the Massachusetts senator's brave remarks might have seemed empty bravado; but on May 29 the congressman from South Carolina challenged Wilson to a duel. The senator disdainfully refused to face Brooks and pronounced duelling "the lingering relic of a barbarous civilization." He refused to retract his words branding Brooks's assault cowardly and brutal and declared himself ready to defend his life. Although Nathaniel Banks snorted "a rat will do that!" when he learned that the senator had refused the challenge, Wilson's stand gained respect and applause throughout Massachusetts. The duelling challenge was not without its emotional effect upon Wilson. He immediately wired his wife: "Have declined to fight a duel, shall do my duty and leave the result to God. If assailed, shall defend my life, if possible, at any cost. Be calm." Then he wrote his good friend Samuel Hunt that "I shall walk the path of duty if it costs me my life."[41]

[39] Wilson to Parker, May 25, 1856, Parker MSS; Natick *Observer,* June 28, 1856; Adelbert Ames to Blanche, May 21, 1871, in Blanche Butler Ames, comp., *Chronicle of the Nineteenth Century: Family Letters of Blanche Butler and Adelbert Ames* (2 vols.; Clinton, Mass., 1957), I, 283; J. B. Alley to Wilson, May 27, 1856, and William Claflin to Wilson, May 24, 1856, Natick Historical Society Museum.

[40] New York *Daily Tribune,* May 28, 1856; Natick *Citizen,* March 1, 1869; Boston *Evening Telegraph,* May 30, 1856; Natick *Observer,* May 31, 1856.

[41] Wilson to Preston Brooks, May 29, 1856, in Nason and Russell, *Wilson,*

Although Wilson was overwrought with excitement over Sumner's attack and Brooks's challenge, he could see that the events of May had provided him with a perfect opportunity to redeem himself with his constituents at home. When Boston newspapers suggested that Wilson was no longer in danger, he dashed off an irate letter to the Boston *Atlas* emphatically insisting that despite his continued insecurity he was willing to "go where duty requires uninfluenced by threats of any kind." He then left the Senate to visit Natick and Boston and tell his constituents how he had stood up to the threats of Southern slaveholders. To his friends at home he promised that he would return to Washington, "perhaps to lose my life." Meetings across the state lauded Wilson's course, and Sumner's constituents flooded his mail with praises of his colleague's fearless stand. Charles Francis Adams proposed to a state Republican convention a resolution thanking Wilson for his role in the Sumner affair. Wilson seemed to have fully regained his constituents' favor.[42]

The congressional debates over Kansas and the Brooks-Sumner incident came just in time to inspire Republicans who met in national conclave in Philadelphia on June 17, to nominate a presidential candidate. Wilson had been eagerly preparing for the convention. Frequently he made public speeches or wrote letters to newspapers urging men of all parties to unite in "cordial union" in behalf of free territories; he would allow "perfect toleration of opinion and action upon all other questions of state and national policy." He told New Jersey Republicans that Whigs, Republicans, and Americans could not defeat the administration party through their own efforts; they

---

188; John Bigelow, *Retrospections on an Active Life* (5 vols.; New York, 1909-1913), I, 170; Wilson to Samuel Hunt, May 29, 1856, Brown University Library, Providence, Rhode Island; Wilson, *Slave Power,* II, 487.

[42] Wilson to editors of *Atlas,* republished in New York *Times,* June 7, 1856; Boston *Daily Telegraph,* June 2, 4, 1856; Natick *Observer,* June 7, 1856; C. F. Adams Diary, June 4, 1856; John Alley to Wilson, May 26, 1856, Henry Claflin to Wilson, May 24, 1856, Natick Historical Society Museum; C. J. Hill to Charles Sumner, June 5, 1856, M. J. Perry to Sumner, June 5, 1856, Hebron Vincent to Sumner, June 16, 1856, Mary Grew to Sumner, June 18, 1856, F. A. Sumner to Sumner, June 24, 1856, Alexander Holmes to Sumner, June, 1856, Lydia Maria Child to Sumner, July 7, 1856, Daniel Henshaw to Sumner, June 6, 1860, all in Sumner MSS.

could succeed only by uniting. The meeting at Philadelphia, he insisted, was not to be a convention of Republicans, "but a gathering of all for freedom."[43]

Wilson actively searched for an available presidential candidate. In the fall of 1855 Nathaniel Banks, who appreciated Wilson's political acumen, talked to him about the possibilities of nominating General John C. Fremont. The general's activities in California during the Mexican War had brought him to the public eye, and he had remained in the news by conducting several explorations through the West. The trips also kept him safely out of the Kansas crisis. In November Wilson, Banks, and several other Republicans met with Fremont in New York and agreed to advance the general as a prime presidential candidate. Fremont "is all right on the Kansas question and is with us," Wilson thought, and he assured an inquiring nativist that the general was "*not* a Catholic but an attendant upon the Episcopal Church."[44]

Wilson and Banks, both former nativists, watched nervously as Northern Know-Nothings gathered at Philadelphia five days before the Republicans. The free-state nativists had abandoned the national party after the Americans had nominated ex-President Millard Fillmore; the group wanted a clear-cut antislavery candidate. Wilson was unable to come to Pennsylvania, as he was busy in Washington attacking Butler and vindicating Sumner by showing that Butler had started the dispute. He sent word to the delegates that he hoped they would either refuse to make a nomination or else choose Banks or Fremont. In the meantime Banks, fearing that a Northern American nomination would hamper the Republicans, agreed to accept the nativist presidential nomination. He then planned to step down in favor of Fremont after the Republicans had chosen the general.[45]

[43] C. F. Adams Diary, Dec. 26, 1855; Wilson to Salmon P. Chase, Jan. 15, 1856, Chase MSS, Historical Society of Pennsylvania; Boston *Evening Telegraph*, May 1, 30, 1856.

[44] Ruhl J. Bartlett, *John C. Fremont and the Republican Party* (Columbus, Ohio, 1930), 14-15; Allan Nevins, *Fremont: Pathmaker of the West* (New York, 1939), 426-27; Harrington, *Banks,* 34-35; Wilson to Dear Well, March 10, 1856, Boston Public Library.

[45] Boston *Evening Telegraph,* June 12, 1856; Harrington, *Banks,* 36-37.

The first part of the scheme went through without serious difficulty; the Americans nominated Banks and William F. Johnson of Pennsylvania. In Washington, Wilson wound up his attack on Butler in a speech Seward thought was "the best possible vindication of Mr. Sumner." Wilson baited Southern congressmen with charges that they sought to govern Washington society as well as politics and condemned their "assumed social superiority" as "piney-woods doctrine." Vehemently he denied the Southern aristocrats could "hold the plantation whip" over him. Wilson then hurried to Philadelphia to make sure the plans for uniting North Americans and Republicans did not go awry.[46]

On June 17, Wilson told the assembled Republicans in convention hall that "I have been more accustomed to look into the stern faces of foes than to meet the kind glances of friends." Repeating his admonition that the Republicans could not win the election unaided, he urged his fellows to "forgive and unite" with Independent Democrats, Whigs, and Americans. He smeared the Democrats with the blood of Kansas and Sumner, and to rousing cheers declared that he and his Republican colleagues in Congress knew that if they were assassinated, Republicans would send "gallant men" to replace them. The following day the Republicans quickly nominated Fremont, and then Wilson helped to name William L. Dayton, a Henry Clay Whig, as Fremont's running mate. Republicans hoped he would draw the support of protectionists in Pennsylvania and his home state of New Jersey. Banks then resigned his Know-Nothing nomination, and Wilson rushed over to the nativist gathering to help persuade them to accept Fremont. The Americans grudgingly agreed.[47]

After helping the Republicans secure a satisfactory presidential ticket, Wilson returned to Washington to stir up the fires of Kansas. Once again he colored his speeches with crimson. The president, he cried, has "the blood of the murdered people of Kansas dripping from his hands—with the lurid light of the sacked and burning dwellings of Kansas flashing upon his brazen brow." Friends in Kansas

[46] Pierce, *Sumner,* III, 481-83; *Congressional Globe,* 34th Cong., 1st sess., 1856, pp. 1399-1403.

[47] New York *Times,* June 18, 1856.

supplied Wilson with concrete evidence of the dastardly blows struck by slave-state forces in the territory. In July he stopped dramatically in the middle of a speech to flourish a rifle ball, which he assured his fellow senators "was shot through a boy eighteen years old, the son of a widow." No peace could be reached, he warned, between "the great contending powers of freedom upon one side, and slavery on the other."[48]

In August Congress finally adjourned, and Wilson rushed off to renew attempts at organizing a fusion movement between Republicans and Know-Nothings in Massachusetts. He shocked many of his friends when he demanded that the Republicans support Gardner for governor instead of nominating a candidate of their own. They could then secure Know-Nothing cooperation in a joint electoral ticket for president. Gardner did not consider Wilson "respectable," but Wilson never allowed personal friction to stand in the way of political success. He assured Republicans that the American organization was about to collapse anyway, and they could afford to be magnanimous. After a bitter argument, the Republican convention accepted Wilson's plan. Some, however, went home in disgust to organize a separate "Honest Men's Ticket." Wilson's friend William S. Robinson was so irate at the senator's course that he frightened his children out of their wits when he stormed home to tear a picture of Wilson from the wall.[49]

In November, worn out from a full year of ardent speech-making, Wilson repaired to his home in Natick to await election results. Although as an adroit politician he customarily appeared sanguine as campaigns came to an end, he could not hide his pessimism about the possibility of Fremont's success. In October state elections in the key state of Pennsylvania had gone Democratic. As he greeted his

[48] *Congressional Globe,* 34th Cong., 1st sess., 1856, p. 1101, appendix, pp. 776, 793, 855; Henry Wilson to A. H. Reeder, March 31, 1856, E. C. French MSS, Massachusetts Historical Society.

[49] Boston *Evening Telegraph,* Sept. 16, 18, 1856; Merriam, *Bowles,* I, 154-56; William G. Bean, "The Transformation of Parties in Massachusetts . . . from 1848 to 1860" (Ph.D. dissertation, Harvard University, 1922), 323; Hamilton Fish to Henry Gardner, Feb. 9, 1857, Fish MSS, Library of Congress; Robinson, ed., *Warrington,* 63-64.

home town Young American Fremont Club, observers found the exhausted politician presented a "perfect picture of despondency." His prescience about the election soon proved correct. The nation's electorate chose Democrat James Buchanan to succeed Franklin Pierce in the president's chair. Wilson sat silently in his library to listen as jubilant Democrats brought a brass band down Central Street to play a dirge in front of his house. They followed the serenade with three groans for the senator.[50]

Despite the disappointment, Wilson could afford to express some enthusiasm about future prospects. By his own role in weakening the American party, stoking up the fires in Kansas, and bravely facing supposed personal dangers in the Senate, he had saved the reputation he had sullied in earlier political bargains. The presidential campaign, although it had resulted in defeat for the Republicans, promised much for the future. Fremont, gathering well over one million votes, had carried Massachusetts and ten other states. The national election had solidified the fusion movement in many areas. Consequently, Wilson could hopefully conclude that "they may have beaten us this time, but we will win in 1860."[51] After searching for twenty years, he had finally found a political home. Before 1856 he had shown slight regard for the integrity of political organizations. Now, however, he would devote the rest of his life to preserving the existence and serving the interests of the Republican party he had helped to create.

[50] Wilson to Sumner, Aug. 3, 1856, Sumner MSS; J. B. Mann in Natick *Bulletin,* Nov. 20, 1885; Natick *Observer,* Nov. 22, 1856.

[51] A. K. McClure, *Recollections of Half a Century* (Salem, Mass., 1902), 45-46.

6

*Hammering out
Republican Policy*

In all of Henry Wilson's wanderings through the Whig, Free Soil, coalition, and Know-Nothing parties, his antislavery principles had often taken second place to considerations of political expediency and political ambition. By 1856 he had the kind of party he wanted, a Northern organization opposed to the Slave Power. Nonetheless, he was still prepared to play the politician, to compromise positions, to soften language, and to conciliate opponents, for the Republican party had not yet won a national election. To build up the strength of the new organization so it could win in 1860, he had to attract more adherents. To do this it would be necessary to reconstruct the image of the Republican party that its opponents had created in the 1856 campaign. They had portrayed the new party members as dedicated abolitionists who would destroy slavery even at the cost of the Union. Such a vision of radicalism drove off many voters who would have readily accepted a weaker position on the slavery question.

To Wilson the solution for the problem was simple. He would mute the more strident antislavery voices of the party and persuade the voters that Republicans, who neither favored violent action against the slaveholders nor threatened disunion, could safely be entrusted with the nation's government. Instead of emphasizing the moral problem posed by the existence of human bondage in the South, he would stress the political and economic effects of maintaining slaveholders in control of the national government. He hoped to convince Western farmers and Eastern industrialists and workers that the Republican party, rather than its Southern-dominated opponent, would best safeguard their economic interests.

Immediately after returning to Congress in December, Wilson began his struggle to rid the Republican party of the odor of abolitionism and disunion. Repudiating the doctrines of William Lloyd Garrison, he advocated a "reasonable and moderate position" on emancipation. He insisted that his party merely sought to destroy slavery's connection with the federal government, not interfere with the institution within the Southern states. If this were done, Wilson was willing to let the citizens of the Southern states settle the question "on their own time, and in their own way."[1]

In January, 1857, when Massachusetts abolitionists invited Wilson to attend a "Disunion Convention" at Worcester, the senator seized the opportunity to reaffirm the views he had expressed to his colleagues. The abolitionists planned to discuss the value of remaining in a federal union that recognized human bondage. Wilson told them he felt "a sincere and profound regret" at reading the convention call. He was certain the meeting would identify disunion with antislavery and thereby array the spirit of nationalism against the Republican party. Vehemently he scored all such movements, "either in the North or the South, as crimes against liberty" and repeated his insistence that emancipation could only come through the consent of the slaveholding states.[2]

Angry abolitionists denounced Wilson for his cowardice. Garrison accused him of trying to advance his own political career rather than the freedom of the slave. Frank Bird charged him with "selling out" the Republican party. Disgusted with his critics, Wilson asserted that "the antislavery cause would be advanced if some of them were ever more to keep silent." Every imprudent word from the Garrisonians weakened the Republican party's chances for victory in 1860. According to Wilson, the radical abolitionists "have but little idea of

[1] *Congressional Globe,* 34th Cong., 1st sess., 1856, appendix, pp. 390, 775; 34th Cong., 3rd sess., 1857, p. 13, appendix, pp. 95-96.

[2] F. W. Bird to Thomas W. Higginson, Jan. 8, 1856, Higginson MSS; Wilson to Higginson, Jan. 10, 1857, in *Proceedings of the State Disunion Convention . . .* (Boston, 1857), 3-4.

the load they put upon our friends in New Jersey, Pennsylvania, Indiana and Illinois. We were beaten by the disunion cry in 1856 and we shall be again if we do not avoid it."[3]

While Wilson moderated his public pronouncements on slavery, he had not changed his private views. As he told Theodore Parker, he hated the institution and thought it a crime to hold a man in bondage. He admitted that "if I had the power to overthrow slavery in the states I would do it," and in a moment of prescience he added that "we may be driven to do it to defend the country." He thought the fact that he had to carry a revolver in his pocket to protect himself against angry slaveholders was proof enough of his loyalty to the cause of freedom.[4]

The continued rumors of Southern threats against him only increased Wilson's animosity toward the "Southern cavaliers." While he admitted that it was possible to be "a kind, generous man and be a slaveholder," he professed contempt for slaveholders as a class. Indignantly he railed at the insolent behavior of the "negro drivers in Washington."[5] Since his childhood the former apprentice and cobbler had harbored resentments against those who claimed exclusive privileges and assumed an artificial superiority over others. As a politician he had stressed the idea that the same spirit that enslaved the black in the South would also degrade the white worker in the North. In March, 1858, Wilson listened in anger and frustration as a Southern senator, James H. Hammond of South Carolina, delivered a

[3] *Proceedings of Disunion Convention,* 6-7, 17-18, 33-34, 43, 54; George E. Baker to Sumner, Jan. 13, 1857, Wilson to Sumner, Jan. 19, 29, 1857, Sumner MSS; Amasa Walker to Thomas W. Higginson, Jan. 30, 1857, Higginson MSS; Wilson to Robert Carter, Jan. 25, 1857, Houghton Library, Harvard University; Wilson to Parker, March 14, 1857, Feb. 28, May 31, 1858, Parker MSS.

[4] Wilson to Parker, March 14, 1857, May 31, 1858, Parker to Sumner, Feb. 27, 1857, Sumner to Parker, March 6, 1857, Parker MSS; Lydia Maria Child to David M. Child, Jan. 7, 1857, in Lydia Maria Child, *Letters of Lydia Maria Child* (Boston, 1853), 80; Wilson to Sumner, Jan. 29, 1857, Sumner MSS.

[5] Wilson to Parker, May 31, 1858, Parker MSS; Wilson to Sumner, Jan. 6, 8, 27, 29, 1857, Jan. 8, 1858, Sumner MSS. In the Senate in 1862, Wilson recalled that "for seven years I have sat in this Chamber and listened to denunciations, reproaches, rebukes, and every manner of indignity and insult by a domineering and insolent majority." *Congressional Globe,* 37th Cong., 2nd sess., 1862, p. 318.

speech that verified his fears. Hammond, who owned four hundred slaves, insisted that all social systems required a class to perform the menial duties of life. Pointing out that the South had slaves to perform such tasks, Hammond suggested that white workers functioned as slaves for Northern society.[6]

The Massachusetts senator immediately prepared an answer to Hammond, in which he planned to "vindicate the 'Northern slaves' and show up the condition of the 'poor whites' of the South." He drafted the services of Sumner's secretary, A. B. Johnson, to help him write out the lengthy address. Johnson thought the speech was the senator's best effort. He found it "excessively Wilsonian, full of words, tautological, sometimes bathetic, somewhat egotistic, but always bold and frank, not uncourteous except where he denounced Hammond as a libelous calumniator of the honest laborers of the North." Wilson compared the backwardness of the Southern economy and culture under slavery with the progress and public spirit manifested in the North under a free labor system. Proudly he paraded himself as a "hireling manual laborer" who had considered himself the peer of his employer. Utilizing Hammond as an example, he condemned Democrats as "hostile to the general progress of the human race."[7] In June, William Gwin, Southern-born proslavery senator from California, took exception to some of Wilson's words in Senate debate and challenged him to a duel. William H. Seward and two other senators were able to work out a settlement between the two antagonists, but not before Wilson had gained new evidence of Southern arrogance.[8]

Wilson voiced the sentiments of the Northern artisan who nursed social grievances against the slaveholder. He also sought to appeal to

[6] The Hammond speech is discussed in William S. Jenkins, *Pro-Slavery Thought in the Old South* (Chapel Hill, N.C., 1935), 286-87.

[7] Wilson to Sumner, March 8, 1858, A. B. Johnson to Sumner, March 25, 27, 1858, Sumner MSS; John M. Forbes to Nassau Senior, May 4, 1858, in Sarah Forbes Hughes, ed., *Letters of John Murray Forbes* (supp. ed., 3 vols.; Boston, 1905), I, 207; *Congressional Globe,* 35th Cong., 1st sess., 1858, appendix, pp. 168-74.

[8] New York *Tribune,* June 11, 12, 14, 1858; Frederick W. Seward, *Seward at Washington* (2 vols.; New York, 1891), II, 346.

Northern yeomen farmers and wealthy capitalists who had economic complaints about Southern political power. He was particularly anxious to attract the support of the latter group, for it had the wealth essential to political success. Money could corrupt, Wilson once admitted, "but if used to spread truth either by speakers or by papers I think it right to use."[9]

In Massachusetts Wilson sought out the wealthy textile manufacturer, Amos Lawrence, to ask him for his political support. The poorly educated former cobbler, whose manners still bore evidence of a crudity that elevation to the society of senators had not erased, appeared to have little in common with the cultured Lawrence, who had degrees from Andover and Harvard. The cotton capitalist had resisted the Free-Soilers and the coalition and had lobbied against Wilson's election as senator.[10] On the other hand, both men wished to keep Kansas free of slavery. Affairs were reaching a crisis in the territory, where free-state inhabitants were growing in numbers every day. Many of the free-state men believed that they could now turn to the polls, outvote their opponents, and wrest control of the territory from the proslavery men. Their leader, "Governor" Charles Robinson, opposed submitting to the territorial government with its proslavery legislature, and his stand threatened to bring further violence. Wilson feared that continued upheavals in the territory would brand the Republicans, who supported Robinson, as agents of violence and disunion. He urged Robinson to avoid force: "We cannot always have what we want; we must take what we can get."[11]

Such a compromising philosophy proved attractive to a conservative man like Amos Lawrence. In the spring of 1857 he sent Wilson on a trip to Kansas to talk to the free-state men. In May the senator visited Lawrence, Leavenworth, and Topeka in Kansas Territory and earnestly pleaded with Robinson and his associates to take part in the fall elections. By promising to return to Massachusetts and raise

[9] Wilson to Gerrit Smith, Oct. 11, 1852, Gerrit Smith MSS, George Arents Research Library, Syracuse University, Syracuse, N. Y.

[10] Lawrence to I. M. L. Williams, Jan. 20, March 2, 1855, Lawrence MSS.

[11] Lawrence to Wilson, Nov. 23, 1858, Lawrence MSS.

funds and send out agents to help organize and run the free-state
campaign, Wilson converted Robinson to his views. He then hurried
East to gather the money. A Boston group headed by Lawrence
selected an emissary to Kansas, gave him $3,000, and sent him West.
Wilson was confident that with proper organization and judicious
use of the funds he had helped to raise, the free-state men could
control the territory.[12]

The results of the October election did indeed give the free-state
men command of the Kansas government. Proslavery forces, however, had controlled an earlier election for a constitutional convention, and the convention delegates, meeting in Lecompton, drew up
a document permitting slavery in Kansas. They then petitioned
Congress for admission to the Union. Wilson was disappointed in the
development but urged Robinson to participate in the government
even if the Lecompton constitution were adopted. He promised the
free-state leader that Republicans in Congress would defeat the
Lecompton scheme.[13]

When the first session of the Thirty-fifth Congress convened in
Washington in December, 1857, President James Buchanan sent the
Lecompton constitution to Capitol Hill with a recommendation that
the legislature accept it, admit Kansas as a slave state, and end further agitation on the subject. Republicans roundly condemned the
scheme. Wilson effectively utilized Buchanan's message to show that
the danger to the Union came not from the Republican party, but

[12] William Lawrence, *A Life of Amos Adams Lawrence,* (Boston, 1889),
105-6; Lawrence to Wilson, April 23, 1857, Nov. 23, 1858, Lawrence to
Robinson, Aug. 17, 1857, Lawrence MSS; James C. Malin, *John Brown and
the Legend of Fifty-Six* (Philadelphia, 1942), 690-700; undated newspaper
clippings, Robinson scrapbooks, pp. 69-71, Amos Lawrence to Robinson, June
6, 1857, in Regional History Department, Spencer Research Library, University of Kansas, Lawrence, Kan.; Wilson to Robinson, June 15, 1857, Charles
Robinson MSS, Kansas State Historical Society, Topeka, Kan.; M. F. Conway
to George L. Stearns, May 29, 1857, Howe MSS, Massachusetts Historical
Society. B. F. Sanborn, one of the leaders of the free-state movement, praised
Wilson's efforts and credited him with the free-state victory in the 1857 elections. See Sanborn, "The Early History of Kansas, 1854-1861," Massachusetts
Historical Society *Proceedings,* 3rd ser., XLI (1907-1908), 495-96.

[13] Wilson to Robinson, Nov. 26, 1857, Robinson MSS.

from the "local, sectional power, that can control this Government, can ride over justice, ride over a wronged people" in the interest of Southern slaveholders.[14]

Although Wilson vociferously condemned Buchanan and the Lecompton constitution, he and his Republican colleagues gladly let Stephen A. Douglas and his Northern Democratic followers carry the brunt of the attack on the slave-state scheme. Douglas had staked his political future on the doctrine of popular sovereignty, by which the population of a territory would decide for itself whether or not to allow slavery to exist within its borders. The frauds inherent in the Lecompton plan were so obviously a violation of popular sovereignty that Douglas had no choice but to oppose it.

Wilson was tremendously pleased by the revelation of a crucial split in the Democratic party. He had always been on the alert for an opportunity to attract Northern Democrats away from their Southern colleagues. A close associate of Douglas noted that Wilson "threw himself with especial fervor among the revolting Democrats. He consulted with us and encouraged us; he travelled far and near to effect cooperation and organization." The Massachusetts senator was sure that Douglas and his followers would ally with opponents of the Slave Power, and he urged his friends to "deal kindly with these men and adopt a liberal policy. We want to carry the entire free states." Wilson was so eager to propitiate Douglas that he joined with Horace Greeley and other Eastern Republicans in recommending that their party colleagues in Illinois let the doughty senator run unopposed for reelection in 1858.[15]

Some of Wilson's friends had always been amazed at his willingness to associate with former political opponents in hopes of adding them to his own party. As a party associate later recalled, Wilson

[14] *Congressional Globe,* 35th Cong., 1st sess., 1858, pp. 387, 542, 545-48, 576-78.

[15] John W. Forney, *Anecdotes of Public Men* (2 vols.; New York, 1873), I, 342; David Donald, *Lincoln's Herndon* (New York, 1948), 109, 114; Amos Lawrence to Charles Robinson, Jan. 2, 1858, Lawrence MSS; Wilson to Schouler, Feb. 19, 1858, William Schouler MSS; A. B. Johnson to Sumner, April 1, 1858, E. L. Pierce to Sumner, Nov. 30, 1858, Sumner MSS.

"never bore malice or seemed to keep angry over night." Unless his impulsiveness got the better of him, he endeavored to "utter not a word that could give reasonable offense to anyone." A Pennsylvania journalist acquainted with the Massachusetts senator found him "warm, generous, and forgiving . . . a thorough commonsense man, and a natural medium between quarreling friends." Despite his frequent and sometimes bitter arguments with Douglas in the Senate, he tried to maintain a cordial relationship with the Illinois senator. Douglas once remarked that if he had any favor to ask of the Republicans "he always preferred going to Senator Wilson, as *he* did not allow *political* differences to interfere with the courtesies of life."[16]

Not everyone associated with Wilson agreed with or even understood his flexible and compromising approach to politics. Even William Henry Seward, well known for his gregarious nature, remarked rather distastefully that he found Wilson "whoring with every decent-looking strumpet he meets." Sumner was quite disturbed at Wilson's associations with political opponents. Samuel Gridley Howe urged him not to doubt his colleague: "[Wilson's] idiosyncracies compel him to a social intercourse with his brother Senators." When Theodore Parker, fearing that Douglas might have personal reasons for opposing Buchanan and the Lecompton constitution, questioned Wilson about his support for the Illinois senator, he replied that "I leave motives to God." He assured Parker, however, that "I know men and their power and I know Douglas is for crushing the slave power to atoms."[17]

Wilson's proposed alliance with Douglas never transpired, for Illinois Republicans chose to contest the Democratic senator's bid for reelection. In August Kansans ended fears that their territory

[16] Hoar, *Autobiography,* I, 217; McClure, *Recollections,* 289; Forney, *Anecdotes,* I, 342-43; F. M. Granger to Mrs. Wilson, Sept. 14, 1868, Wilson MSS, Library of Congress.

[17] Seward quoted in Frank Bird to Charles Sumner, June 8, 1857, Sumner MSS; Samuel Gridley Howe to Sumner, July 27, 1858, Howe MSS, Houghton Library, Harvard University; Wilson to Theodore Parker, Feb. 28, 1858, Parker MSS.

might become a slave state when they overwhelmingly rejected statehood under the Lecompton constitution. Continuing to search for
new allies and issues, Wilson now drew closer to "Cotton Whig"
Amos Lawrence. Frequently he visited the industrialist's Boston
office to discuss Bay State politics and even borrowed small sums of
money from him when his bank account grew short. Lawrence was
pleased with the promptness with which Wilson repaid the loans. He
began to discuss the future of the Republican party with the senator.
Lawrence had recently joined the Know-Nothing party, hoping that
the nativist movement would prevent political agitation over slavery
and at the same time forward Northern industrial interests. As the
Know-Nothing organization dissolved, Lawrence urged Wilson to inspire the Republican party with concern for a "free labor policy."[18]

The senator needed no encouragement. He had already been
introducing in the Senate a variety of proposals to develop the
manufacturing and commercial resources of the country. Such activity would help convince voters that the Republicans sought a government that comprehended the whole country, "including the seventeen millions of Northern free men." He defended fishing bounties
for New England, advocated river improvements in the Mississippi
Valley, and strongly supported liberal land grants to railroads in the
Western states. At the same time, he wanted to make it easier for
settlers to obtain land within the railroad grants and also demanded
that Congress pass a homestead bill. He admitted that "we of the
Atlantic coast, who are engaged in manufactures and commerce, all
have a direct interest in the settlement and development, growth and
prosperity, of the new States of the interior." Viewing nations south
of the United States borders as potential markets for Massachusetts
goods, he urged the federal government to establish "reciprocal
commercial intercourse" with them. He assured his colleagues that
"I shall vote for all measures that have a tendency to take off restrictions on trade, liberalize our commercial connections, and prepare

[18] Thomas H. O'Connor, *Lords of the Loom: The Cotton Whigs and the
Coming of the Civil War* (New York, 1968), 119-31; Lawrence manuscript
journal, Oct. 23, 1858, Lawrence to Wilson, Nov. 23, 1858, Wilson to Lawrence, Dec. 8, 1858, Lawrence MSS; Lawrence, *Lawrence*, 139.

that portion of our continent for intimate commercial and perhaps in time, political relations with us."[19]

Wilson also stood ready to satisfy the country's demands for telegraph and rail connections with the Pacific coast. Railroads to California, he thought, should be built by the federal government. He suggested that the government sell federal lands for the needed revenue rather than donate the domain to private companies. When his proposal failed to gather much support in Congress, Wilson agreed to give government lands and bonds to aid private companies in constructing the road, but he sought to amend the suggested bills in order to insure the road's completion. Wilson joined his Republican colleagues in refusing to build a Pacific railroad that would benefit the South; instead he insisted that the eastern terminus of the road be located in the central region of the Mississippi Valley.[20]

Wilson's speeches on various economic issues in the Senate gained Amos Lawrence's approval. He noted with pleasure that the Republicans had "abandoned the cry of no more slave states" and were turning to more practical questions. "I like your business speeches best," he told Wilson, "but they are all good, when you don't ram down the slavery question too hard." He confided to the senator that "providence has brought you up for some good purpose, and I hope and believe that you will not act contrary to that purpose."[21]

Lawrence watched carefully to see if Providence would act through Wilson to change the tariff laws; but distrustful of the efficacy of divine intervention, the industrialist took it upon himself to advise Wilson on the subject. Wilson needed the advice. Many Northern industrialists blamed the panic of 1857 on the tariff of that year, which enacted the lowest duties the country had seen since

[19] *Congressional Globe,* 34th Cong., 1st sess., 1856, pp. 1170-71, 1312, 1980, 2128-29; 34th Cong., 3rd sess., 1857, pp. 463, 556, 568, 590, 613; 35th Cong., 1st sess., 1858, pp. 41, 132, 135, 1152, 1618, 2071-72; 35th Cong., 2nd sess., 1859, pp. 907-8, 1327, 1622-23.

[20] *Ibid.,* 34th Cong., 3rd sess., 1857, appendix, p. 298; 35th Cong., 1st sess., 1858, pp. 1559-60; 35th Cong., 2nd sess., 1858-1859, pp. 304-10, 374-77, 577-78.

[21] Amos A. Lawrence to Henry Wilson, April 28, Nov. 26, 1858, Feb. 1, 1859, Lawrence to Charles Hale, Oct. 8, 1858, Lawrence MSS.

1816. Not all who wanted tariff revision, however, wanted the rates pushed upward. Pennsylvania ironmasters and Ohio sheep raisers demanded heavy rates on imported iron and wool; on the other hand, New England textile manufacturers seemed willing to forego higher duties in return for lower rates on imported raw materials.[22]

To find his way out of the dilemma, Wilson consulted both Lawrence and his own political compass. Pennsylvania, whose iron-masters demanded protection, was an important political plum. In 1858 the newly organized People's party promised to provide the higher rates, and that fall they carried the state elections against the Democrats. Wilson told archprotectionist Henry Carey that "we are all rejoicing over the victory in your state as a victory for Free Labor." He did ask Carey to take a moderate view on tariff revision, rather than endanger Republican success by trying to force high duties on the party. Encouraged by the People's party sweep in Pennsylvania, Wilson assured the convalescent Sumner that the Republicans would carry New York, New Jersey, and Illinois too. He admitted that "these results will not be purely antislavery" but insisted that "antislavery sentiment will be the leading one."[23]

Although Wilson was confident that his cause "must extend and spread over the country," he took no chances in insuring his reelection for the Senate in 1859. In 1857, over the protests of some of his friends, he had encouraged Republicans to nominate Nathaniel Banks for governor, and he advised the same strategy in 1858, for Banks could still gather a good deal of Know-Nothing support and thus swell the Republican vote. Wilson hoped that Banks would be grateful enough for Wilson's efforts in his behalf to refuse to contest

[22] Richard Hofstadter, "The Tariff Issue on the Eve of the Civil War," *American Historical Review*, XLIV (1938-1939), 50-56; *Congressional Globe*, 34th Cong., 3rd sess., 1857, appendix, pp. 333, 342-43; 35th Cong., 1st sess., 1857-1858, pp. 85-87, 90.

[23] Wilson to Henry Carey, Oct. 18, 1858, Henry Carey MSS, Historical Society of Pennsylvania; C. F. Adams Diary, Oct. 28, Dec. 2, 1858; Wilson to Amos Lawrence, [Nov., 1858], Lawrence to Wilson, Feb. 1, 1859, Lawrence MSS; Wilson to Gardner Brewer, Feb. 23, 1859, Boston Public Library; *Congressional Globe*, 35th Cong., 2nd sess., 1859, p. 1312; Wilson to Sumner, Oct. 19, 1858, Sumner MSS.

the Senate seat. The Republicans did renominate and elect Banks in 1858, and his victory annihilated the last remnants of the American party and secured a Republican majority in the 1859 legislature. Wilson's reelection seemed certain. At the last moment, Know-Nothings threatened a coalition with the Democrats to defeat him, but Banks refused to be a candidate for the Senate and the Americans had no one else to suggest. Therefore, in January, 1859, the state legislature reelected Wilson for a full six-year term.[24]

The senator, who had been quite upset at criticisms of his course in Congress, found vindication in his reelection. In a moment of personal reflection, he confessed to his wife that "if any man ought to be thankful to God for His goodness, I am that man. Sustained with such generous unanimity by my state, applauded by my personal and political friends, out of debt with a home for the wife and son I love so much and blessed with health and strength surely I ought to be grateful for the goodness of my Maker." The senator might also have thanked his own political maneuverings for securing such blessings.[25]

Henry Wilson's personal success was dimmed by continued difficulties with the Republican party. He was particularly dismayed at the nativist tendencies in the Republican state legislature. In 1859 it proposed requiring immigrants to live in the state two years after naturalization before they could vote. Wilson, who had just toured some of the Western states and had found much feeling among immigrant peoples there against nativist legislation, returned home "thoroughly frightened." He attacked the proposed amendment as "an invidious and offensive distinction" harmful to men who were born in other lands. Despite his efforts, citizens of the state ap-

[24]C. F. Adams Diary, June 11, 1857, Jan. 13, 1858; Duberman, *Adams*, 210; Amos Lawrence to Wilson, July 13, 1857, Lawrence MSS; F.W. Bird to Sumner, June 8, 1857, E. L. Pierce to Sumner, Oct. 10, 1858, Wilson to Sumner, Aug. 26, 1857, J. W. Stone to Sumner, March 13, May 21, 1858, A. B. Johnson to Sumner, Oct. 15, 1858, Sumner MSS; Wilson to Schuyler Colfax, July 25, 1857, Schuyler Colfax MSS, Library of Congress.

[25]Wilson to "My Dear Wife," Jan. 13, 1859, Natick Historical Society Museum.

proved the proposal. Wilson, however, had cleared himself of responsibility for its success, and he was much pleased to learn that "his praise is in all the West." E. L. Pierce was certain that "General Wilson has thoroughly dispossessed himself of his Americanism and admits that he is wiser than he once was."[26]

Although the action of the Massachusetts legislature greatly concerned the Republican leader, even more discouraging was the fact that his appeals to the economic interests of Massachusetts had met with failure. He complained that Bay State manufacturers who would raise $50,000 for tariff lobbies "might also give money to defeat us." Despite his earnest efforts to divorce the Republican party from association with violence and disunion, businessmen were skeptical of the party's new approach.[27] And then, late in 1859, came a sudden and horrifying event that seemed to justify their fears and also the suspicions of the South concerning the Republican party. On October 16, an abolitionist named John Brown, accompanied by a band of whites and free Negroes, seized the federal arsenal at Harper's Ferry, Virginia, in a bold but unsuccessful attempt to inspire a slave insurrection that they hoped would spread across the South.

Wilson, who had just returned from an electioneering trip into Pennsylvania, was resting at home when he first heard of the Brown raid. Horror-stricken, he rushed to Boston to confer with William Lloyd Garrison, Amos Lawrence, and fellow Republicans. Fearing that the country would associate "Black Republicanism" with the attempted insurrection, he roared in anguish: "Brown's invasion has thrown us, who were in a splendid position, into a defensive position ... if we are defeated next year we owe it to that foolish and

[26] Anderson, "Slavery Issue," 241-46; Wilson to E. L. Pierce, March 12, April 23, 1857, Houghton Library, Harvard University; Mann, *Wilson*, 56-58; Natick *Observer*, May 7, 1859; Wilson to Salmon P. Chase, May 18, 1859, Salmon P. Chase MSS, Library of Congress; Wilson to ?, Aug. 12, 1859, Historical Society of Pennsylvania; E. L. Pierce to Sumner, [April, 1859], May 31, 1859, Frank Bird to Sumner, April 17, 1859, Sumner MSS; C. F. Adams Diary, May 9, Dec. 17, 1859.

[27] Wilson to D. Robner, Sept. 10, 1859, Republican State Central Committee MSS, Minnesota Historical Society, St. Paul, Minn.

insane movement of Brown's." He had heard of the insurrectionist before. The grizzled abolitionist had been active in Kansas, where he had led retaliatory raids on proslavery camps and had personally aided in murdering several white settlers. Wilson, who had constantly advised against the use of violence, had flown into a rage at news of Brown's depredations in Kansas and had cursed him as a "damned old fool."[28]

But Wilson had more personal reasons for becoming so upset at the news of Brown's raid on Virginia. His thoughts flashed back to a scene in the United States Senate in the spring of 1858. At that time, a nervous, excitable young man had forced his way onto the Senate floor during a recess to spill out to him a flood of jumbled accusations concerning the activities of Brown, who was then in Kansas. Gesticulating wildly, Wilson's visitor insisted that some rifles sent from Massachusetts to Kansas to aid settlers in protecting themselves had fallen into Brown's hands; Brown threatened to use the rifles to strike a blow into Southern territory. Wilson, startled and dismayed by the confused tale and thinking that Brown probably planned a retaliatory raid into Missouri, repeated the story to Samuel Gridley Howe, one of the members of the committee that had supplied the arms to Kansas. Attacking the whole policy of sending rifles to the territory, Wilson demanded that Howe reclaim the guns. Howe assured him that "no countenance has been given to Brown for any operations outside of Kansas by the Kansas committee." Wilson then forgot the incident; but in the spring of 1859 he ran into Brown in Boston and exchanged some sharp words with the free-state warrior.[29]

[28] Lawrence, *Lawrence,* 131; Wendell Phillips Garrison and Frances Jackson Garrison, *William Lloyd Garrison, 1805-1877* (4 vols.; New York, 1889), III, 488; C. Vann Woodward, *The Burden of Southern History* (Baton Rouge, La., 1960), 46; Eli Thayer, *A History of the Kansas Crusade* (New York, 1899), 194; Amos Lawrence to Wilson, June 14, 1859, Lawrence MSS; New York *Times,* Nov. 29, 1875; Natick *Bulletin,* Nov. 20, 1885.

[29] *Senate Report No. 278,* 36th Cong., 1st sess., 1859, pp. 140-45, 160, 176, 232; J. B. Mann in Natick *Bulletin,* Nov. 20, 1885; Samuel Gridley Howe to Wilson, May 15, 1858, Jan. 23, 1860, Howe MSS, Massachusetts Historical Society.

As matters turned out, ownership of the guns had been transferred from the Kansas Committee to one of its members, George Luther Stearns, and although the committee may have refused to encourage any act of violence on the part of Brown, Stearns neither reclaimed the rifles nor advised Brown against using them. Wilson, who felt he had been tricked by the committee, feared he might be dragged into an investigation of the Harper's Ferry raid and accused of having had prior knowledge of the attack. In a fit of passion he angrily declared he would not care if Howe and Stearns were hanged for conspiring with Brown.[30]

Wilson's first burst of anger soon gave way to concern for shielding the Republican party from the shock of the Brown raid. Wasting not a day, he left on a hurried speaking tour to convince voters in the East that Brown's raid "was not a consequence of the teachings of Republicanism." All good party members, he insisted, were horrified by the events at Harper's Ferry.[31] Despite Wilson's frantic activity, when he returned to Washington for the opening of Congress Southern senators accused him of condoning slave insurrections in the South. Newspaper reports of Wilson's speech at Syracuse, New York, had garbled his language to quote him as saying Brown's raid "was the legitimate consequence" of Republican teachings.[32]

Although Wilson managed to correct the Senate's false impressions of his speeches, he still had to appear before a Senate committee appointed to investigate the Harper's Ferry raid. He was still

[30] Oswald Garrison Villard, *John Brown, 1800-1859* (New York, 1943), 317-18, 339-42; F. B. Sanborn to Henry Richards, May 15, 1908, Higginson MSS; Frank P. Stearns, *Life and Public Services of George Luther Stearns* (Philadelphia, 1907) 168-71.

[31] New York *Times,* Oct. 26, 1859; New York *Tribune,* Oct. 27, 1859.

[32] Wooster Sherman to R. M. T. Hunter, Dec. 10, 1859, in C. H. Ambler, ed., "Correspondence of R. M. T. Hunter, 1826-1876," in *Annual Report* of the American Historical Association, 1916 (2 vols.; Washington, D. C., 1918), II, 278; *Congressional Globe,* 36th Cong., 1st sess., 1859-1860, pp. 12-13; 38th Cong., 1st sess., 1864, p. 704; Natick *Observer,* Nov. 24, Dec. 10, 1859. Wilson's mangled quote has been incorrectly utilized in Laurence T. Lowery, *Northern Opinion of Approaching Secession,* Smith College Studies in History, III (July, 1918), 213, and in J. G. de R. Hamilton, "Lincoln's Election an Immediate Menace to Slavery in the States?" *American Historical Review,* XXXVII (1931-1932), 701.

angry with the men in Massachusetts who had supplied Brown with money and arms, but he tried to calm their fears and encourage them to appear before the committee, because he needed their testimony in order to clear himself of charges of complicity in the raid. Fortunately for the senator, Howe, Stearns, and one of John Brown's personal secretaries were able to prove that he had had no foreknowledge of Brown's attack into Virginia.[33]

Although the Harper's Ferry raid failed to harm Wilson's personal career, his hopes for an easy Republican victory in 1860 were dashed. He could only hope that with hard work, judicious use of campaign funds, good organization, thorough canvassing, and an available candidate, he and his party colleagues could overcome the handicap imposed upon them by John Brown.

[33] F. B. Sanborn to T. W. Higginson, Dec. 20, 25, 1859, Jan. 2, 1860, Wilson to Higginson, Dec. 24, 1859, Boston Public Library; Wilson to Amos Lawrence, Dec. 19, 1859, Lawrence MSS; Sumner to Samuel Gridley Howe; Dec. 8, 1859, Sumner MSS; *Congressional Globe,* 36th Cong., 1st sess., 1859-1860, p. 11; Natick *Observer,* Jan. 28, 1860; *Senate Report No. 278,* p. 15.

7

*From Ballots
to Bullets*

The winter following John Brown's raid was one of the longest seasons in Henry Wilson's life. In Washington he faced the withering attacks of angry Southerners, knowing full well that "the Slave Power intends to excite and alarm the conservative men of the North and thus defeat our course for four years longer." All he could do was urge his party colleagues to keep silent. The proslavery men must "get up a panic if they can alone."[1]

Convinced that without the votes of moderate men Republicans could not hope to win in 1860, Wilson continued to urge his friends to soften their antislavery sentiments. He told abolitionist Lydia Maria Child that "the people are not *ready* for the truth on the subject of slavery." He explained he often had to be silent lest he alienate Republicans who represented "dark sections of the country where the people are growing up to our position but doing it slowly." Mrs. Child decided Wilson was "too much of a politician to trust him entirely. Always he is looking to the immediate effect on some party . . . not to the ultimate and universal effect on the character and motives of the country."[2]

Late in January, charges of timidity provoked Wilson into abandoning his defensive pose. In a lengthy speech he scored Southern Democrats for threatening to dissolve the Union if they lost the coming election. Branding the Democratic party as treasonous, Wilson called upon the North to insist on preserving the Union. Friends congratulated him on his speech; Mrs. Child's husband praised him "for making the Southern blusterers *run* the *gauntlet.*"

While Wilson had pleased those who wanted someone to attack the Slave Power, he also had managed to reassert that Republicans were not abolitionists; they only desired to exclude slavery from the territories. The mildly antislavery Samuel Bowles found the speech "a full, free, and frank declaration of the principles of the North," and throughout the year various Massachusetts papers referred to it as the best exposition of the party's position.[3]

Searching for ways to keep the pressure on the Southerners, Wilson accused them of seeking to reopen the slave trade. His old antagonist, James Hammond, branded Wilson's charges as "sheer fudge," but the determined senator, insisting that the whole South desired to resume the trade, read to his colleagues a spate of newspaper abstracts to prove his point. At this Louis Wigfall snorted that "there is nothing you cannot prove on anybody by . . . the system of keeping a pair of scissors in one's pocket and cutting out newspaper articles." Undaunted, Wilson kept up his agitation.[4]

In April Wilson's spirits were lifted with the news that the Democratic party, meeting in national conclave in Charleston, South Carolina, had divided over the question of slavery in the territories. Now it was more important than ever for the Republicans to choose a man to run in 1860 who could attract a wide following. Since Fremont's defeat in 1856, Wilson had contemplated the merits of possible presidential candidates. Personally, he preferred Salmon P.

[1] Wilson to Reverend James Freeman Clarke, Jan. 29, 1860, Houghton Library, Harvard University.

[2] Wilson to Henry C. Carey, April 16, 1860, Carey MSS; Lydia Maria Child to Charles Sumner, June 17, 1860, Sumner MSS; Wilson to James F. Clarke, Jan. 29, 1860, Houghton Library, Harvard University.

[3] Henry Wilson, *Democratic Leaders for Disunion* (New York, 1860); C. Cleveland to Charles Sumner, Jan. 29, 1860, Sumner MSS; Samuel Goodrich to Wilson, Jan. 31, 1860, Rutherford B. Hayes Library, Fremont, Ohio; R. A. Chapman to Henry L. Dawes, Jan. 27, 1860, Dawes MSS; David Lee Child to Wilson, March 13, 1860, Boston Public Library; Edith Allen Ware, *Political Opinion in Massachusetts During the Civil War and Reconstruction* (New York, 1916), 22.

[4] Wilson's efforts to get American sloops of war to patrol the African coast for slave traders were successful. On his bills against the slave trade, see *Congressional Globe,* 36th Cong., 1st sess., 1860, pp. 1118, 1245, 1610, 1721, 2029, 2207-11, 2269, 3099, 3102.

Chase of Ohio or Seward of New York, but he feared candidates "so mixed up in the conflict" would alienate moderate men. Although the Massachusetts senator insisted on someone "fully committed" to Republican principles, his search for an available candidate led him to a man Southern-born and Southern in his social sympathies— General Winfield Scott. Wilson, who knew that the former Whig presidential nominee was stubbornly loyal to the Union, visited the aging general during the Christmas recess. Scott was impressed by his visitor's "manliness and conservatism" but refused to be associated with the Republican party. Wilson had to abandon his plans to resurrect the old hero.[5]

In the spring of 1860 Massachusetts Republicans selected a delegation to represent the state in May at the party's national convention in Chicago. Desiring to give the delegation a tone of moderation, Wilson invited a former Webster lieutenant, George Ashmun, to attend. Ashmun, who confessed "a desire to rebuke Southern impudence," agreed to go. Too busy in Washington to attend the convention, Wilson kept himself informed of developments. He was pleased to find his name included in the lists of possible presidential nominees. In the great convention hall, the contest centered on William H. Seward, and opponents of the New York senator finally settled on the prairie politician and lawyer from Illinois, Abraham Lincoln. On the first ballot the Massachusetts delegation gave the gangling Springfield attorney a few votes; on the third, John Andrew transferred the state's entire vote to Lincoln, thereby adding to the landslide that gave him the nomination.[6]

[5] Wilson to Schouler, Feb. 19, 1858, William Schouler MSS; Wilson to Amos Lawrence, Nov. 25, 1858, Lawrence MSS; Wilson to E. A. Stansbury, Jan. 25, 1859, Wilson MSS, Library of Congress; Wilson to George Julian, Jan. 20, 1860, Giddings-Julian MSS; Wilson to Salmon P. Chase, Oct. 14, 1859, Feb. 5, 1860, Chase MSS, Historical Society of Pennsylvania; Wilson to Henry C. Carey, April 16, 1860, Carey MSS; E. L. Pierce to Charles Sumner, July 12, 1859, Sumner MSS; Charles Winslow Elliott, *Winfield Scott: The Soldier and the Man* (New York, 1937), 672-74; Scott to J. J. Crittenden, Jan. 6, 27, Feb. 1, 1860, and Scott to Wilson, Jan., 1860, all quoted in Mrs. Chapman Coleman, ed., *The Life of John J. Crittenden* (2 vols.; Philadelphia, 1871), II, 182-85.

[6] Wilson to Herndon, May 30, 1867, Herndon-Weik Collection, William Herndon MSS, Library of Congress; George Ashmun to Wilson, April 22,

Upon learning of the decision of the Chicago convention, Wilson wrote to Lincoln's law partner, abolitionist William Herndon, asking him for his impressions of the nominee. Herndon, who had met Wilson two years earlier, assured the senator that Lincoln hated slavery and was determined to see justice and liberty prevail. Wilson was satisfied with the reply. He was worried about the effects of Lincoln's nomination in Seward's home state, but he was sure that "The West will go it with a rush." When the vanquished Seward returned to Senate halls, his Republican colleagues were embarrassed to speak to him about his defeat. Wilson, however, who had made political maneuvering a way of life, hovered eagerly about Seward's desk, thirsting for explanations for his failure.[7]

In August Wilson departed for an extensive tour around Massachusetts and into neighboring states. He traveled thousands of miles and delivered one hundred speeches. In his campaigning he found meetings well attended, but he feared Republicans were overconfident and neglectful of proper organization. Anxiously he urged Abraham Lincoln to alert the party's leaders to "the duty of work, organization, system." He hoped Republicans would not rely solely on mass meetings, but would "go into the school districts, into the out of the way places and organize our friends." In his own speeches Wilson bitterly denounced the newly formed Constitutional Union party as an attempt to ignore "the living issues of the age" and "delude, deceive, and cheat" the Northern people. He told an audience of workers in East Boston that John Bell, the party's nominee, was an abject servant of the Slave Power. Noting that many Massachusetts businessmen supported Bell, Wilson warned the workers not to entrust their interests to "the nerveless conservatives, the dry goods traffickers, who are eager to sell their principles as well as their goods." He told laborers wherever he went that the

1860, Wilson MSS, Library of Congress; Henry G. Pearson, *The Life of John A. Andrew* (2 vols.; Boston, 1904), I, 112-13; Emerson D. Fite, *The Presidential Campaign of 1860* (New York, 1911), 122.

[7] Wilson to E. A. Stansbury, May 21, 1860, Wilson MSS, Library of Congress; William H. Seward to Mrs. Seward, May 30, 1860, in Seward, *Seward at Washington,* II, 455.

presidential contest was an "irrepressible conflict" between those who benefited from the toil of others, and the toiling men themselves. He reminded them that the Democratic party represented the interests of slaveholders who were contemptuous of free labor and laboring men. The Republican party, on the other hand, was concerned about the rights of laboring classes and the equality of mankind.[8]

In November the exhausted campaigner returned to Natick to await the outcome of the election. In the few days before he received the verdict of the voters, Wilson had time to ponder his political career. He had experienced triumphant successes and dismal failures, but on the whole, he had gone far toward satisfying his ambition. The struggling cobbler of 1840 was now in his second term as United States senator; he was a leading figure of a new political party. He had reason to be complacent. However, holding high public office was not enough. During the last twenty years he had demolished one political organization after another, searching for a party that would drive the Slave Power from Washington. Until that goal was accomplished, he could not be satisfied.

Now, in November, as the votes began to roll in from across the North, the hardened political battler realized that the greatest success of his twenty-one year political career was about to dawn. Abraham Lincoln, profiting from the existence of three rival candidates that divided his opponents, was about to become the sixteenth president of the United States. The "Negro drivers" had finally felt the lash themselves—they had been whipped in the political arena! Exulting, Wilson rushed to Boston to join his exuberant comrades. His friend J. B. Mann later recalled that "any success at the polls made a new man of him. It was a sight to be long remembered, to

[8] Lawrence, *Lawrence,* 154; Boston *Daily Advertiser,* Aug. 14, Sept. 7, 11, 12, 19, 20, 1860; Wilson to Abraham Lincoln, Aug. 25, 1860, Robert Todd Lincoln MSS, Library of Congress; Wilson to Sumner, Sept. 25, 1860, Oct. 24, 1860, Sumner MSS; Wilson, *Position of John Bell and His Supporters* (Boston, 1860); Natick *Observer,* Sept. 29, 1860; Henry Wilson, *How Ought Working Men to Vote in the Coming Election?* (Boston, 1860); New York *Times,* March 29, 1860.

see Wilson triumphant. . . . His whole figure showed a transformation . . . his eyes, naturally bright, flashed with an unusual fire, and
his voice acquired a louder and steadier tone."[9]

The victory in 1860 was the greatest triumph of all, and Wilson
savored it to the fullest. Torrential rains had left the city sodden, but
muddied streets did not deter the surging crowds and blaring bands
that marched about trumpeting campaign tunes. Members of the
victorious party jammed Music Hall to listen to their leaders gloat
over election returns. The senator sat in the middle of the crowded
platform, and when his turn came to speak, he stepped jubilantly to
the podium. "Tonight, thanks be to God," he began, "we stand with
the Slave Power beneath our feet." The crowd roared its approval.
"That haughty power which corrupted the Whig party, strangled the
American party, and used the Democratic party as a tool, lies
crushed to the dust tonight, and our heel is upon it." Wilson's audience stopped him short with wild applause. The speaker, encouraged
by such enthusiasm, grew defiant as he addressed himself to the
slaveholders who were threatening to secede from the Union: "Go
on, if you dare. We intend to stand by the Union, come what
may."[10]

Later in the month, Massachusetts Democrat Caleb Cushing spoke
in Newburyport and, in referring to Wilson's earlier remarks in
Boston, charged the senator with proposing to crush the Southern
states and their citizenry beneath the heel of the Republican party.
By this time, Wilson's impulsiveness had given way to more practical
considerations; he was growing increasingly disturbed by movements
toward secession in some Southern states. Consequently he published an open letter to Cushing, admitting that his language in
Boston, "uttered in the first flush of our brilliant national triumph,"
was "unpremeditated and unguarded." He insisted that the people of
Massachusetts bore no hate for the South, and he reminded Cushing
that the Republican party recognized the doctrine of states' rights

[9] J. B. Mann quoted in Natick *Bulletin,* Nov. 20, 1885.
[10] Boston *Daily Advertiser,* Nov. 10, 1860; Boston *Daily Courier,* Nov. 10,
1860.

and did not propose to attack slavery in the states where it existed.[11]

Unfortunately for Wilson and the nation, the South did not listen to his assurances. At news of Lincoln's election South Carolinians began preparing to take their state out of the Union, and many of her neighbors watched sympathetically. Wilson had long ridiculed Southern threats of secession. As he left for Washington in late November he could hardly believe South Carolina was serious. Once in the nation's capital, however, he became convinced that the threat was fast becoming a reality. On December 20 South Carolina left the Union and was quickly followed by several of her sisters. In the Senate, the Massachusetts legislator watched silently as representatives of the seceded states strode out of the chamber. One of them, Jefferson Davis, had served as chairman of the military affairs committee; Wilson, who was one of the committee members, had managed to stay on good terms with him. As Davis prepared to leave, Wilson walked over to ask if he really was following his state. Davis confirmed his suspicions and then, grasping his fellow senator by the hand, tersely remarked: "Wilson, you and I have always been friends; I hope we shall meet in calmer times." Then the tall Mississippian made his last exit from the Senate. In a few months he would be president of a people at war with the United States.[12]

Wilson had no doubt about the proper course for the Republican party to follow in the secession crisis. The North, acting through the Republican party, had to show its determination to stand by its principles and maintain the Union and thereby "frighten southerners away from their object." He encouraged Salmon P. Chase to take a cabinet post if Lincoln offered it to him. By doing so the Ohioan could make sure that the administration would be conducted on "*Republican* principles."[13]

[11] Boston *Daily Courier,* Nov. 28, 1860; *Letter of Senator Wilson to Honorable Caleb Cushing* (Washington, 1860).

[12] E. C. Cowdin, *A Tribute to the Memory of Henry Wilson* (New York: Union League Club, 1875), 11; reminiscences of Mary Thomas, in Natick *Citizen,* March 21, 1879; Mrs. Wilson to Mrs. Claflin, Jan. 14, 1861, Claflin MSS.

[13] Boston *Daily Courier,* Nov. 27, 28, 1860; Salmon P. Chase to Wilson,

Wilson's own devotion to the principles of his party was soon tested. As the secession crisis grew more serious, worried Northerners pressured Congress to adopt Union-saving compromises. Since much of the demand for a peaceful settlement came from Massachusetts, Wilson could not ignore it. In December local elections in the state had reversed earlier Republican victories; in January, the political crisis prompted a series of business failures. Amos Lawrence circulated petitions favoring compromise, and some towns gave more signatures than they had given votes to the Republican party. In Boston, a city of 19,000 voters, Lawrence gathered 14,000 names. Boston capitalists also joined with ex-Whig politicians, former governors, and state judicial officers to recommend repeal of the Massachusetts personal liberty law. This legislation, which had been designed to block the execution in Massachusetts of the federal fugitive slave law, was especially obnoxious to the South. According to the Massachusetts law, state courts, jails, and militia were not to be used in the case of any Negro claimed as a fugitive.[14]

To some degree Wilson bent to the pressure. He had always believed that the personal liberty law was embarrassing to the Republican party, and in the Senate he angered many of his constituents by questioning the constitutionality of the enactments. He insisted again that Massachusetts harbored no ill feeling toward the South and denied that the Republican party was filled with abolitionists. Some observers thought that Wilson might support Seward's frantic attempts to find a compromise suitable to the South. In late January, the Massachusetts senator united with the rest of the Massachusetts congressional delegation—except Sumner—to urge Governor Andrew to send representatives to the peace conference in Washing-

---

Dec. 13, 1860, Chase, "Diary and Correspondence," 293-94; Wilson to Chase, Dec. 15, 1860, Chase MSS, Historical Society of Pennsylvania; Carl Schurz to wife, Dec. 27, 1860, in Joseph Schafer, trans. and ed., *Intimate Letters of Carl Schurz, 1841-1869* (Madison, Wis., 1928), 238; Wilson to William S. Robinson, Dec. 16, 1860, in Robinson, ed., *Warrington*, 93.

[14] David M. Potter, *Lincoln and His Party in the Secession Crisis* (New Haven, Conn., 1942), 124, 190, 198; Pearson, *Andrew*, I, 131-38; Ware, *Political Opinion*, 47, 49-56; Anderson, "Slavery Issue," 303-5; George Morey to John Andrew, Jan. 29, 1861, Andrew MSS, Massachusetts Historical Society.

ton called by Virginia to propose a settlement between the sections.[15]

Although Wilson outwardly gave in somewhat to compromise pressure, he never really abandoned a hard line toward the secessionists. When he advised Andrew to send commissioners to the peace conference, he asked him to send "able and firm men." After Andrew asked Wilson and Sumner to visit the Massachusetts commissioners in Washington and "surround them with the best influence," Wilson readily complied. Most important, the senator was determined to resist any attempt to allow slavery in the territories of the United States or in any new lands annexed in the future. During the 1860 campaign he had repeatedly defined the establishment of free territories as the basis of the Republican platform.[16]

In February John J. Crittenden, senator from Kentucky, proposed a compromise that sorely tested Wilson's convictions on the territorial issue. Crittenden suggested drawing the Missouri Compromise line to the Pacific; such a proposal would permit slavery below the line. In Massachusetts, supporters of the measure found over 35,000 people favoring it. When Crittenden presented the petitions in the Senate, he took occasion to notice that 259 of the signers lived in Natick. Eyes turned to Wilson as he rose to answer the Kentuckian. Almost ten years earlier, he had reminded Sumner that "the people above all things love a man of iron will." Now he chose to demonstrate such fortitude by condemning the proposal. It was not a compromise, he charged, but a complete surrender of all practical issues concerning slavery in the territories. According to him, the Crittenden compromise was a "cheat, a delusion, a snare." It would protect slavery, and it was the proponents of slavery who had

[15] Wilson, *Letter to Caleb Cushing;* H. L. Dawes to J. D. Colt, Dec. 23, 1860, Dawes MSS; E. L. Pierce to Charles Sumner, Feb. 10, 1861, Sumner MSS; Henry Adams to Charles Francis Adams, Jr., Jan. 17, 1861, in Worthington C. Ford, ed., *Letters of Henry Adams, 1858-1891* (2 vols.; Boston, 1930), 79; Garrison, *Garrison,* IV, 9; C. F. Adams Diary, Jan. 28, 1861.

[16] Wilson to Andrew, Jan. 29, 1861, Andrew to Charles Sumner, Feb. 6, 1861, Andrew MSS; C. F. Adams Diary, Feb. 8, 1861; Wilson to George Julian, Jan. 19, 1860, Giddings-Julian MSS; Wilson to Theodore Parker, June 5, 1858, Parker MSS.

brought the nation to the verge of calamity. He insisted that the South had nothing to secede from, since no one threatened slavery in the states. Finding that "madness and folly rule the hour, and treason holds its carnival here in the national capital," he refused to give way. The "wicked conspiracy against the rights of man and democratic institutions" inspired by the South would get no assistance from him.[17]

Wilson and his Republican colleagues managed to defeat every compromise proposal presented in the Senate. His own position instead became more militant. In March, when Stephen A. Douglas suggested that the federal government had no right to preserve itself by holding or recapturing federal forts in the South, Wilson charged him with making a "mischievous, wicked, and . . . unpatriotic speech." It was not that he avoided the alternative of war—rather, he accepted it. Nine years earlier he had confided to Sumner: "I would shun war if I could do so with honor but war is not the worst of evils. Cannon Balls are yet required to demolish the works of tyranny." In 1853, at the Massachusetts constitutional convention, he had declared "I am not one of those . . . who cry peace when there is no peace, without slavery, injustice, and wrong." His motto then was "Liberty first—peace afterwards." Nothing had happened since to change his convictions.[18]

Four days before South Carolina seceded, Wilson had admitted: "it may come in a few weeks to blood." "If so," he added, "let it come, be the consequences what they may." He believed that a war would not last long. In February he busily inspected United States militia laws and applauded an act passed by the Massachusetts legislature allowing the governor to enlarge the state's militia. He urged his friend William Schouler, now adjutant general of Massachusetts, to put state forces in good order. He and Sumner advised Governor Andrew to pledge the state's endorsement for federal treasury notes. Wilson thought it was important for Massachusetts to uphold the

[17] *Congressional Globe,* 36th Cong., 2nd sess., 1861, pp. 862, 1088-94.

[18] *Ibid.,* pp. 1459, 1461; Wilson to Charles Sumner, Jan. 5, 1852, Sumner MSS; *Official Report of Debates,* I, 551.

credit of the government; if it came to fighting, "men can be easily found anywhere."[19]

Congress adjourned in March without recommending any kind of compromise settlement for the newly inaugurated president to implement. When Lincoln grappled with the problem of the federal fortifications in the South that Wilson and his colleagues insisted he protect, his solution prompted the Confederates to fire on Fort Sumter in Charleston harbor. The blood-spilling that Wilson had predicted had occurred; the war he foresaw had begun. Unfortunately, neither the Massachusetts senator, nor his Republican colleagues, nor anyone else in the divided nation anticipated the awesome dimensions of the conflict that was beginning. Wilson, who in February predicted that if war came Massachusetts would be called upon for money but not for men, would find that his state would pour out both in large quantities. Boston's capitalists might reclaim the money thus expended, but Massachusetts would never regain the thousands of lives she dedicated to the Union cause. Within two years, Wilson, who had just declared that "if it came to fighting, men can easily be found anywhere," would ask Congress to fill Union armies by conscripting men from their homes and fields.

In the uncertain days just before the war broke out, Wilson, who was always subject to emotional extremes, was unusually despondent. The news of Sumter, however, aroused a spirited determination in him. He immediately raced to the War Department where he learned with dismay that Lincoln had asked for only 75,000 volunteers to put down the rebellion. He rushed off to beg the president and Secretary of War Simon Cameron to increase the call to 300,000 men. Cameron termed the request preposterous but agreed to double the Massachusetts quota. Disgruntled, Wilson left the capital for Boston in order to hurry troops on to Washington.[20]

[19] Wilson to W. S. Robinson, Dec. 16, 1860, in Robinson, ed., *Warrington,* 93; Carl Schurz to wife, Boston, Dec. 27, 1860, in Schafer, ed., *Schurz Letters,* 238; Harrison Ritchie to John Andrew, Feb. 6, 8, 1861, Sumner to Andrew, Jan. 24, 1861, Andrew MSS; Wilson to William Schouler, Feb. 1, 1861, William Schouler MSS; Kenneth Stampp, *And the War Came* (Baton Rouge, La., 1950), 93.

[20] James L. Bowen, *Massachusetts in the War, 1861-1865* (Springfield,

Although the president hesitated to call Congress into session, Wilson returned to the capital, holding long interviews with Lincoln and paying daily visits to the War Department to urge determined action. He also busied himself inspecting hospitals, reviewing applications for military commissions, preparing bills for Congress, inspecting shipyards, touring Union camps, scolding Andrew for failing to provide adequately for Massachusetts soldiers, and urging the administration to begin at once an active campaign. He told Lincoln that Massachusetts stood for "prompt and earnest action" and hoped the president would do all in his power to "put down treason."[21]

Even after Lincoln called Congress into special session in July, Wilson continued to scuttle hither and yon in the city; small wonder that Adam Gurowski, a State Department lackey who himself was rather frenetic, found the senator "too mercurial." The first excitement of the war had released his natural impetuosity, a characteristic he usually restrained. Wilson joined with others in Washington in demanding an immediate march on Richmond, and he often hurried across the Potomac River to visit army encampments in Virginia. On the day Congress convened, he promised William H. Russell, a British correspondent, that General Irwin McDowell "would positively attack the rebels in front of Washington."[22]

In the middle of July the popular pressure for war, which Wilson had helped to create, pushed the hesitant McDowell into a forward movement against the Confederate forces south of the capital. Wilson was overjoyed. On July 20, when a battle seemed imminent, he hired a carriage, loaded it with sandwiches and an attendant to

Mass., 1889), 87; J. B. Mann in Natick *Bulletin,* Nov. 20, 1885; Boston *Daily Advertiser,* May 15, 1861.

[21] New York *Daily Tribune,* May 2, 6, 19, 24, 27, June 1, 1861; P. C. Headley, *Massachusetts in the Rebellion* (Boston, 1866), 49; Bowen, *Massachusetts,* 87; E. R. Hoar to John Andrew, May 7, 1861, Andrew MSS; Wilson to Abraham Lincoln, May 16, 1861, Robert Todd Lincoln MSS; E. F. Jones to Benjamin Butler, May 2, 1861, in Jessie Ames Marshall, ed., *Private and Official Correspondence of General Benjamin F. Butler* (5 vols.; Norwood, Mass., 1917), I, 64.

[22] Adam Gurowski, *Diary* (3 vols.; Boston, 1862-1866), I, 43; New York *Tribune,* July 8, 1861; William Howard Russell, *My Diary North and South* (Boston, 1863), 378.

serve them, and trotted off for Centerville. He soon found himself caught up in a gigantic procession of Washingtonians, all bent on seeing the Yankees chase the Confederates to Richmond. Working his way free of the mob, the senator found his way to McDowell's headquarters. His conversation with the general was interrupted when Ambrose Burnside, a brigade commander, burst into the tent to plead with McDowell not to advance. Wilson said nothing but fixed the disheveled visitor with a cold stare that plainly implied he thought the general a coward. Upon learning that McDowell shared Burnside's fears, Wilson strode out of the tent and spent a sleepless night wondering if the Union army would ever fight.[23]

On July 21 McDowell did move forward and soon engaged the enemy. Wilson later said he had journeyed up to the front, had become satisfied that the Union troops were carrying the day, and then had turned back to Centerville. Unfortunately for the senator and the Union cause, his impression as to the tide of the battle was wrong. First retreating soldiers and then frightened civilians, fleeing down the Centerville road, served notice that the Confederates were winning. Quickly the hurrying individuals became a terrified mob. Wagons overturned, horses reared, and shouts and curses filled the air. In the melee Wilson lost his carriage, his horse, his servant, and his sandwiches. One observer saw the honorable senator begging a teamster for a ride on his wagon; another recalled "Henry Wilson's memorable display of bareback equestrianship on a stray army mule." Apparently Wilson soon fell off the mule, for Albert G. Riddle, a congressman from Ohio who valiantly tried to stop the rout, saw him roar by in a sulky bound for Washington.[24]

[23] For a full account of events at Bull Run from a congressman who accompanied Wilson, see Elihu B. Washburne to Wilson, Sept. 7, 1874, Wilson MSS, Library of Congress. For Wilson's account, see *Congressional Globe*, 38th Cong., 1st sess., 1861, p. 183. On Wilson and Burnside, see Ben: Perley Poore, *Life and Public Services of Ambrose Burnside* (Philadelphia, 1882), 110; see also correspondence between the senator and the general in New York *Times*, Aug. 16, 1861.

[24] Mrs. Cornelia McDonald, *A Diary with Reminiscences of the War...* (Nashville, Tenn., 1934), 31; James G. Randall, *Lincoln the President: Midstream* (New York, 1952), 9; Albert Gallatin Riddle, *Recollections of War Times* (New York, 1895), 52.

William H. Russell hoped Wilson was satisfied; by urging an attack "he and those like him have inflicted a heavy blow on their cause." In the Senate, the harassed legislator suffered a convenient loss of memory which enabled him to declare he had never joined that cry that "has probably forced us prematurely into a conflict." When Wilson went so far as to attack the officers responsible for the "Bull Run stampede" John Sherman rebuked him, and the New York *Herald* reminded its readers that the senator himself had "made double quick time" from Bull Run. The criticism had its effect upon the sensitive Wilson. Immediately he sobered, and his voice was heard no more complaining of Union military forces.[25]

Wilson had yet another reason for ceasing to carp about the war effort. The staid and respectable senator was embarrassed by rumors that a rebel spy, Rose Greenhow, had used her feminine wiles to gain secret information from him. Fortyish, but still indomitable and dignified, with a certain beauty and charm that attracted a wide variety of admirers, Rose indeed had made Wilson's acquaintance. And she was indeed a rebel spy. She was able to warn Confederate General P. G. T. Beauregard of McDowell's advance, but her source of information was not Wilson but rather a clerk on his committee. The Massachusetts senator was only one of many of Rose's highly placed friends. She also was well acquainted with William H. Seward and many of Wilson's fellow senators. In late August federal authorities imprisoned Rose and seized her papers. She had destroyed many, but she had preserved a packet of love letters signed with the initial "H." Many in Washington chuckled at the embarrassment caused the righteous senator, who had been associated with the letters, but few believed the charges.[26]

[25] William H. Russell to John Bigelow, July 27, 1861, in John Bigelow, *Retrospections of an Active Life* (5 vols.; New York, 1909-1913), I, 359; *Congressional Globe,* 37th Cong., 1st sess., 1861, pp. 239-40; New York *Herald,* July 26, 1861.

[26] Ishbel Ross, *Rebel Rose: Life of Rose O'Neal Greenhow, Confederate Spy* (New York, 1954), 77-80, 110-11, 113, 123, 147, 227. Perhaps Ross is correct when she suggests that Rose left the love letters in hopes of incriminating the senator. Certainly she was quite angry with him when he told her that "the country had been ruled long enough by Southern aristocrats" and that his party would enforce its principles "at the point of a bayonet." See Rose

In early August Congress adjourned, leaving the capital to marching troops, rumbling artillery wagons, and dusty cavalry. Wilson stayed in Washington to observe the activity of the newly arrived commander-in-chief of the armies, George B. McClellan. The senator took an instant liking to the young general from Ohio. Wilson was eager to do more for the war effort and McClellan agreed to appoint him as a volunteer aide-de-camp on his staff. Much pleased, Wilson headed home "to get up a series of meetings to enliven the people, and wake up their patriotism."[27]

Wilson gloried in his new role as a war leader. In Massachusetts people flocked around him to hear news from Washington, and state officials consulted with him about the intentions of the administration. From the capital came word that the cabinet, anxious for volunteers, wanted the senator to raise a regiment in the Bay State. Highly flattered, he plunged into the work with enthusiasm and soon had gone $1,000 into debt; but by the first week of October he had raised 2,300 men. Proudly, he accepted a commission as colonel of the 22nd Massachusetts Volunteers, and on October 8 prepared to

---

O'Neal Greenhow, *My Imprisonment and the First Year of Abolition Rule at Washington* (London, 1863), 77, 105, 249, 298, 306-7.

Five years after the end of the war further evidence appeared incriminating Wilson, when General Thomas Jordan, who in 1861 had been with the Confederate forces at Manassas, said Wilson had told Rose about the planned Union offensive. This information is recorded in Hamilton Fish's diary, May 12, 1870, and he got the news secondhand from James Watson Webb; it had been Webb who had talked to Jordan. See Allan Nevins, *Hamilton Fish* (2 vols.; New York, 1936), II, 609-10. Thus Fish's diary is thirdhand evidence. At any rate, it was hardly a secret that McDowell was going to advance about the time that he did. Certainly the love letters signed "H" (which can be found in RG 59, "Political Prisoner Records," National Archives, Washington, D.C.) were not written by Henry Wilson. They are not in his handwriting; and they were written by a congressman favoring the Pacific railroad bill, which at that time Wilson strongly criticized in the Senate. Neither is there any reason to doubt Wilson's fidelity to his wife, Harriet, who was with him in Washington at the time. If the charges had been at all supportable, Wilson's political and personal enemies would have been glad to use them; yet never did anyone but Rose Greenhow and Jordan imply that they were true—and Rose herself never claimed it.

[27]C. F. Adams, Jr., to C. F. Adams, Sept. 3, 1861, in Worthington C. Ford, ed., *A Cycle of Adams Letters, 1861-1865* (2 vols.; Boston, 1920), I, 38-39; John B. Alley to Henry L. Dawes, Aug. 27, 1861, Dawes MSS.

leave for Washington. Despite a rather heavy rain, a large crowd gathered on Boston Common to see the regiment depart. Wilson appeared, resplendent in a new uniform and riding a black Morgan horse. It was one of the grandest moments of his life. Even the rain stopped as if nature wished to accommodate him. The proud colonel, who sat on his horse somewhat gingerly, brought loud hurrahs from the crowd as he trotted before his men. Many had to look again to make sure it was Wilson they saw, for in the tailored blues, the stocky, graying senator looked young, lean, and athletic. The crowd grew silent as he prepared to accept the regimental standard; then a murmur arose as they realized Wilson's long-time political enemy, Robert Winthrop, would present it. Wilson had asked that his old antagonist make the gesture, and Winthrop graciously agreed. Flushed with pride, the new colonel of the 22nd accepted the flag, read a short speech, and led his men through the cheering throng to the railroad station.[28]

Wilson's train rolled through Natick, where his fellow citizens fired an artillery salute in his honor. Inhabitants of Springfield and New Haven, Connecticut, did likewise. Bridgeport citizens found their celebration spoiled by a spiked gun. On October 9, the Massachusetts men reached New York, where great preparations had been made to use Wilson's regiment to stir patriotism and enlistments. Even then events moved slowly, and a welcome breakfast became a welcome dinner, as the Massachusetts troops were forced to wait in the train station until all the dignitaries could assemble. New York Governor E. D. Morgan gave Wilson yet another flag, and the crowd hushed as he delivered his reply. In a vigorous voice, the Massachusetts solon-turned-soldier insisted that he and his men were actu-

[28] For a complete account of Wilson's association with the 22nd Regiment, see John L. Parker, *Henry Wilson's Regiment: A History of the Twenty-Second Massachusetts Infantry* (Boston, 1887), 1-48. See also Headley, *Massachusetts*, 50-52; Mann, *Wilson*, 104; Charles Sumner to the President, Sept. 8, 1861, RG 94, Adjutant General's Office, National Archives; Wilson to Amos A. Lawrence, Dec. 8, 1861, Lawrence MSS; Winthrop, *Memoir*, 220. There is a picture of Colonel Henry Wilson in full uniform in a scrapbook by Abram Cutter, "Three Massachusetts Worthies," in the Rare Book Room of the Boston Public Library.

ated by no spirit of revenge; then to roars of applause he called upon his troops to save their powder and give the cold steel to the traitors of the country.[29]

Wilson led his troops on to Washington. The train moved slowly between Baltimore and the capital, and the colonel, angry at the delay, threatened to commandeer the train at the point of a bayonet. His soldiers were duly impressed at his determination and vigor and were sorry to see him resign his commission and return to McClellan's staff upon his arrival in Washington. The general sent him scurrying about from one regiment to another, investigating complaints and inspecting conditions. Wilson did not object, but after one particularly long and arduous trip on horseback, he went to bed for a week. On January 9, 1862, he resigned his post in order to give full attention to his congressional duties.[30]

[29] New York *Times,* Oct. 9, 10, 1861; letters of Frank E. Howe to John Andrew, Sept. and Oct., 1861, Andrew MSS. Howe was the Massachusetts recruiting agent in New York.

[30] Wilson to Reverend Elias Nason, Aug. 15, 1862, Morse Institute; Henry Lee, Jr., to John Andrew, Oct. 31, Nov. 1, 1861, Andrew MSS; Ben: Perley Poore, *Perley's Reminiscences of Sixty Years in the National Metropolis* (2 vols.; Philadelphia, 1886), II, 99-100. On Oct. 28, 1861, "believing that I can render more service to the country in another military position," Wilson begged leave to resign. See Wilson to George B. McClellan, Hall's Hill, Va., in RG 94, Adjutant General's Office, Commission Branch, National Archives.

8

Raising an Army

Wilson's responsibilities in Washington demanded his undiverted attention. Upon the departure of the Southern senators, he became chairman of the Senate Committee on Military Affairs, and he held this important post until he assumed the vice-presidency in 1873. Thus the senator, who heretofore had played a largely negative role as an opponent of the administration, was called upon to take a constructive part in mobilizing the army and putting the country on a war footing. Except for bills revising the tariff, levying taxes, and authorizing loans, the seventy-six acts passed in the twenty-nine-day special session of Congress in July all related to the organization of military and naval forces.[1]

To get his bills through Congress Wilson relied on a complete presentation of facts rather than on stirring rhetoric. A reporter in the Senate gallery found him "rather loose and ramshackle in his manner of speech: his enunciation was not distinct, his delivery was slipshod, and he was neither precise nor fortunate in his choice of words." Yet Wilson impressed the observer as a man "of great mental power." Others acquainted with Senate affairs found the amount of work Wilson performed was prodigious: "he was a real break of day man—a sleepless, untiring, and unmurmuring patriot." At the end of the session several newspapers praised the senator for his work. He also received thanks from Secretary of War Simon Cameron and from General in Chief of the army Winfield Scott, who declared that "Senator Wilson had done more work in that short session than all the chairmen of the Military Committees had done for the last twenty years."[2]

The former militia commander and aide-de-camp was able to take

advantage of his experiences in military organization in drawing up
his bills. For the moment the Civil War was his war, and the Union
army his army. He failed to understand why his colleagues wanted to
examine his proposals and question his judgment. He had always
been sensitive to criticism, and his normally benign temper flared as
some senators took him to task. James W. Grimes of Iowa complained there were so many military bills he could not keep the run
of them and charged that Wilson expected the Senate to pass everything that came from his committee. According to John Sherman,
Wilson was inaugurating a dangerous policy by introducing important legislation and demanding votes without previous discussion.
The Massachusetts senator complained at the changes made in his
bills and petulantly announced that if he introduced the Lord's
Prayer his colleagues would attempt to amend it.[3]

Major difficulties arose between Wilson and his fellow senators
over questions of executive prerogative. After Sumter, the president
had called out volunteers, increased the regular army, declared a
blockade of Southern ports, and suspended the writ of *habeas
corpus* in certain localities, all without the approval of Congress. In
July, when Wilson introduced a resolution to approve Lincoln's
actions, he met a determined resistance. Sherman, along with many
others, was sure the president lacked the requisite powers. Lyman
Trumbull condemned the resolution as a "pet measure" of Wilson's
and insisted the Republicans had no obligation to support it. The
Massachusetts senator had no quarrel with Lincoln; he only felt the
president had not acted with enough vigor. He could not understand

[1] James G. Blaine, *Twenty Years of Congress* (2 vols.; Norwich, Conn.,
1884), I, 337.

[2] Noah Brooks, *Washington in Lincoln's Time* (New York, 1895), 23;
Harriet Beecher Stowe, *Men of Our Times* (Hartford, Conn., 1868), 274;
Pierce, *Sumner*, IV, 87; Forney, *Anecdotes*, I, 342; New York *Tribune*, May 6,
July 17, 1861; Washington *Star* quoted in Natick *Observer*, Aug. 17, 1861;
Scott's letter quoted in Headley, *Massachusetts*, 50; Simon Cameron to
Wilson, Jan. 27, 1862, The Henry E. Huntington Library and Art Gallery, San
Marino, Cal.; John Sherman, *Recollections of Forty Years in House, Senate,
and Cabinet* (2 vols.; Chicago, 1895), I, 314.

[3] *Congressional Globe*, 37th Cong., 1st sess., 1861, pp. 82, 435.

why his colleagues refused to vote for the resolution. Finally, after lengthy debates, he got the Senate to approve Lincoln's actions regarding the army and navy, but his colleagues refused to sanction the suspension of the writ.[4]

Wilson also jousted with Trumbull over the right of Secretary of State Seward to authorize the arrest of Northern civilians for interfering with the war effort. Trumbull wanted the prisoners released unless their activities could clearly be proven dangerous to the Union cause. Wilson contemptuously charged this would result in "a jail delivery of traitors." He added that rather than being too harsh, the executive department had dealt too gently with men hostile to the country. Wilson also approved of military interference in border-state elections, saying that otherwise traitors who failed on the battlefield would "rush to the ballot-box, hoping there to win what they could not conquer." Garrett Davis of Kentucky continually exasperated Wilson with his criticism of the administration and its infringements on civil liberties, and in 1864 the Massachusetts senator sought unsuccessfully to have him expelled from Congress as disloyal to the Union.[5]

Wilson engaged in even sharper conflict with his colleagues over legislation concerning the Federal armies. The senator was an impressionable man. As chairman of the military committee he listened sympathetically as enlisted men and officers brought their demands and requests to his rooms. He had never shared his colleague Sumner's pacifism, and he admired the gaudily uniformed men who proposed to crush the rebels. Military men soon found that their wish was Wilson's command.[6] Many of his colleagues, however, did

[4] T. Harry Williams, *Lincoln and the Radicals* (Madison, Wis., 1960), 24-27; George Clark Sellery, *Lincoln's Suspension of Habeas Corpus as Viewed by Congress,* Bulletin of University of Wisconsin History Series, Vol. I, No. 2 (Madison, Wis., 1907), 223-38; *Congressional Globe,* 37th Cong., 1st sess., 1861, pp. 41-46, 144, 332, 391-93, 441-42, 452-53.

[5] *Congressional Globe,* 37th Cong., 2nd sess., 1861-1862, pp. 90-98, 3359-60; 37th Cong., 3rd sess., 1862-1863, pp. 17-18, 27-28, 35, 554, 1162-65; 38th Cong., 1st sess., 1864, pp. 105, 139, 174, 392-94; Sellery, *Suspension,* 242-45, 266.

[6] Headley, *Massachusetts,* 48; Bowen, *Massachusetts,* 87. Early in 1862,

not share his enthusiasm for the military and suspected he was overly solicitous of the army's welfare. The incensed committee chairman denied the accusation but then insisted the government was not watching over the interests of army officers as it should.[7]

From the time the special session of Congress adjourned until the regular session met in December, 1861, criticism of the administration and the army mounted. Many senators chafed at McClellan's unwillingness to advance on Richmond. They were determined to force the Federal armies to attack the rebels, and they were also eager to purge Union generals who had refused to free fugitive slaves entering their lines. Fearing Democratic control of the military forces, the senators agreed that Congress's power over the army should be unqualified. Many hoped to utilize the recent military disaster at Ball's Bluff to remove McClellan and replace him with a general of their own choice.[8]

Henry Wilson was more disappointed than angry at Union military failures and inaction. He was determined to defeat the Confederates, yet his recent association with McClellan and the attentions which that general had given to the impressionable senator kept him from attacking the Union commander-in-chief. He insisted to friends that "the safety of the country demands that the General should

Wilson backed down before military pressure and refused to support a bill he had previously promised members of the United States Sanitary Commission he would back. A New York merchant active in the commission was convinced that Wilson lacked "straightforwardness and sincerity and reliability," but Samuel Gridley Howe, who knew Wilson well, denied he had been guilty of double-dealing. He insisted the senator was honest and earnest but admitted he was "very impressionable." For the dispute, see W. Q. Maxwell, *Lincoln's Fifth Wheel* (New York, 1956), 18-19; Allan Nevins and Milton H. Thomas, eds., *The Diary of George Templeton Strong* (4 vols.; New York, 1952), III, 165, 173, 203 (July 15, Aug. 2, 1861, Jan. 29, 1862).

[7] *Congressional Globe,* 37th Cong., 1st sess., 1861, pp. 41, 52, 89-90, 123-25, 158, 164, 180-84, 239-41; 37th Cong., 2nd sess., 1862, pp. 844, 1283; 37th Cong., 3rd sess., 1862-1863, pp. 447-48, 536-37, 823, 1304, 1416-17.

[8] Williams, *Lincoln and the Radicals,* 53-58. Williams's work should be used in connection with the later study by Hans L. Trefousse, *The Radical Republicans* (New York, 1969). Williams stresses the antagonisms between the Radical Republicans and the administration, whereas Trefousse contends that despite their differences the Radicals and Lincoln cooperated effectively to further the war effort.

Senator Henry Wilson (ca. 1856)

U.S. Signal Corps Photo No. B-4159 (Brady Collection),
courtesy of the National Archives

Colonel Wilson (1861)

*U.S. Signal Corps Photo No. B-6040 (Brady Collection),
courtesy of the National Archives*

Wilson as Vice President

*U.S. Signal Corps Photo No. B-4171 (Brady Collection),
courtesy of the National Archives*

Harriet H. Wilson

Courtesy of the Rutherford B. Hayes Library,
Fremont, Ohio

have his time."[9] Wilson found, however, that his Senate colleagues were in no mood to listen to his admonitions. As soon as Congress convened in December, Zachariah Chandler moved to create a joint committee to investigate the conduct of the war, past, present, and future. Both houses of Congress had military committees with jurisdiction over subjects relating to the military establishment and public defense. Administration critics, however, refused to entrust the job of investigating the army to either group.[10]

Radical senators not only bypassed Wilson's committee; they also failed to appoint him to the new investigatory body. Although he had given his blessing to its organization, Wilson had not provided the radicals with any reason to believe they could depend on him during an investigation of the North's military organization. On the day before Vice-President Hannibal Hamlin named the Senate members of the committee, Wilson rose to answer complaints about McClellan's inactivity. Using the general's own argument, he contended that during the past few months Confederate forces had consistently outnumbered those of the Union. When Benjamin Wade sourly retorted that Union defeats resulted from bad generalship rather than insufficient numbers, Wilson asserted that "wild and unregulated impatience" did not help the Union cause and asked his colleagues to have "some faith, some trust, some confidence in the Administration and in the men who lead the armies." Wilson also sought to defend the Army of the Potomac against charges that it was overloaded with Democratic generals who refused to fight. Admitting that most army officers were Democrats, he insisted that these men opposed the administration, not the war. Lincoln had appointed them because most of the experienced military men in the country happened to be members of the opposition party.[11]

[9] Tyler Dennett, ed., *Lincoln and the Civil War in the Diaries and Letters of John Hay* (New York, 1939), 32; Henry Lee to John Andrew, Nov. 1, 1861, Andrew MSS.

[10] Williams, *Lincoln and the Radicals,* 62-65; Trefousse, *Radicals,* 177-82; *Congressional Globe,* 37th Cong., 2nd sess., 1861-1862, pp. 16, 17, 29-32, 110.

[11] *Congressional Globe,* 37th Cong., 1st sess., 1861, pp. 159, 239; 37th Cong., 2nd sess., 1861-1862, pp. 32, 75, 94-95, 156, 164.

As the war wore on, Wilson became more disenchanted with the military forces and more critical of the administration's policy. By March of 1862 he had lost patience with McClellan; during a visit with the provost marshal general of the Army of the Potomac, Wilson "pitched into McClellan and all connected with the war." Yet, as usual, Wilson restrained his personal feelings when he thought they might endanger a larger cause and sought to keep his criticism out of the public record. He firmly believed that public carping and complaining only weakened the government, the war effort, and the army, and he frequently took his colleagues to task for using the time of the Senate to criticize the administration.[12]

In reply to questioning from his colleagues, Wilson insisted he had never advised the president, or the secretary of war, or anyone else to withdraw or appoint any officer in high command. As chairman of the Senate military affairs committee, however, he did refuse to confirm the appointments of any officers who returned fugitive slaves to their masters. Recommendations crossing his desk often stressed the antislavery views of the officer in question. When Governor Andrew asked Sumner about some appointments, the senator promised that he and Wilson would investigate: "How," he asked, "can any Hunker or doubtful character pass this ordeal where we hold seats?"[13] Wilson did claim he avoided partisanship on his committee. During the war his committee considered over ten thousand recommendations for appointments; he frequently remarked,

[12] David S. Sparks, ed., *Inside Lincoln's Army: The Diary of Marsena Rudolph Patrick* (New York, 1964), 50; *Congressional Globe,* 37th Cong., 2nd sess., 1862, pp. 1896, 2037, 3221; 37th Cong., 3rd sess., 1863, p. 328; 38th Cong., 1st sess., 1864, pp. 793, 797, 899, 2219; Boston *Commonwealth,* March 18, 1864; Wilson to Abraham Lincoln, Oct. 25, 1863, Robert Todd Lincoln MSS.

[13] Poore, *Reminiscences,* II, 99-100; O. O. Howard to Wilson, April 28, 1864, Historical Society of Pennsylvania; Montgomery Blair to Wilson, March 10, 1863, Brown University Library; J. I. Forman to Wilson, [1862], Yale University Library; W. J. Murtagh to Wilson, Feb. 27, 1865, Rutherford B. Hayes Library; Charles Sumner to John Andrew, June 21, 1862, Andrew MSS; W. A. Gorman to Wilson, Dec. 22, 1861, Wilson MSS, Library of Congress. Wilson also made it clear he would not vote for any man guilty of intemperance. *Congressional Globe,* 37th Cong., 2nd sess., 1862, p. 1773; S. L. Pierce to Wilson, Feb. 19, 1863, in Senate Military Affairs Committee records, National Archives.

without being contradicted, that although three Democrats sat on his committee, never did its members divide politically when voting on an appointment.[14]

By the spring of 1862, Wilson found himself more concerned about the size of the Union forces than about the views of their officers. The number of men volunteering to fill the Northern army was rapidly dwindling. State governors valiantly encouraged their citizens to sign up to fight, but after a year of war they had developed an immunity to patriotic appeals. As a result, Wilson, along with many others in policy-making positions, had to consider abandoning the reliance on volunteers and instead using the federal government to draft men. Choosing the best policy involved much more than evaluating military considerations. Wilson would have to take into account political and economic issues involving states' rights, governors' prerogatives, and the labor supply for Northern factories. The solution the Massachusetts senator reached was typical of his whole political and legislative career; he compromised.[15]

His service as militia general and Massachusetts legislator had given Wilson several ideas about the proper manner of raising troops. In the Bay State, he had seen a voluntary program work quite well in creating an efficient and active militia full of "young men of spirit and enterprise." He believed that the states, rather than Congress, should have the responsibility of maintaining a military organization.[16] As a United States senator during a national crisis, Wilson might well have abandoned his concern for states' rights; however, during the Civil War Bay State authorities, jealous of their dwindling powers, pressured him to protect their interests.[17]

[14]*Congressional Globe,* 37th Cong., 3rd sess., 1863, p. 1163; 38th Cong., 1st sess., 1864, p. 108; Boston *Commonwealth,* March 10, 1866.

[15]For a discussion of states' rights versus nationalism in raising troops, see Fred A. Shannon, *The Organization and Administration of the Union Army, 1861-1865* (2 vols.; Cleveland, Ohio, 1928), and William B. Hesseltine, *Lincoln and the War Governors* (New York, 1948).

[16]*Official Report of the Debates,* I, 525, 550-51.

[17]*Congressional Globe,* 37th Cong., 1st sess., 1861, pp. 240-42, 369; William Schouler, *A History of Massachusetts in the Civil War* (2 vols.; Boston, 1868), I, 226, 320; John T. Morse, Jr., *Memoir of Colonel Henry Lee* (Boston, 1905), 246.

When Congress reconvened in December, 1861, James Wilkinson of Minnesota introduced a bill to abolish the distinctions between the regular and volunteer military forces of the United States. Such a proposal would give the president power to raise, organize, and support all troops used in the war and would also provide him with the power to appoint all commissioned officers in the service. The bill was sent to Wilson's committee, and within two weeks the Massachusetts senator returned an adverse report on the proposal. According to Wilson, volunteers should be recruited under state authority, with the governors retaining the right to appoint officers and train the men according to discipline prescribed by Congress. Later the same month, when federal officers sought to displace the state governors as recruiting agents, the Massachusetts adjutant general bitterly complained to Wilson that "the old and good doctrine of State Rights has been tabooed." He supplied the senator with a long list of objections to the order. Governor John A. Andrew was extremely jealous of his prerogatives and constantly insisted upon his right to raise troops without outside interference.[18]

Wilson sought to meet Andrew's every need. In May, 1862, the governor was struggling to raise three-year volunteers, and he wanted permission to pay a $2 premium to recruiters bringing them in. He also wanted to offer recruits one month's pay in advance. When Secretary of War Edwin M. Stanton refused both requests, Wilson immediately introduced legislation to provide for Andrew's wishes. He insisted the bill had to pass immediately and, despite one senator's warning that Wilson's "terrible haste . . . has led us into errors of expenditure," he quickly got it approved. On June 30, Lincoln asked the Northern governors to approve a new call for volunteers. Andrew refused to sign without permission to offer recruits a $25 bounty. Stanton hesitated, pleading lack of legal authorization; after continued pressure from Andrew he agreed to take responsibility for issuing the bounty money. Wilson again came to the rescue, amend-

[18] Frank Moore, ed., *The Rebellion Record* (11 vols.; New York, 1862-1868), XI, 118-21; Henry Lee to John Andrew, Nov. 1, 1861, Andrew MSS; William Schouler to Wilson, Jan. 15, 1862, [Jan., 1862], William Schouler MSS.

ing a House appropriation bill to authorize immediate payment of $25 of the $100 bounty established by the volunteer acts of 1861.[19]

With the money thus obtained, Wilson and Andrew hoped Massachusetts would meet her quotas, but once again response to pleas for enlistment was meager. In Washington congressmen noted that all Northern states were struggling to obtain volunteers and began to talk of a national draft. In an effort to stimulate volunteering, in 1861 governors in Iowa and Missouri had already threatened a draft, and early in 1862 the executives of Maine, Indiana, and Illinois expressed similar thoughts. The leaders of Massachusetts, however, felt otherwise about conscription. The state's adjutant general later recalled that "from the beginning to the end of the Rebellion, the Governor, the city and town authorities, and the people of the Commonwealth, were opposed to a draft, and labored to avoid it." Andrew stated that a draft would produce a "mere paper army, unorganized, ineffectual, discontented, valueless."[20]

Caught between the need for troops and the need to protect Andrew's prerogatives, Wilson came up with a compromise. On July 8 he introduced a new militia bill, sternly declaring that although he preferred raising men voluntarily, he was ready to "draft every last man who can carry a musket." Despite his impressive language, his bill made no mention of conscription. Its chief innovation lay in permitting the president to call out the militia for any length of time up to nine months. If states could not meet their quotas, drafting could take place; but states could avoid application of a draft by making "adequate provisions" of their own for calling out the militia. If the state's militia legislation was defective, the president could provide the necessary regulations, which, if broadly interpreted, would permit a draft. The bill, based on state authority and the

[19] Pearson, *Andrew*, II, 27, 30; *War of the Rebellion . . . Official Records of the Union and Confederate Armies* (128 vols.; Washington, D. C., 1880-1901), ser. 3, vol. II, pp. 97-98, 100, 182, 187 (hereafter cited as *Official Records);* Shannon, *Union Army,* II, 56; *Congressional Globe,* 37th Cong., 2nd sess., 1862, pp. 2452-53; Henry Wilson, "Military Measures of Congress," in Frank Moore, ed., *The Rebellion Record* (11 vols.; New York, 1862-1868), X, 30-31.

[20] Schouler, *Massachusetts,* 355, 501.

concept of state militia rather than a national army, passed Congress.[21]

Volunteering continued at its slow pace, so on August 4, Stanton, acting under the authorization of the new militia act, ordered a draft of 300,000 militia for nine months. Governors across the North joined Andrew in taking advantage of the ambiguous nature of Wilson's legislation in order to postpone an actual draft while they struggled valiantly to raise more volunteers. By the end of the year, it was clear that a new, stronger draft law would have to be passed. Wilson was getting calls from all parts of the country for firm congressional action on conscription. Even leading Democratic newspapers were demanding a draft as the fairest way to obtain troops. As Congress met in Washington in December, 1862, attention centered on the Senate military affairs committee, and senators awaited news of a conscription bill.[22]

For well over a month, the Massachusetts senator labored over the measure he planned to present. He received advice on conscription laws from a great many quarters, both military and civilian, but the bill that he presented on February 4, 1863, represented his own attempt to find a solution for the manpower shortage in Union armies. The measure authorized the president "to make all proper rules and regulations for enrolling and drafting the militia for a period up to two years." In order to enforce compliance with the draft, the act provided that men were to come under the jurisdiction of the federal authorities as soon as they were conscripted, and before they were mustered into federal service.[23]

[21] Shannon, *Union Army*, I, 274-77; *Congressional Globe*, 37th Cong., 2nd sess., 1862, pp. 3198-205, 3227, 3250, 3254.

[22] Pearson, *Andrew*, II, 39-43; *Congressional Globe*, 38th Cong., 1st sess., 1863, pp. 64-65.

[23] Howard K. Beale, ed., *The Diary of Gideon Welles* (3 vols.; New York, 1960), I, 397, 407 (Aug. 10, 15, 1863); General William S. Rosecrans to Wilson, Feb. 5, 1863, in *Official Records*, ser. 1, vol. XXIII, pt. 2, p. 47; Henry Lee to Wilson, Jan. 28, 1863, General S. R. Curtis to Wilson, Feb. 17, 1863, in records of the Senate Committee on Military Affairs, National Archives; Frank Freidel, *Francis Lieber* (Baton Rouge, La., 1947), 348; *Congressional Globe*, 37th Cong., 3rd sess., 1863, p. 705.

Despite outward indications that Wilson was giving up the idea of state control over troop raising, and despite protests of Senate conservatives who found the bill destructive of states' rights, the measure was in fact only a halting and hesitant step toward organizing a national army. It referred frequently to the "militia" of the states and recognized the governors' right to appoint draft officials. When some senators objected to a clause giving the president power "to make all proper rules and regulations" for drafting the militia, preferring instead to have Congress enact the regulations, Wilson demurred. Instead of having Congress draw up specific rules to govern the procurement of soldiers, he insisted that "we must to a considerable degree adapt ourselves . . . to the rules and regulations adopted in the several states." Such a view, coming from the man chiefly responsible for a national conscription bill, served fair notice that the draft would not greatly embarrass state executives.[24]

Many congressmen insisted on a stronger measure, and Wilson agreed to send the bill back to committee. On February 16, he introduced new legislation that moved a step closer to a national draft. This measure gave the president power to call out or draft the national forces, defined as consisting of able-bodied men ages twenty to forty-five. Various provisions exempted a restricted number of government officials, the physically and mentally unfit, and sole supporters of infirm parents or orphaned children. For purposes of the draft, the whole country was divided into enrollment districts roughly corresponding to congressional districts; provost marshals appointed by the president were to superintend the enrollment and drafting of the national forces in each district. Wilson declared that the bill was "an enrollment of the population of the country, and not of the militia." The phrasing of the enrollment act, as it came to be known, carefully avoided use of the word "state."[25]

Reluctantly, Wilson had produced a bill which favored direct

[24] *Congressional Globe,* 37th Cong., 3rd sess., 1863, pp. 708-15, 729-37; see also Shannon, *Union Armies,* I, 308 ff.

[25] *Congressional Globe,* 37th Cong., 3rd sess., 1863, pp. 976-78; 38th Cong., 1st sess., 1864, p. 239.

conscription by the national government. Before the measure passed Congress, however, he managed to weaken its effect. When it reached the floor of the Senate, he immediately sought to amend it to permit a draftee to avoid conscription by payment of a commutation fee of $300, or by furnishing a substitute. Wilson had been unable to get his committee's approval for the provisions, so he carried his fight onto the Senate floor and successfully added them to the bill. Congress, prompted by the pressure of war, quickly passed it and thus protected men of wealth from the draft.[26]

As sponsor of the conscription act, Wilson had to defend it against public criticism. Since the loudest complaints came from militant anti-administration Democrats, Wilson branded their complaints as treasonable. When Congressman Fernando Wood of New York led his fellow Democrats in a violent denunciation of conscription, Wilson sent him a public letter attacking the "foul, shameless, and damnable libel upon the law and its framers." His warnings to the New Yorkers that the draft would be enforced did not prevent a three-day riot in the city in July, in which at least seventy-five men were killed. From Washington, D.C., to Kennebunk, Maine, Wilson defended his law and attacked fractious Copperheads for opposing it. In every critic he saw a demogogue, "with shameless brow and malignant heart . . . hissing his poisoned lies, his wicked perversions." He urged citizens of the North to vote down the bill's critics in the fall elections.[27]

In his public speeches Wilson preferred to attack critics of the law rather than to praise its provisions. The only part of the measure he proved willing to defend to the last was the commutation clause. This provision created violent opposition from the moment Wilson

[26] Fred Shannon called the commutation clause a "concession to the bourgeoisie." See Shannon, *Union Armies,* II, 1-25. For examples of the pressures from Massachusetts politicians and capitalists urging Wilson to secure commutation privileges, see Horatio Woodman to Wilson, Feb. 15, 1863, Horatio Woodman MSS, Massachusetts Historical Society; John Murray Forbes to Wilson, Feb. 11, 1863, in Hughes, ed., *Forbes Letters* (supp. ed.), II, 67-68.

[27] New York *Times,* April 2, 1863; Boston *Morning Journal,* Sept. 8, 1863; Henry Wilson, *The Draft,* speech at Goshen, Orange County, N. Y., Oct. 22, 1863 (n. p., 1863).

introduced it, and it was to be repealed a year after the passage of the bill. The Massachusetts senator stoutly maintained that commutation was in the best interest of "the masses of people." He claimed that, without it, the price of substitutes would rise beyond the reach of working men. He failed to say how farmers and laborers could afford to pay $300 to avoid the draft. During the year commutation was in effect, Wilson had to force Stanton and Provost Marshal General James Fry to apply it. At first, by use of a technicality, Stanton sought simply to ignore commutation; Wilson protested bitterly and forced the secretary to recognize it. Then Fry decided that the fee relieved a man only from the current draft and not for the whole period of three years. Wilson immediately protested to Fry, pointing to "the great feeling in Boston" against his decision. The thought of his rich constituents being drafted clearly made him uncomfortable.[28]

The draft not only threatened Wilson's wealthy constituents; it also presented a great problem for the Bay State's industries. Massachusetts was the most highly industrialized state in the Union. In 1860, 25 percent of her male population worked in manufacturing establishments, compared to 13 percent in Pennsylvania and 9 percent in New York. Although the state's cotton industry suffered during the war, her woolen and shoe manufacturers prospered. The draft, if continuously and rigorously applied, would destroy the state's labor supply. The Massachusetts adjutant general noted that on October 17, 1863, when Lincoln called for 300,000 troops, "business, in all its branches, was in a highly prosperous condition. Money was plentiful, wages high, and labor in great demand; so that

[28] New York *Times*, May 23, 31, 1863; Boston *Commonwealth*, May 2, 1863; John Murray Forbes to John Andrew, June 1, 1863, and to Chauncey Smith, Aug. 6, 1863, in Hughes, ed., *Forbes Letters* (supp. ed.), II, 122-23, 132-33; John Murray Forbes to John A. Andrew, Aug. 18, 1863, Andrew MSS; Provost Marshal General Fry to Wilson, July 25, 1863, in *Official Records*, ser. 3, vol. III, 570-71. Recent scholarship has upheld Wilson's contention that commutation kept down the price of substitutes and made it possible for workers to avoid the draft. See Eugene C. Murdock, "Was It A 'Poor Man's Fight'?" *Civil War History*, X (1964), 241-45, and Hugh G. Earnhart, "Commutation: Democratic or Undemocratic?" in *ibid.*, XII (1966), 132-42.

it was difficult to fill our army, and meet the calls of the President."[29]

From the very month that drafting began, Wilson deluged Fry with criticisms of the draft and its administration. He condemned doctors for taking bribes to release conscripted men and attacked provost marshals for being "uncivil and insulting." He passed along to Fry every complaint he encountered, capping his revelations with an assertion that a provost marshal in Boston "demanded criminal intercourse with wives of two recruits enlisted by him as a condition of giving them or their husbands, the bounty to which they were entitled." In September, 1863, he insisted to Fry that the whole draft law had become "a mere farce, shame, and disgrace." The Massachusetts senator hoped no more drafts would be necessary; the abuses of the program, he believed, justified the abandonment of the whole enactment. Fry tartly replied that "so far as I can see there was quite as much to find fault with in the construction of the law as in its administration. It is essentially a law not to secure military service, but to exempt men from it."[30]

Since revoking the conscription act was an impossibility, Wilson, charging that "the federal government does not know much about enlisting men," lent his support to John Andrew's attempts to gain more state control over recruiting in Massachusetts. The governor persuaded Fry to withdraw his federal recruiters and let Andrew obtain volunteers through his own agents, who had their premiums paid from federal funds. Fry did so reluctantly; he was bitter at Wilson's criticisms and insisted the federal government had con-

[29] United States Census, 1860: *Manufactures* (Washington, D. C., 1865), 729; *ibid., Population* (Washington, D. C., 1864), 592-93; Emerson D. Fite, *Social and Industrial Conditions in the North during the Civil War* (New York, 1910), 84, 86, 91; Schouler, *Massachusetts,* I, 501.

[30] For Wilson's letters to Fry's office attacking administration of the draft, see Provost Marshal General's Office, Letters Received, 1863, vol. III, letters dated July 28, Aug. 4, Sept. 14 (2 letters), Sept. 19, Nov. 16, Dec. 18; for Fry's replies, see Provost Marshal General's Office, Letters Sent, vols. III-IV, Aug. 8, Oct. 22, 1863, Feb. 10, 15, June 20, 1864, March 5, 1865, all in War Department, National Archives. See also Fry to Wilson, Sept. 16, 1863, in *Official Records,* ser. 3, vol. III, 799-801.

ducted recruiting with great success. He asserted that in Massachusetts, the only state where the governor controlled the procurement of troops, the results were "very unfavorable."[31]

Wilson worked hard to encourage volunteering in order to avoid a draft. In October, 1863, when Stanton was about to call for 300,000 more troops, Wilson suggested to him that increased federal bounties would be a great enticement to volunteers. Stanton agreed, and at the same time he issued the call he authorized payment of bounties of $400 to veterans and $300 to new recruits. This was a sizable increase over the original $100 bounty Congress had approved in 1861. When that body convened in December, John Sherman condemned the granting of the new bonus without legal authorization as "the greatest stretch of power that has been exercised during this war." Wilson defended Stanton's action and demanded legislation to appropriate the necessary funds for the bounties, but he did not tell his colleagues he had been the first to suggest their payment. Congress agreed to his request.[32]

Governor Andrew, supplied with the bounties Wilson had provided, sought out new supplies of men to meet his state quotas. Amos Lawrence set up a recruiting system that garnered a few men in neighboring states and Canada, and John Murray Forbes went to Germany to seek immigrants to fill the state's regiments.[33] Yet the state still failed to provide the required numbers of troops. Then, in January, 1863, Abraham Lincoln issued his Emancipation Proclamation, in which he suggested that slaves freed by his order could be "received into the armed forces." Wilson, Andrew, and other Massa-

[31] Pearson, *Andrew,* II, 136 n; James B. Fry to James W. Grimes, April 5, 1864, in *Official Records,* ser. 3, vol. IV, 217; and Fry to Brigadier General R. A. Peirce, Assistant Quartermaster General of Massachusetts, Oct. 26, 1863, in *ibid.,* ser. 3, vol. III, 928-29; and Andrew's General Orders No. 32, quoted in ser. 3, vol. III, 1086-88.

[32] Provost Marshal General Fry to E. M. Stanton, Dec. 25, 1863, in *Official Records,* ser. 3, vol. III, 1192-93; *Congressional Globe,* 38th Cong., 1st sess., 1864, pp. 59-60, 65.

[33] John Murray Forbes to Zachariah Chandler, Dec. 28, 1863, Zachariah Chandler MSS, Library of Congress; John Murray Forbes to John Andrew, March 24, 1863, Andrew MSS; Pearson, *Andrew,* II, 138-39.

chusetts leaders, along with other politicians and humanitarians across the North, had long been urging the Lincoln administration to destroy slavery and enlist Negroes in the Union armies. Such action would encourage the North to support emancipation, strengthen the Northern war effort and weaken the Confederacy, and establish a claim for equal treatment for all men of black skin. And, as Wilson and Andrew well knew, Negroes could help fill the state's quotas and keep her laboring force at home.[34]

In an attempt to use Negro manpower, Congress had included a provision in the 1862 militia draft act for recruiting slaves for constructing trenches and performing camp services. The act also freed the Negro and his family if they belonged to a disloyal owner. Although Wilson was eager to free the bondsmen regardless of their owners' loyalty, he was pleased with the result and noted that had Congress passed the bill sooner, "we could have employed thousands of colored men at low rates of wages to do ditching, and thus saved the health, and strength, and the lives of our brave soldiers." Wilson's enthusiasm quickly turned to disappointment when the federal government refused to make use of the militia bill for obtaining Negro recruits. The administration likewise ignored Andrew's pleas that he be permitted to raise a regiment of free Negroes in Massachusetts.[35]

In January, 1863, shortly after issuing his Emancipation Proclamation, Lincoln authorized Andrew to recruit Negro troops. By May Andrew had found enough blacks in Massachusetts and in neighboring states, Canada, and Virginia to fill a regiment, and Wilson journeyed to Boston to join the governor in reviewing the new troops. He returned to Washington to spur on the government to induct even more blacks into federal armies. He knew that many white Northerners would oppose the use of Negro troops, and he

[34] See Richard H. Abbott, "Massachusetts and the Recruitment of Southern Negroes, 1863-1865," *Civil War History*, XIV (Sept., 1968), 197-210.

[35] *Congressional Globe*, 37th Cong., 2nd sess., 1862, p. 3203; Hesseltine, *War Governors*, 202-3.

reminded such critics that "the draft cannot be averted, except by promptly weaponing the willing hands of the loyal men in the rebel states."[36] The conscription act would be particularly useful, he hoped, in freeing slaves in the border states, which had been exempted from Lincoln's proclamation. He intended to have federal authorities include such bondsmen in their enrollment lists and was greatly irritated at the War Department's hesitation to implement the idea. He insisted to Lincoln that he intended the enrollment act to *"fill our armies and destroy slavery."* In December he asked Stanton to explain why he had not enrolled border-state slaves. Receiving the reply that the War Department did not feel it had the requisite power under the 1863 law, Wilson helped guide through the Senate a House-sponsored amendment to the enrollment act that specifically provided for drafting slaves. He then obtained an additional amendment to explicitly guarantee freedom to any slave drafted, be he a servant of a loyal or rebel master. Wilson noted with satisfaction the passage of the bill, which would both "augment our armed forces" and "demoralize and break up slavery in the border states."[37]

Wilson continued to criticize the federal government for its failure to actively recruit Southern blacks. He suggested that the states could do a better job and presented legislation to the Senate authorizing Northern governors to send agents into the South to seek black recruits to apply against their state quotas. In October, 1863, Lincoln called for 300,000 more troops, and Wilson, insisting that "we need all the men we have on our farms, in our workshops, and in our manufacturing establishments," pleaded with the Senate to pass the recruiting bill. Senators from the West who did not want

[36] Pearson, *Andrew,* II, 81, 91-94; Stearns, *George Luther Stearns,* 287-91, 330; Benjamin Quarles, *The Negro in the Civil War* (Boston, 1953), 8-11; New York *Times,* April 2, 1863.

[37] Wilson to Abraham Lincoln, Oct. 25, 1863, Robert Todd Lincoln MSS; James B. Fry to Edwin M. Stanton, Dec. 25, 1863, in *Official Records,* ser. 3, vol. III, 1191; Henry Wilson, *History of the Antislavery Measures . . . of Congress* (Boston, 1864), 305; *Congressional Globe,* 38th Cong., 1st sess., 1863-1864, pp. 93, 160; 39th Cong., 1st sess., 1866, p. 3964.

their states to compete with the richer states of the Northeast in recruiting Southern slaves with bounty money blocked Wilson's proposal.[38]

Early in 1864 Wilson sought approval of a joint resolution to equalize the pay of black and white soldiers. Black men were dissatisfied with receiving $10 per month while their white counterparts received $13; Wilson feared the disparity discouraged Negro enlistments. Some senators noted that in 1862 it was his own anxiety to pass the militia bill providing for Negro enlistments that had led Wilson to approve the $10 pay provision. Two years later, the senator apparently thought the time had come to make amends, and he sought to provide the Negro troops with equal pay retroactive to the time of enlistment. Since some of his colleagues strenuously resisted the retroactive clause, Wilson agreed to demand equal pay only from January, 1864. His compromise brought a rash of criticism from the Bay State, for most of the troops excluded were serving in Massachusetts regiments. In 1865 Wilson returned to the matter and finally obtained equal pay dating from the time of enlistment.[39]

Even as Wilson sought approval for equal pay for black troops and state recruitment of Southern slaves, he was forced to deal with yet another problem—attempts to repeal the commutation clause of the 1863 conscription act. In December, 1863, a dozen bills and resolutions were introduced in the House alone seeking to amend or repeal the provision. John Murray Forbes frantically protested against the threatened repeal and begged Wilson and the War Department to encourage commutation rather than substitution. There was little Wilson could do, however, to delay the inevitable. He did manage to pigeonhole several amendatory proposals, thus angering Provost Marshal General Fry, who was a dedicated opponent of commutation. Determined to abolish the provision, Fry got Lincoln

[38]*Congressional Globe,* 38th Cong., 1st sess., 1863-1864, pp. 85-86, 240-47, 820-24, 1403-5, 2025.

[39]Wilson, *Antislavery Measures,* 293-312; Quarles, *Negro in Civil War,* 202; Pearson, *Andrew,* II, 98-120; *Congressional Globe,* 38th Cong., 1st sess., 1864, pp. 482, 869-73; Boston *Commonwealth,* Feb. 19, 26, 1864; Wilson to William L. Garrison, Feb. 22, 1864, Boston Public Library.

to support him. On May 23, Edwin Morgan of New York, a member of Wilson's own committee, introduced a bill to abolish commutation. Wilson, who frantically argued against the bill in committee hearings, chose not to attack it on the floor of the Senate, since it was now an administration measure. He did claim that commutation was "a humane provision" which had been "very wickedly misrepresented." He denied that commutation resulted in reducing the number of soldiers available for duty. Speaking on June 23, 1864, he declared that "since the 17th day of October we have put 700,000 men into the field." Once again Fry objected to Wilson's tactics; he told Stanton that the 700,000 men Wilson referred to had been furnished since July, 1862, rather than since October, 1863. Since the latter date, Fry claimed the federal government had mustered in only 300,000 "white men."[40]

Realizing that his battle was lost, Wilson skillfully bargained for a satisfactory compromise. In March he reported from committee a House resolution authorizing states to recruit in the South. He did this in the face of violent criticism from two members of his committee, who complained that Wilson had held an unscheduled meeting, attended by only a few members, in order to obtain approval for the bill. Of the seven committee members, only two stood by Wilson consistently in voting for state recruitment in the South. At the same time, Wilson and Sumner revived a battle that they had begun early in 1863—to give states credit for sailors enlisting in the Union navy. Critics of the proposal had heretofore successfully resisted it, arguing that it would be impossible to decide where the sailors held residence, and consequently, since most men enlisting in the navy did so in Massachusetts ports, the state would benefit unfairly at the expense of her sisters.[41]

[40] John Murray Forbes to Charles Eliot Norton, Dec. 26, 1863, and New England Loyal Publication Society, Publication No. 152, both in Boston Public Library; Hughes, *Forbes Letters* (supp. ed.), II, 68; Shannon, *Union Army,* II, 29-33, 35-37; *Congressional Globe,* 38th Cong., 1st sess., 1864, pp. 64, 122, 143, 2804, 3094; James B. Fry to Edwin M. Stanton, June 23, 1864, in *Official Records,* ser. 3, vol. IV, 450.

[41] *Congressional Globe,* 37th Cong., 3rd sess., 1863, p. 985; 38th Cong., 1st sess., 1864, pp. 119-21, 3383-86.

Wilson bargained frantically and successfully during a hectic series of debates in June and July to obtain a new enrollment bill acceptable to himself and to Massachusetts. He was forced to surrender the sacred provision of commutation, but in return he obtained, again over the strong objections of his own committee members, a clause reducing the time of service under the draft from three years to a minimum of one year, subject to the president's discretion. The Massachusetts senator was also able to beat down an attempt to repeal substitution. "The country is not in any such distressed condition as to require it," he claimed. "We have got the business interests of the country to take care of as well as the military interests." Finally, Wilson secured inclusion of his two pet measures: the Senate agreed to permit individual states to recruit Negroes in occupied areas of the South, and, after a due amount of pressure from Wilson and Sumner and a visit to Washington by Andrew, Congress consented to allow states credit on their draft quotas for naval enlistments.[42]

During the long delay of the state recruiting bill, its supporters had attached undue value to it as a panacea. When at last it passed, Andrew acted quickly, sending agents to six cities in the South to enlist Negroes. The substitute brokers thus unleashed on federally held territory were dishonest and corrupt. The abuse of the law led to its repeal in February, 1865. By that time, Northern governors had sent a total of 1,405 agents South; they raised only 5,052 recruits. Massachusetts agents secured 1,257 of that total for their own state.[43]

On the other hand, the Bay State reaped great benefit from the provision of the law concerning naval enlistees. Stanton appointed Andrew himself as chairman of a two-man commission to ascertain the number of men Massachusetts had sent into the navy and assured him that "the state in which naval enlistments were made is entitled to credit for them." Andrew, with his fellow committee member,

[42] *Ibid.*, 38th Cong., 1st sess., 1864, pp. 3097, 3381, 3383-86.

[43] Pearson, *Andrew*, II, 143-46; Bell I. Wiley, *Southern Negroes, 1861-1865* (New Haven, Conn., 1938), 306-7; Bowen, *Massachusetts*, 75.

ex-Massachusetts governor John A. Clifford, drew up a list of names, and the War Department accordingly credited Massachusetts with 16,000 sailors against her quotas. In the meantime, Andrew got Fry to accept his figures on the scattered groups of troops his state had furnished since the beginning of the war which had not been credited properly; as a consequence of the various credit revisions, Massachusetts filled her deficiencies and had enough surplus to drastically reduce her troop quotas for the rest of the war.[44]

In the final accounting, Massachusetts oversubscribed her quotas in the Civil War. However, her constant search for recruits outside her own borders and Andrew's steady resistance to federal attempts to control the raising of troops within the state had given Massachusetts a tarnished reputation for patriotism.[45] In the Senate, despite frequent objections from his own committee, Henry Wilson had kept up a constant warfare against an effective national conscription. He was largely responsible for delaying conscription until 1863 and then for drawing it up in an emasculated form. Then he watched contentedly as the government, instead of raising troops directly through a draft, used the new law to stimulate volunteering.[46] The Union obtained the troops needed to win the war, and governors like Andrew were able to maintain some of the prerogatives of their position. Finally, by depending on volunteering rather than drafting, Bay State industrialists had not lost their labor force. Wilson's compromises served his purposes well.

[44] James B. Fry to Andrew, July 7, 1864, in *Official Records*, ser. 3, vol. IV, 476-77; Pearson, *Andrew*, II, 140-42.

[45] *Congressional Globe*, 37th Cong., 3rd sess., 1863, p. 1363; 38th Cong., 1st sess., 1864, pp. 2807-8, 2833, 2842, 3197, 3274, 3489.

[46] On several occasions Wilson noted with satisfaction that the draft had not raised men directly but had instead stimulated state and local efforts to raise volunteers. *Congressional Globe*, 38th Cong., 1st sess., 1864, pp. 64-65, 143, 633.

9

The Politics of Abolition

Henry Wilson's duties as chairman of the Senate Committee on Military Affairs stretched his great industry to its limits. He once admitted to his friend William Schouler that he was "pressed beyond endurance with work."[1] The senator did not shirk his responsibilities, for he had visions of a goal far greater than that of raising and organizing troops. To him the Federal armies and the Republican party were instruments to achieve that which he had sought for thirty years, but which he had once thought could not be accomplished in his lifetime: the abolition of slavery. At first he moved against slavery carefully, for he knew that Northern opinion was not ready to countenance abolition, and the Lincoln administration desperately needed political support. After the war pushed on into its second year, however, and Lincoln seemed unwilling to do anything at all about slavery, Wilson risked a breach with the administration in order to wage his own war on the institution.

Before the war the Republicans had continually pledged that slavery in the states was protected by the Constitution. As late as the secession crisis Wilson himself had uttered such assurances. In 1857, however, he had remarked to Theodore Parker that "we may be driven to [overthrow slavery] to defend the country." Four years later, when the smoke of battle rolled over the land and Southern planters seemed bent on destroying the American republic, Wilson knew the time had come. In September, 1861, he assured a friend that "events are inevitably shaping themselves for a more antislavery policy" and he hoped that in December Congress would forever abolish the institution.[2]

The senator was overenthusiastic. The North, and even his home state of Massachusetts, proved reluctant to accept emancipation as a war aim. For the moment even John Andrew agreed to remain publicly silent on slavery. In September Charles Sumner tried and failed to get the state Republicans to demand emancipation. The results of such a cautious policy seemed fruitful when in November Andrew won reelection by an increased vote. That fall, when Wilson received his regimental flag from Robert Winthrop, he did not choose to argue when the old Whig asked the troops not to destroy the constitutional rights of any section or state. Wilson was a smart and practical politician, and he realized the administration could "only expect to follow events and the popular will." Years later, the Massachusetts senator admitted that proslavery sentiments "pervaded not merely the North, but the Republican party as well." Large numbers of voters who loved the Union and opposed the Slave Power "had no very strong desires for the emancipation of the slaves. They would accept abolition rather than disunion, but they did not desire it."[3]

Strongly aware of the limited Northern support for freedom for the Negro, Wilson returned to Washington in December, 1861, prepared to move in a cautious yet determined fashion to strike at slavery wherever he found an opportunity. He was careful not to attack the institution directly but instead to weaken it where Congress's control seemed incontestable. He seized upon any expedient or compromise proposal that moved toward freedom, fearing that stronger and more thorough measures might never be passed. He even proved willing to endorse bills that included gradual or compensated emancipation, with provisions for voluntary colonization of freed Negroes, fearing that he could obtain nothing more at the moment.

[1] Wilson to Schouler, Feb. 1, 1863, James Schouler MSS, Massachusetts Historical Society.

[2] Wilson to Parker, March 14, 1857, Parker MSS; T. W. Higginson to James F. Fields, Sept. 18, 18[61], Higginson MSS.

[3] Ware, *Political Opinion,* 79-80; Pearson, *Andrew,* I, 320-21; Robert C. Winthrop, *Addresses and Speeches on Various Occasions* (4 vols.; Boston, 1895), II, 511; T. W. Higginson to James F. Fields, Sept. 18, 18[61], Higginson MSS; Wilson, *Slave Power,* III, 233.

Wilson was especially eager to attack slavery in the District of Columbia, where Congress had immediate control. After his trip to Washington in 1836, he had returned to New Hampshire to demand the abolition of slavery in the nation's capital. Twenty-five years later, in December, 1861, Senator Wilson introduced legislation that would achieve that purpose. He did not win his victory for four long months; but he was ready to pursue the arduous task of gaining Senate approval for his proposal. At first, praising the accomplishments of free Negroes in Washington, he refused to consider colonizing the emancipated slaves. Realizing, however, that without such a qualification the bill might not pass, he agreed to provide for the voluntary colonization of freedmen. He also was willing to compensate loyal slaveowners for the loss of their bondsmen. Finally, on April 3, 1862, the Senate agreed to vote on the bill, and Wilson watched thankfully and proudly as his colleagues approved the measure by a vote of 27-10; it then passed the House and Lincoln signed it into law. It was a victory Wilson would remember the rest of his life. He was the author of the first practical act of emancipation.[4]

Praise poured in from his constituents, but Wilson was not ready to stop with his first accomplishment. A month before passage of his District emancipation bill, he had suggested abolishing slavery in Maryland on the same terms of voluntary colonization and compensation: "then we can clear this thing out of our neighborhood." A few days later, President Lincoln recommended to Congress the appropriation of money for compensated emancipation in the border states. In the Senate, Wilson promptly introduced a bill to grant aid to Maryland and Delaware. His measure was then absorbed by a more comprehensive joint resolution which promised aid to any state undertaking gradual emancipation. Not too pleased with a paper victory, Wilson turned with his colleagues to examine West Virginia's petition for statehood. He was willing to admit the state provided she freed the children of slaves within her own borders. Sumner, who demanded immediate emancipation of all slaves, refused to vote for the bill. Wilson sympathized with his colleague but,

[4] *Congressional Globe*, 37th Cong., 2nd sess., 1861-1862, pp. 1050-53.

realizing Sumner's proposal would not pass, he cast his vote for the original bill. As one of his friends recalled, if Wilson could not take two steps forward, he would "take one, and bide his time for further advance."[5]

By the spring of 1862, however, Wilson was chafing impatiently for some more universal measure to destroy slavery. Little had been done to threaten the institution where it was strongest of all: in the Confederate states. There slavery had destroyed the patriotism of the masses and impelled its supporters "to raise the banners of bloody insurrection." The leaders of the Confederacy, claimed Wilson, were not the cause of rebellion: they were "simply the hands, the tools; the heart, the brain, the soul, is slavery." The Confederate army could be destroyed and its leaders imprisoned, but unless slavery was abolished, "we will not change the hearts that hate our institutions, hate our flag." With such convictions as these, Wilson would spare no effort to kill "the great criminal."[6]

Early in the year, Wilson joined Charles Sumner and Congressman Thaddeus Stevens in a concerted campaign to persuade Abraham Lincoln to proclaim the freedom of all slaves in the country. The president joked with visitors about the three legislators; he compared himself to a poor schoolboy rereading a Bible and meeting again the unpronounceable names of Shadrach, Meshach, and Abednego, and wailing "Look! There comes them same damn three fellers again!" Sumner and Wilson also encouraged Susan B. Anthony, an ardent feminist, to organize Women's National Loyal Leagues and petition Congress and the president in favor of universal emancipation. In May, the Senate discussed a bill to confiscate and free the slaves of all rebel owners. Wilson heartily endorsed the proposal, stating that

[5] R. S. Storrs to Wilson, May 20, 1862, C. W. Storey to Wilson, April 26, 1862, Wilson MSS, Library of Congress; *Congressional Globe,* 37th Cong., 2nd sess., 1862, pp. 917, 1132, 3308, 3320; O. O. Howard, *Autobiography of Oliver Otis Howard* (2 vols.; New York, 1907), II, 198.

[6] Wilson made these points in a variety of speeches beginning in 1862. For example, see Wilson, *The Death of Slavery Is the Life of the Nation* (Washington, D. C., 1864); New York *Times,* March 7, 1862; Boston *Commonwealth,* Nov. 1, 1862; *Congressional Globe,* 37th Cong., 2nd sess., 1862, pp. 1895-97, 1955; 38th Cong., 1st sess., 1864, pp. 1323-24.

releasing slaves from bondage would "make a bond for the peace and repose of the country hereafter." In order to force the president's hand on emancipation, Wilson sought to amend the confiscation bill to require Lincoln to issue an emancipation proclamation within thirty days. The Senate, however, refused to accept his proposal.[7]

Lincoln seemed immovable on emancipation. Wilson continued to visit him but apparently to no avail. In late August, Wilson spoke to an enthusiastic crowd in Boston that had convened to welcome abolitionist John C. Fremont. The senator praised the general for his earlier attempt to emancipate slaves in Missouri and told the audience that the administration was lagging behind the people in demanding abolition. On September 10 the state Republican convention passed resolutions favoring emancipation. Antislavery congressmen increased their agitation in Washington, while some of the Northern state governors, led by Andrew, prepared to meet at Altoona, Pennsylvania, to urge the president to undertake more drastic measures to bring the war to a speedy conclusion.[8]

Wilson, Andrew and their radical associates did not know that Lincoln had already decided to issue an emancipation proclamation. Seward had persuaded him to postpone the announcement until the Union won a military victory, and that came at Antietam on September 17. Five days later Lincoln issued a public pronouncement promising that on January 1, 1863, he would proclaim the abolition of slavery in rebel areas of the country. The tentative and somewhat ambiguous nature of the proclamation did not satisfy Wilson. In a speech in Boston on October 7, he praised Lincoln's action but noted that Congress itself had already done more than the president to set the slaves free. Also, he noted that the proclamation made no mention of the border states.[9] Since Lincoln was apparently willing to free border-state slaves through a process of voluntary,

[7] Carl Sandburg, *Lincoln: The War Years* (4 vols.; New York, 1939), I, 566; Ida H. Harper, *The Life and Work of Susan B. Anthony* (3 vols.; Indianapolis, 1898-1908), I, 238; *Congressional Globe*, 37th Cong., 2nd sess., 1862, pp. 1896-97, 1953-54, 2200, 2201.

[8] Boston *Commonwealth*, Sept. 6, 1862; Hesseltine, *War Governors*, 249-55.

[9] Boston *Commonwealth*, Nov. 1, 1862.

compensated emancipation, Wilson began planning a Senate bill to provide for such a program in Missouri. When the House sent over a similar proposal, he dropped his own measure and sought to amend the House bill to include the other border states in its provisions. Since he wanted Missouri made a free state "in my day and generation," he opposed amendments to graduate emancipation until 1885. Defending the compensation proposals, Wilson stated that "existing institutions around us are practical facts to be dealt with . . . if a little money will smooth the way in this work of emancipation, I am willing to vote it."[10]

Wilson's efforts to secure compensated emancipation for Missouri failed, and, as he had feared, Lincoln did not include the border states in his final proclamation of January 1. Rather than giving up, the Massachusetts senator increased his efforts. Now he sought to free border slaves by drafting them into the army and thereby releasing them and their families from bondage. When John Sherman suggested that a constitutional amendment was a safer way to abolish slavery everywhere, Wilson replied: "it is sound policy to strike at this system of slavery whenever and wherever you can get a blow at it." To aid the passage of his bill, he remained ready to compensate loyal masters for their slaves; the editors of the Boston *Commonwealth* condemned this as another example of Wilson's "irresistible tendency to a calculating electicism that so often misleads him." Wilson had to battle until early 1864 to gain an explicit legislative guarantee of freedom to any drafted slave whether of rebel or loyal master. He called the bill "the greatest emancipation measure ever to pass the Congress of the United States."[11]

While Wilson worked for emancipation by congressional enactment, he kept an anxious eye on the president to see if he was determined to make a reality of his proclamation. In September, 1863, when Lincoln declared that the promise of emancipation,

[10] *Daily Missouri Democrat* (St. Louis), Dec. 9, 1862; B. Gratz Brown to Wilson, Dec. 6, 1862, Wilson MSS, Library of Congress; *Congressional Globe,* 37th Cong., 3rd sess., 1863, pp. 357-58, 618-19; 38th Cong., 1st sess., 1864, p. 824; 39th Cong., 1st sess., 1866, p. 702.

[11] Boston *Commonwealth,* March 20, 1863, April 8, 1864; Wilson, *History of Antislavery Measures,* 203-23, 305, 313-27.

"being made, must be kept," the senator expressed his thanks for
"the noble, patriotic, and Christian words." Still he chafed with
doubt, for conservative Montgomery Blair remained in the cabinet.
In the middle of October the postmaster general bitterly attacked
"ultra-abolitionists" who aimed at ruling the South by the sword. He
criticized Charles Sumner and condemned all Republicans out of
harmony with Lincoln's policy. Wilson was furious. Speaking in
Pittsburgh, he declared that Blair had insulted the country. Repeatedly he implored Lincoln to remove the obnoxious cabinet
member.[12]

As the city and state elections of 1863 approached, Wilson decided to close Republican ranks and criticize Democrats instead of
Lincoln. Union victories at Vicksburg and Gettysburg increased his
confidence and helped ease his dismay at the violent draft and race
riot that occurred in New York in July. In August he urged an
audience in Boston to be thankful for Northern victories; he scorned
Copperhead Democratic opponents and promised to put them down
along with the hated institution of slavery. The following month he
called upon delegates to the Massachusetts Republican convention to
support Lincoln "without qualification or reservation" and insisted
the president was "as ardent a lover of human liberty as we have." In
October he journeyed to New York to tell a large Cooper Institute
audience that if they voted Democratic, they might as well shoot
down from behind the loyal Union soldiers.[13]

In the fall Wilson was immensely pleased to see Republican Union
tickets carry every Northern state except New Jersey. Friends
congratulated him for his contributions to "the late political Gettys-
burgs of the North."[14] Yet the senator knew the final battle to end
slavery once and for all was still to be won. Early in December he
journeyed to Philadelphia to attend the thirtieth anniversary of the
American Anti-slavery Society. Although he was not on the pro-

[12] Wilson to Lincoln, Aug. 21, Sept. 3, 5, Oct. 25, 1863, Robert Todd
Lincoln MSS; Boston *Commonwealth,* Oct. 16, 1863.

[13] New York *Times,* Aug. 9, Oct. 18, 1863; Boston *Commonwealth,* Oct. 2,
1863.

[14] General James C. Rice to Wilson, Nov. 11, 1863, in Robert Todd Lincoln
MSS.

gram, attending abolitionists quickly spotted the sturdy form of the graying Massachusetts senator and invited him to the platform. It was one of the greatest moments of the Natick cobbler's life. He had been on record as an opponent of slavery for almost thirty years. During that time he had borne the brunt of bitter criticisms coming not only from proslavery Whigs and Democrats, but from many of his own antislavery associates who felt that his course was too ambiguous or too cautious. Despite his frequent flirtations with compromise, Wilson had never lost sight of the ultimate goal of emancipation, and on the evening of December 4, the country's foremost abolitionist, William Lloyd Garrison, acknowledged that fact. In past years he had frequently criticized Wilson's course; yet now, when the emancipation movement was at last succeeding, Garrison could freely admit that Wilson had taken his stand against slavery long before it was popular to do so. The abolitionist editor then introduced the senator as the man responsible for the first practical act of emancipation, the freeing of the slaves in the District of Columbia.

Wilson's heart swelled as the audience responded to Garrison's introduction with long peals of applause. At long last it seemed that he was receiving his due recognition as a leader of antislavery reform. For the moment, he was free to enjoy the fruits of his own accomplishments and relish the plaudits of the crowd. He rose to speak and with the crowd reminisced about the antislavery movement of the past thirty years. He told his listeners that although in the past two decades he had no doubt made errors in judgment, "I have ever striven to write my name in ineffaceable letters on the Abolition record." After reminding the crowd of his own legislative contributions to ending slavery, Wilson promised to go back to Washington, "where antislavery men are to be tried as perhaps they were never tried before," determined to do all he could "to break the last fetter of the last slave in the United States."[15]

Back in Washington Wilson anxiously watched the progress of

[15] *Proceedings of the American Antislavery Society at its Third Decade* (New York, 1864); New York *Times,* Dec. 6, 1863; Garrisons, *Garrison,* IV, 90.

the war effort, as well as the attitude of the Lincoln administration, for signs that both the generals and the president were united and determined to crush the rebellion and abolish slavery. Throughout the war, the impulsive senator was beset by moments of panic and doubt, alternating with periods of fatuous confidence, concerning the success of the war effort.[16] In December he listened carefully to the president's annual message and rejoiced to hear Lincoln renew his promise to stand by the emancipation proclamation. Exultantly he rushed up to Lincoln's secretary, John Hay, to exclaim that "the president has struck another great blow. Tell him for me, 'God bless him.'" Yet doubts about Lincoln continued to plague him. He still worried about the influence Montgomery Blair had upon the president and continued to question Lincoln's determination to raise Negro troops. Late in January, seized by a moment of despair, he declared that "the whole government is so mean it would go to pieces were it not for the great cause that props it up." Three months later, the impetuous senator startled Ohio Congressman Albert G. Riddle by erupting in Lincoln's very anterooms in a bitter tirade against the president.[17]

In the elections of 1863 Wilson had stood behind the administration; but in 1864 he wondered if Lincoln should be renominated for the presidency. Some Republicans wanted to select instead Salmon P. Chase, the secretary of the treasury, for they felt his dedication to abolitionism was unquestioned. As early as December, 1863, these Republicans began organizing a committee to obtain the honor for Chase and sought Wilson's support for the movement. The senator briefly weighed the alternatives; then he decided to stay with Lincoln. Early in his career, when he had nothing to lose and everything to gain by breaking party discipline, he had not hesitated to challenge his party leaders. By 1864, however, he was a leading member of a strong Northern party, and he did not care to risk his position in

[16] Beale, ed., *Welles Diary,* I, 118 (Sept. 10, 1862); Sparks, ed., *Inside Lincoln's Army,* 234; C. F. Adams to father, Dec. 18, 1864, in Worthington C. Ford, ed., *A Cycle of Adams Letters, 1861-1865* (2 vols., Boston, 1920), II, 233.

[17] Dennett, ed., *Hay Diary,* 132 (Dec. 9, 1863); G. L. Stearns to wife, Jan. 23, 1864, in Stearns, *George Luther Stearns,* 326; Riddle, *Recollections,* 267.

a reckless political maneuver. The following year the Massachusetts legislature would consider his reelection to the Senate. Since the legislature would be chosen in the 1864 election, Wilson would take no action that would risk a Republican rupture or raise dissatisfaction with his own political course. Thus, when Riddle reprimanded Wilson for his vehement denunciation of the president, the senator admitted that the entire North stood with the administration and would renominate Lincoln and declared that "bad as that would be, the best must be made of it."[18]

As matters turned out, Wilson was wisely cautious, for the Chase boom quickly perished. Yet as the summer dragged on in 1864, Northern fortunes declined and with them went Republican hopes. General Ulysses S. Grant's advance into Virginia slowed down as Union casualty lists mounted; in early July a Confederate force led by General Jubal Early reached the outskirts of Washington itself. Depression and defeatism settled over the capital, and Democratic opponents of the war stepped up their efforts to bring about peace. Wilson may have been affected by the pessimistic atmosphere. In August rumors spread associating his name with a desperate movement to secure Republican victory in November by negotiating an armistice and postponing drafts until after the election. Massachusetts Republicans reprimanded Wilson, and he issued a public denial of the rumor. The senator then consulted with Lincoln and found him determined to stand by his principles, restore the Union, and end slavery; Wilson left the conference with renewed confidence.[19]

The Massachusetts senator's determination to present a unified Republican front during the campaign was increased by the results of the Democratic convention in Chicago, for the party platform included a "peace plank" which Republicans interpreted as a pre-

[18] James G. Randall and Richard N. Current, *Lincoln the President: Last Full Measure* (New York, 1955), 96; Riddle, *Recollections,* 267.

[19] John Murray Forbes to John Andrew, Aug. 3, 1864, Andrew MSS; Forbes to Wilson, Aug. 4, 1864, in Hughes, ed., *Forbes Letters* (supp. ed.), II, 282-83; New York *Herald,* Aug. 19, 1864; New York *Times,* Aug. 21, 1864; Boston *Commonwealth,* Aug. 21, 1864; Wilson to William G. Herndon, May 30, 1867, Herndon-Weik Collection, Herndon MSS, Library of Congress.

lude to stopping the war. On the other hand, Wilson was highly gratified to see Lincoln demand and get a Republican platform promise to seek passage of an amendment abolishing slavery. Through September and October the Massachusetts senator spared no effort to solidify party ranks. He tried to persuade John C. Fremont to decline an independent nomination for the presidency, and then he asked Lincoln to encourage Chase and Benjamin F. Wade, two of the president's bitterest critics, to enter the canvass. Warning Lincoln that many New Englanders were critical of the administration, Wilson insisted the only way to gain their support was to dismiss Montgomery Blair from the cabinet. He reminded the president that "if we are beaten our friends will place the blame wholly on you, for they believe they can carry the country easy with another candidate."[20]

Wilson campaigned vigorously through ten states and continued to supply Lincoln with suggestions on the direction of the campaign. In November, after doing all he could to insure Republican success, Wilson retired to Natick to await the election returns. The results could not have been more satisfactory. Not only did Lincoln sweep to victory, but he got almost three out of every four votes in Massachusetts, thereby assuring solid Republican control of the state legislature. The road seemed clear for the return of the junior senator from Massachusetts for another six-year term in Washington.

During the summer and fall of 1864, Wilson had carefully avoided any action that might have endangered his reelection. Fellow members of the Massachusetts delegation in Washington promised him that no one intended to contest his return to the Senate, and he received similar assurances from state and local politicians. Consequently, when the state Republican convention met in the summer, he decided not to ask the delegates to pass a resolution supporting his candidacy, feeling the gesture would be unnecessary. The only rumble of any opposition to Wilson came from vitriolic Charles

[20] William F. Zornow, *Lincoln and the Party Divided* (Norman, Okla., 1954), 146; Wilson to Abraham Lincoln, Sept. 5, 1864, Robert Todd Lincoln MSS.

Wright, an old Free-Soiler who had never forgiven the senator for flirting with the Know-Nothings.[21]

Wright had sounded the only note of opposition in Massachusetts against Wilson until the state legislature convened in January, 1865. Then the Boston *Advertiser* published a series of editorials recommending that the House of Representatives avoid any "unseemly haste" in choosing the next senator. On January 10, the House delegates delivered a rousing vote of support for Henry Wilson, electing him by a vote of 207 to 12. According to the editor of the Boston *Transcript,* the House's action was "a deserved tribute to a hardworking, patriotic and able public servant." Most observers expected the Senate to confirm the election the following day, but several legislators managed to postpone voting until January 20. A wave of surprise and puzzlement swept the state. The *Transcript,* contending that Wilson "represented the great *middling interest* of this Commonwealth, and has a stronger hold upon the public than almost any other public man," did not see how the Senate could avoid ratifying the choice of the House. The *Worcester Spy* also attacked the Senate for trying to defy the will of the people of the state. Wilson was as shocked as most other people in Massachusetts at the developments. He refused to make any public statements, but he told friends that the Senate's action "touched me at a tender point." He admitted that "Massachusetts has been more than kind to me and I would not occupy a seat in the Senate a day longer if she desired to retire me." The people of the state had, according to Wilson, expressed their will the previous November, when they had indicated no disposition to replace him. He was certain that "just and fair dealing will triumph in the end."[22]

[21] *New Bedford Mercury* quoted in Boston *Commonwealth,* July 15, 1864; Wilson to Dawes, Aug. 22, 1864, Dawes MSS; Wilson to William P. Robinson, Jan. 12, 1865, Historical Society of Pennsylvania; Charles Wright, *Our Political Practice* (Boston, 1865).

[22] Boston *Advertiser,* Jan. 4, 7, 9, 10, 11, 1865; Boston *Transcript,* Jan. 10, 11, 12, 1865; *Worcester Spy* quoted in *Transcript,* Jan. 13, 1865; Wilson to William P. Robinson, Jan. 12, 1865, Historical Society of Pennsylvania; Wilson to H. B. Claflin, Jan. 13, 1865, Claflin MSS.

Some observers speculated that Benjamin Butler was maneuvering for the Senate seat, but he quickly denied the rumor. Others suspected that supporters of Massachusetts House speaker A. H. Bullock hoped to elevate John Andrew to the Senate so that Bullock might take the governor's chair. As it turned out, most of the men seeking to hold back the election did hope that Andrew might emerge as the new senator. Frank Bird noted that "a few gentlemen friends of Andrew . . . who can never breathe freely so long as a shoemaker is in the Senate" hoped to displace the Natick cobbler. Andrew himself issued disclaimers, but according to William Robinson, he "looked with a considerable degree of complacency upon the anti-Wilson movement." Consequently the governor's supporters, acting upon what they thought were the governor's secret wishes, frantically sought to defeat Wilson's reelection. Lacking any sign from Andrew, however, their delaying tactics collapsed, and on January 20 the state Senate returned Wilson to Congress by a vote of 37 to 3.[23] The reelected former shoemaker had never really doubted his eventual success, for he knew he had the support of most of the state's Republican voters, newspapers, and politicians. He had indeed served his state well, and the men who had opposed his reelection amounted to a mere handful.[24]

As usual with the benign senator, he refused to hold any grudges against his former opponents, and he willingly supported the unsuccessful efforts of others to gain Andrew a portfolio in Lincoln's cabinet.[25] He was secure in Washington for another six years, and he

[23] Butler to Wilson, Jan. 15, 1865, in Marshall, ed., *Butler Correspondence,* V, 498; Boston *Commonwealth,* Aug. 26, 1864, Jan. 14, 1865, Feb. 1, 1868, Jan. 28, 1871; Pearson, *Andrew,* II, 177-78, 181-83, 185-88; J. G. Robinson to Henry L. Dawes, Jan. 20, 1865, Dawes MSS; George Baty Blake to John Andrew, Jan. 13, 1865, Andrew to Blake, Jan. 16, 1865, Oakes Ames to Andrew, Jan. 14, 1865, Frank Howe to Andrew, Jan. 14, 1865, all in Andrew MSS; John M. Forbes to William P. Fessenden, Jan. 11, 1865, in Hughes, ed., *Forbes Letters* (supp. ed.), II, 121; New York *Times,* Jan. 21, 1865.

[24] E. R. Hoar to Charles Sumner, Jan. 11, 24, 1865, Sumner MSS; Boston *Commonwealth,* Jan. 28, 1865; James A. Dix to Wilson, Jan. 20, 1865, Wilson MSS, Library of Congress; Boston *Transcript,* Jan. 21, 31, 1865.

[25] W. L. Burt to Andrew, Feb. 1, 1865, Forbes to Andrew, Feb. 7, 1865, William Schouler to Andrew, Feb. 23, 1865, and Charles Ingersoll to Andrew, March 6, 1865, all in Andrew MSS.

seemed equally secure in the hearts of his constituents. Amos Lawrence even suggested to E. Rockwood Hoar that Harvard grant the
junior senator an honorary degree. Hoar agreed that such an action
would be fitting but indicated that it was too late for the governing
board to act in time for the coming commencement. Thinking back
to Wilson's attacks on Harvard during the days of the coalition, Hoar
chuckled: "think of the sensation which the suggestion of Wilson
would have had when we were first members of the corporation."[26]

As if to complete Wilson's contentment, Abraham Lincoln used
his executive powers to encourage Congress to approve the Thirteenth Amendment, and Congress then sent it out to the states for
ratification. At the same time that Northern state legislatures began
to write the last chapter in the history of slavery in the United
States, the Southern Confederacy, launched to prolong the existence
of the institution, entered its final stages. By March, 1865, when
Congress adjourned, the end of the war seemed imminent. Sherman
was pushing up through the Carolinas, and Grant had begun to close
in on Robert E. Lee's Army of Northern Virginia. On April 3,
Richmond, the war-long target of repeated Union advances, finally
was abandoned to federal troops. Six days later, at Appomattox,
Virginia, Lee surrendered his army to Grant, thereby virtually ending
the Civil War.

Wilson agreed to join Garrison, English reformer George Thompson, and other assorted abolitionists, politicians, generals, and
reporters in an expedition to Charleston, where they planned to
commemorate the end of the war by visiting the fort wherein it
started. The steamer reached the South Carolina city on April 13,
and on the following day a solemn and impressive ceremony took
place in Fort Sumter. Once again the United States flag was raised
over its ramparts.[27]

On April 16 Wilson left the city along with other members of the
entourage to continue on to Florida. The ship was leisurely steaming
southward, and the passengers were enjoying the variegated colors of

[26] Hoar to Lawrence, May 15, 1865, Lawrence MSS.

[27] Garrisons, *Garrison*, IV, 137-39; Charleston *Daily Courier*, April 16,
1865; New York *Tribune*, April 20, 22, 1865.

the sunset, when Senator Wilson received a telegram. He took the message to his cabin; few noticed his departure. Suddenly the senator reappeared. Stumbling on deck, choked with emotion, he cried, "Good God! The President is killed!" The stunned vacationers listened in silence as Wilson read the contents of the dispatch and thereby learned that Abraham Lincoln had been shot by an assassin two nights earlier and had died early the following morning.[28]

The ship immediately set about to return to the North. As the somber passengers gathered quietly in small groups to discuss the tragedy and its meaning, Wilson had time to think about the former president. With the success of the Thirteenth Amendment, the Republican victory of 1864, his own reelection to the Senate, and the collapse of the Southern Confederacy, the Massachusetts senator no longer had reason to harbor his earlier irritation with Lincoln. Perhaps now the assassination finished the process of softening Wilson's image of the martyred president. Certainly he was not one to dwell on personal disagreements anyway. On May 3, when he delivered a brief eulogy of the president before the New England Historical and Genealogical Society, he spoke of himself as much as of the people of the country, when he stated: "The nation has failed to comprehend fully the character of Abraham Lincoln in all its proportions, but now that he has suddenly fallen, the people are beginning to do justice towards their fallen leader. He will pass into history as the foremost man of the age." Two years later, the Massachusetts senator told Lincoln's former law partner that the president, although perhaps being too flexible concerning moral principles, was "a genuine democrat in feeling, sentiment, and action."[29]

[28] Garrisons, *Garrison*, IV, 151.

[29] *New England Historical and Genealogical Register*, XIX (1865), 279; Wilson to William Herndon, May 30, 1867, Herndon-Weik Collection, Herndon MSS, Library of Congress. When Wilson later discussed Lincoln in his history, he portrayed the president as a well-meaning, humble, God-fearing, and unselfish man, who had prejudices against Negro equality and opposed immediate emancipation. Wilson showed some appreciation however for the many forces working on Lincoln and praised his final decision to seek unqualified emancipation for all slaves. See Wilson, *Slave Power*, III, 556-57, 575-77, 589-90.

In the late spring of 1865, Henry Wilson had little time to ponder the merits of the deceased president. Pressures of reconstruction now mounted, and he was forced to turn his attention to the many problems facing the country at the conclusion of the great civil conflict.

10

The Spirit of
Slavery Still Lives

The problems of reuniting a nation severed by civil war, dealing justly with the opponents of the government, and guaranteeing the equality of almost four million ex-slaves were without precedent in the history of the United States. Henry Wilson later recalled that "no Congressional wisdom less than inspired, even if such wisdom were possible, could have known exactly what was required." Looking back upon the process of reconstruction after ten years had elapsed, he admitted that he and his contemporaries had underestimated the difficulties which confronted them, particularly as they attempted to protect the rights of the freedmen in the South.[1]

At the end of the war Wilson hoped that the abolition of slavery, by removing the cause of sectional discord and allowing reason "to assume its mild sway again over our now maddened, poisoned, and intoxicated countrymen of the South," would pave the way toward national and racial reconciliation. Yet even as the Thirteenth Amendment was passed, he was realist enough to recognize that many who voted for it were opponents of racial equality. Such prejudice, "which was the result of the teachings of demagogues and politicians who had for years undertaken to delude and deceive the American people," existed even in Republican ranks and endangered the complete freedom of the blacks.[2]

Wilson's own views on the question of the racial equality of blacks were ambivalent. At times before the Civil War, under pressure from Southern senators, he had stated that whites were superior to blacks intellectually, physically, and morally. Yet he also condemned the prejudice of "this proud and domineering white race of ours" that kept blacks from enjoying the full fruits of liberty. He insisted that Negroes should be given full equality before the law, so that they would have the opportunity to "improve all the faculties that God has given them." As a state legislator he had striven to provide the blacks of Massachusetts with equal rights. He praised them for their intelligence and industry and claimed that they were little if any inferior to the average population of his state or of the country. He called upon the free states of the North that legally discriminated against Negroes to join with Massachusetts in "putting our own States and our own public sentiments right, before we arrange others."[3]

During the Civil War Wilson struggled to enlarge the opportunities available for free blacks. In every session of Congress after he first entered the Senate, Wilson had introduced bills to appropriate money from federal land sales to finance education in the District, which he insisted should be provided for "children of every class and description, of every race." In 1863 he did manage to incorporate a private institution in Washington to educate black children, and in 1867 he helped a group of Congregationalists incorporate a Negro university in Washington named after Union General O. O. Howard. He and Sumner cooperated to repeal the black codes in Washington and give freedmen there equal rights under the law. Wilson demanded that Negroes be licensed along with whites to do business in the District, and he heartily supported Sumner's resolution aimed at eliminating discrimination in street railways of the city. He insisted he did not want to force social intercourse between the races, but he

[1] Wilson, *Slave Power,* III, 503-4, 604.

[2] *Ibid.,* III, 233, 453, 503-4; *Congressional Globe,* 37th Cong., 2nd sess., 1862, pp. 1895-96, 3203; 38th Cong., 1st sess., 1864, pp. 554, 1320, 1322-24; 39th Cong., 1st sess., 1866, p. 340; Wilson, *The Death of Slavery, passim.* See also *Memorial Addresses on the Life and Character of Henry Wilson* (Washington, D. C., 1876), 66.

[3] *Congressional Globe,* 33rd Cong., 2nd sess., 1855, p. 239; 34th Cong., 1st sess., 1856, appendix, pp. 393-94; 35th Cong., 1st sess., 1858, p. 1966; 36th Cong., 1st sess., 1860, pp. 1636-37, 1684; Wilson to James Freeman Clarke, April 11, 1860, and Clarke to Wilson, April 17, 1860, Houghton Library, Harvard University.

did want men "to have the privilege of making out of themselves all that God and nature intended they should be."[4]

Wilson took a special interest in the Negroes inducted into the federal armies, for he had played a large role in putting them there. He showed concern for their health and safety and spoke out against their unjust treatment by officers. When black troops were criticized in Congress, he asserted that "they have suffered, toiled, and worked as no troops in the service." Although many criticized him for his tardiness in seeking legislation providing retroactive equal pay for black soldiers, he persisted until Congress passed such a measure in 1865. "At last," Wilson could remark, "justice has been done."[5]

Wilson was also instrumental in obtaining legislation creating the Freedman's Bureau in 1865. The federal agency was charged with feeding, clothing, and housing hundreds of thousands of former slaves who found themselves destitute. The bureau was also to settle freedmen on abandoned lands in the South and seek to safeguard their civil rights. Wilson kept informed about the operations of the bureau and struggled to get Congress to keep it in operation. He frequently demanded investigations of charges that the bureau was ignoring its responsibilities and sought the dismissal of officials guilty of abusing rather than assisting the freedmen.[6]

[4] Every year from 1857 to 1869 Wilson introduced bills to provide revenue for schools in the District. On his bill for the institution incorporated in 1863, see Wilson, *Antislavery Measures,* 188; on Howard University, see *Congressional Globe,* 39th Cong., 2nd sess., 1867, p. 674, and Howard, *Autobiography,* II, 396-97. For his efforts to secure legal and social equality for Negroes in the District of Columbia, see *Congressional Globe,* 37th Cong., 2nd sess., 1863, pp. 917, 2020; 38th Cong., 1st sess., 1864, pp. 554-55, 817.

[5] *Congressional Globe,* 38th Cong., 1st sess., 1864, pp. 1664, 2766-67; A. F. Augusta to Wilson, Camp Birney, N. C., April 5, 1864, and Wilson to Bureau of Colored Troops, Dec. 28, 1863, both in Letters Received, Bureau for Colored Troops, War Department, National Archives; James A. Hardie to Wilson, April 15, 1864, Letters Sent, Office of the Secretary of War, War Department, National Archives; F. W. Bird to Charles Sumner, Feb. 24, 1864, Charles Sumner to F. W. Bird, Feb. 22, 1864, Sumner MSS; Wilson to Benjamin F. Butler, Dec. 18, 1863, in Marshall, ed., *Butler Correspondence,* III, 227; Wilson to T. W. Higginson, March 26, 1865, Houghton Library.

[6] John Eaton, *Lincoln, Grant, and the Freedman* (New York, 1907), 222-29; George F. Bentley, *History of the Freedman's Bureau* (Philadelphia,

As the war ended, Wilson was under no illusions that with emancipation and the creation of the Freedman's Bureau the struggle for human rights had ended. He told a crowd assembled in Faneuil Hall to celebrate the fall of Richmond, that "the sooner we resolve to do justice to all our countrymen of every clime and race, the sooner we shall have a great, united and free Republic." In South Carolina he told a Negro audience that solving the problems created by the war and emancipation would "take all the resources of statesmanship and philanthropy in the country."[7]

At Charleston Wilson for the first time clearly indicated that he thought the path of "statesmanship and philanthropy" should lead to enfranchisement of the freed Negroes. To protect the former slaves in their freedom he promised temporary help from the Union army, and he urged the freedmen to trust in God, be faithful and true to the country, industrious and courteous, and to educate their children. But he also promised them that such industry and education would prepare them to "use the ballot in the cause we have maintained." When the senator returned to Massachusetts, he learned that antislavery societies were preparing to disband since their original purpose had been realized. Early in May he spoke to the American Anti-slavery Society in Boston, and later in the month he appeared before the members of the city's Emancipation League. To both groups he brought the same message: "The dark spirits of slavery still live." He pointed out that one house of the Tennessee legislature had just passed a set of black codes severely restricting the rights of freedmen in that state. Wilson told his listeners that their duty was "as clear as the track of the sun across the heavens." To

1955), 40-43, 48-49; *Congressional Globe,* 38th Cong., 1st sess., 1864, pp. 253, 3300, 3307-8, 3332-33; 40th Cong., 2nd sess., 1868, pp. 2769-70, 3056; Wilson letters to Freedman's Bureau, dated April 9, 29, May 19, 27, June 17, 18, [June], Dec. 9, 1868, in Letters Received, and E. Whittlesey to Wilson, Aug. 15, 1868, and O. O. Howard to Wilson, July 13, 1867, Letters Sent, Bureau of Refugees, Freedmen, and Abandoned Lands, War Department, National Archives.

[7] Boston *Transcript,* April 5, 1865; Charleston *Daily Courier,* April 16, 1865; New York *Tribune,* April 20, 1865.

insure the freedmen's rights and to secure the loyalty of the South, friends of the Negro must endeavor to enfranchise "every black man in the Republic."[8]

Wilson saw a twofold purpose in enfranchising Southern Negroes. The ballot would first of all help the freedman safeguard his new-found freedom. Secondly, since according to Wilson Negroes by their behavior during the war had demonstrated their loyalty to the Union, their vote would offset the political power of the white Southern rebels. In May he told Boston abolitionists that the con-quered South could be "kept in subjection by the bayonet of the white man or the ballot of the black man." Wilson preferred the latter alternative; he sought no cruel penalties for white Southerners. The war had punished them enough. According to him, Jefferson Davis and his followers, rather than causing the rebellion, had been helpless tools of slavery. In 1864 the passions of the great struggle had led Wilson momentarily to advocate confiscation, but before and after that time he consistently opposed taking anything from Southerners but their slaves. "After the conflict," he said, "when the din of battle has ceased, the humane and kindly and charitable feel-ings of the country and of the world will require us to deal gently with the masses of the people who are engaged in this rebellion."[9]

After the war Wilson opposed death penalties or any lengthy imprisonment for Confederate officials. In August, 1865, he visited the former vice-president of the Confederacy, Alexander H. Ste-phens, who was incarcerated in a prison in Massachusetts. Wilson found him sick and very uncomfortable in a damp, unheated room. Immediately the senator asked President Johnson to permit Ste-phens to return to Georgia on parole. Although the prisoner was not immediately released, he was removed to a better room, and he sent Wilson his thanks. Likewise, in November the senator recommended

[8] Charleston *Daily Courier*, April 17, 1865; New York *Times*, May 11, 1865; Boston *Commonwealth*, June 3, 1865.

[9] New York *Times*, May 11, 1865; *Congressional Globe*, 37th Cong., 2nd sess., 1862, pp. 1895-96, 1954; 38th Cong., 1st sess., 1864, p. 824; Wilson, *The Death of Slavery*.

the release of Robert Mallory, Confederate secretary of the navy, and pressed the president to release all other rebel leaders held on charge of treason. In April, 1866, he personally intervened to obtain the parole of Clement C. Clay, former Alabama senator who had been charged with conspiring in the assassination of Lincoln. At the time he told Mrs. Clay he thought Jefferson Davis, also accused of taking part in the conspiracy, was innocent of the charge. A year later, he recommended to Congress that the imprisoned Davis be brought to a speedy trial or released. His speech prompted the Richmond *Enquirer* to commend Wilson for exhibiting "a humane and conciliatory spirit."[10]

If Wilson was determined to oppose any cruel or unusual punishment for the rebel leaders, he was equally determined to keep them from reviving their former political power. His whole career of campaigning against the Slave Power had convinced him that prominent Southern planters had not only dominated the people both black and white of their own section, but had also ruled the whole nation through their control of the federal government. After working for twenty years to drive the slavemasters from Washington, he was not prepared to see them resume political power. Unless Congress took steps to avoid it, he was sure that as the war ended "traitors would rush to the ballot box, to save their lives and their property, and direct and control public affairs." He had little faith in the efficacy of administering an oath of loyalty to former Confederates before letting them vote or hold office. He believed enfranchising Southern

[10] *Congressional Globe,* 37th Cong., 2nd sess., 1862, p. 2197; 40th Cong., 1st sess., 1867, pp. 267-68; Increase N. Tarbox to Henry L. Dawes, June 9, 1865, H. B. Jackson to Dawes, June 16, 1865, Dawes MSS; Wilson to Andrew Johnson, Aug. 14, 1865, March 3, 1866, Andrew Johnson MSS, Library of Congress; Alexander H. Stephens to Wilson, Sept. 13, 1865, Wilson MSS, Library of Congress; Wilson to Andrew Johnson, March 5, 1866, Letters Received, Adjutant General's Office, War Department, National Archives; William Henry Seward to Wilson, Nov. 16, 1865, William Henry Seward MSS, University of Rochester Library, Rochester, N. Y.; Ada Sterling, ed., *A Belle of the Fifties: Memoirs of Mrs. Clay of Alabama* (New York, 1904), 358-61; New York *Times,* April 25, 1866; Richmond *Enquirer* quoted in Natick *Times,* April 6, 1867.

blacks would more effectively eliminate the danger of resurrecting the old Southern political dominance.[11]

It is difficult to say when Wilson first became convinced of the necessity for Negro suffrage in the South, or how he thought it might be obtained. Certainly he had long advocated enfranchising free Negroes in the North. In 1858 and 1864, in considering statehood bills for the Minnesota and Montana territories, he had tried without success to guarantee Negroes there the ballot. He was well aware of Northern prejudices against enfranchising Negroes, however, and he moved with caution in advocating congressional support for the idea. In May, 1864, Charles Sumner tried to provide for equal suffrage in the District of Columbia. Wilson, who knew his colleague's proposal was doomed, sought to alter it to give the vote to Negroes who had fought in the Union army or possessed $250 worth of property. He was eager to "begin the work of elevation which the extension of the ballot to colored men would give to that long-oppressed race," but he was certain that "we cannot extend the right of suffrage to the masses of colored men in the District upon conditions which permit white men to exercise the right." Wilson's proposal was quickly defeated, for the 1864 election was in the offing and Republicans could ill afford to antagonize Northern voters. In July, when Sumner and a few other senators sought to amend the Wade-Davis reconstruction bill to provide for Negro suffrage in the South, Wilson helped vote down the proposed alteration.[12]

In keeping with his pragmatic approach to problems of reconstruction and suffrage, Wilson had little patience with debates over constitutional theories about restoring the Union. He agreed with those of his colleagues who insisted that Congress should control the reconstruction process, and in 1864 he voted without comment for the Wade-Davis bill, which spelled out congressional terms for read-

[11] *Congressional Globe,* 37th Cong., 2nd sess., 1862, p. 1785; 38th Cong., 1st sess., 1864, pp. 106, 2903; 38th Cong., 2nd sess., 1865, p. 499; New York *Tribune,* Dec. 8, 1863; Boston *Commonwealth,* Sept. 9, 1864.

[12] *Congressional Globe,* 35th Cong., 1st sess., 1858, p. 1513; 38th Cong., 1st sess., 1864, pp. 1361, 2243, 2244, 2351, 2512, 2543, 3449.

mitting the Southern states. When Abraham Lincoln sought to reconstruct state governments in the South under his own plan, however, Wilson seemed to fear that refusal to recognize the new governments might discourage loyal men in their efforts to "put their State right." Wilson eventually voted with the rest of his colleagues against counting the electoral votes cast in 1865 by the states reconstructed under Lincoln's plan. He later contended, however, that the state governments created under Lincoln's auspices "went for freedom" and adopted a "progressive policy." He admitted they were not moving "so fast as we desired, nor so far, but still it was all in the right direction."[13]

If Wilson was somewhat uncertain about the true meaning of Lincoln's plan of reconstruction, he was not hesitant about opposing the program of his successor, Andrew Johnson. After Lincoln's assassination, much of the nation's future depended upon Johnson's attitude toward reconstruction and the freedman. Wilson had no reason to suspect Johnson's loyalty to the Union, for as senator and military governor of Tennessee he had spared no effort to prosecute the war. More important, Wilson remembered with satisfaction that Johnson had championed the cause of emancipation in the Volunteer State. In September, 1863, at the Massachusetts Republican convention Wilson had praised Johnson, "that glorious old Roman who has stood by the unity of the Republic with unsurpassed courage and fidelity." The next year the Massachusetts senator had approved placing Andrew Johnson on the Republican ticket with Abraham Lincoln.[14]

[13] For Wilson's comments on constitutional disputes over the status of Southern states, see *Congressional Globe,* 39th Cong., 1st sess., 1865-1866, pp. 111, 701-2. On his attitude toward state governments reconstructed by Lincoln, see *Congressional Globe,* 38th Cong., 1st sess., 1864, pp. 2903-4; 38th Cong., 2nd sess., 1865, pp. 583, 848, 1065; Boston *Commonwealth,* March 11, 18, 25, 1865. For remarks on Louisiana, see Henry Wilson, *Executive Patronage* (Washington, D. C., 1866), 6-7.

[14] Boston *Commonwealth,* Oct. 2, 1863. There is a controversy over whom Wilson supported for vice-president in 1864. Charles Eugene Hamlin, on the basis of interviews and letters obtained almost thirty years after the nomination of Johnson, claims that Lincoln authorized Wilson to stop the Johnson boom and keep Hamlin. See Charles E. Hamlin, *The Life and Times of Hanni-*

Wilson had no assurances, however, that Johnson was determined to protect the freedman's rights and liberties. He and the rest of the nation had to wait until May 29 before the new president issued his first proclamations concerning reconstruction. He promised the Southern states an early return to the Union after they had reconstituted their governments, abolished slavery, and repudiated their war debts and secession ordinances. State officials were to be selected by voters who could pledge future loyalty to the Union. In the meantime, Johnson appointed military governors to maintain order in each Southern state. His policy put no serious impediments in the way of a rapid return of the South; he did not inquire as to past loyalty to the nation and apparently was ready to commit the freedman to the care of the white South without any provisions for protecting his newly acquired freedom.[15]

When Wilson learned of Johnson's proclamation, he impulsively promised a group of friends that New England would repudiate the president's policy and make an open issue with him in the next Congress. He was quite critical of Johnson's appointments to fill the provisional governorships, and he was bitterly opposed to readmitting Southern states without protecting the Negro with the ballot. Convinced that Johnson's policy would abandon the freedmen "to the hatred of their disloyal masters," Wilson pleaded with his friend General O. O. Howard, head of the Freedman's Bureau, and Secretary of State Seward to protect the blacks. Then Wilson rushed off to Washington to consult with Republicans in the capital. One of his

---

bal Hamlin (Cambridge, Mass., 1899), 467. In 1866, however, Wendell Phillips attacked Wilson for using his influence to replace Hamlin with Johnson. Boston *Commonwealth,* Nov. 10, 1866. Taking into account Wilson's tendency to endorse nominations on the basis of political expediency, the more contemporaneous nature of Phillips' remarks, and Charles Hamlin's admission that several Massachusetts delegates to the Republican convention who spoke with Wilson denied he had given his support to Hamlin, it seems clear that he supported Johnson.

[15] I have found the following two books immensely helpful for their review of the events of Johnson's presidency: Lawanda and John H. Cox, *Politics, Principles, and Prejudice, 1865-1866: Dilemma of Reconstruction America* (Glencoe, Ill., 1963), and Eric L. McKitrick, *Andrew Johnson and Reconstruction* (Chicago, 1960).

associates there was sure the senator "was bent on making trouble with the President," and Johnson himself complained that Wilson was "dictatorial and insolent." In June the president irritated Wilson by insisting that only the states could determine suffrage qualifications and by asserting that if the Negro could vote, he would vote as his former master dictated.[16]

On July 4, Wilson had a chance to reply publicly to Johnson's claims and declare his own position on reconstruction. On that day a large group of Negroes gathered in Washington to celebrate the national holiday had asked Wilson to address them. The senator willingly complied. As he rose to speak, the audience enthusiastically applauded him as the man who had abolished slavery in the District. Slavery was gone, Wilson admitted, but its effects remained. Southern Negroes were still being denied their basic rights. Wilson assured his listeners that he had faith in the motives and purposes of Andrew Johnson in dealing with the problem and insisted he had no desire to find fault with the government.

Then, without directly condemning Johnson's program, Wilson set forth his own solutions to the reconstruction problem. First of all, he promised to present to Congress on the first day of its December session a bill to secure the personal liberty "of every freedman on the continent." But he would not stop there. Every Negro, promised Wilson, would receive the ballot. Denying "one of the greatest falsehoods ever uttered"—Johnson's statement that the Negro if enfranchised would vote as his former master wished— Wilson insisted the freedman would vote as he had fought, guided by his heart rather than his master. According to the senator, had Johnson told the white Southerners right after Appomattox that they could not return to the Union until the Negro could vote, the terms would have been accepted. Now, Wilson had to admit that it was too

[16] A. W. Campbell to Francis H. Pierpont, June 16, 1865, in Charles H. Ambler, *Francis H. Pierpont* (Chapel Hill, N. C., 1937), 430-31; Wilson to O. O. Howard, June 15, 1865, O. O. Howard MSS, Bowdoin College Library, Brunswick, Me.; Wilson to William Henry Seward, June 15, 1865, Seward MSS; Henry J. Raymond to Thurlow Weed, June, 1865, in Thurlow Weed Barnes, *Memoir of Thurlow Weed,* (Boston, 1884), 451.

late; Johnson's program had already begun. Congress, however, still had control over the reconstruction process, for it had passed a law barring Confederate supporters from holding office. Consequently Wilson offered a bargain to the Southerners. If they gave the Negro the vote, he would permit the former rebels to hold office. Foreseeing that Johnson might resist the bargain, Wilson, after reminding his listeners that for thirty years he had acted with men "who put up parties and put down parties," promised that "I . . . *can do it again*."[17]

If Wilson was firmly convinced of the rightness of his own position on reconstruction, as an able politician he knew he could not act without the support of public opinion. Republican officeholders, fearing party dissension, objected vociferously to his July 4 speech. Party leaders even in Massachusetts were slow to agree on the need for Negro suffrage. The North was clearly unwilling to lend full support to the idea; as late as 1865 most Northern states denied their Negro inhabitants the ballot. Feeling the force of these opinions, Wilson began to search for compromise solutions.[18] He hoped to reach an agreement with Johnson. The president had given some indication that he would favor limited suffrage for the Negro, although he wanted the states themselves to grant the privilege. Wilson, uneasy at the sight of Washington "full of Rebels seeking pardon and power," waited somewhat impatiently to talk to the chief executive. "We are in a critical position and must commit no false step," he warned Sumner. "While we stand firm as a rock for suffrage for the Negro, we must not weaken the cause of the poor and oppressed by saying or doing imprudent things." Admitting that Johnson refused "to go as far as we do in the right direction," Wilson concluded that the only solution was to "stand by the administration and endeavor to bring it right." If Johnson refused to be

[17] Boston *Commonwealth,* July 8, 13, 1865; *Daily National Republican* (Washington, D. C.), July 5, 1865.

[18] Boston *Commonwealth,* Aug. 5, 1865; Eliphalet Traske to Benjamin Butler, June 13, 1865, Benjamin F. Butler MSS, Library of Congress; New England Loyal Publication Society, Publication no. 289, in Boston Public Library; Boston *Transcript,* June 21, July 21, Sept. 14, 1865; Amos Lawrence to Andrew Johnson, July 1, 1865, Lawrence MSS.

moved, "then we must follow where our principles lead whether to victory or to temporary defeat."[19]

In September Wilson finally gained an interview with Johnson. He asked the president if he planned to ostracize party members who advocated Negro suffrage. Johnson assured him he would not and added that he favored the fullest, freest discussion of all questions concerning reconstruction. Thus reassured, Wilson left the capital to journey North through Pennsylvania and New York to speak for Union Republican candidates in the fall state elections. To audiences in Philadelphia, New York, and Brooklyn he brought the same message; he admitted there were differences between Republicans over Johnson's program, but he promised there would be no trouble with the president. In Brooklyn he even predicted that Congress would pass a law giving the black man the ballot, and Johnson would sign it.[20]

In late October the senator returned to Natick to ponder the results of the campaign. His tour had convinced him that public opinion would not support congressional attempts to gain universal suffrage for all races. Republican conventions in several large Northern states had refused to endorse any resolutions favoring Negro suffrage. In addition, during the fall Connecticut, Wisconsin, and Minnesota citizens had all voted against enfranchising Negroes in their own states. Consequently, Wilson decided to abandon for the present any hope of action on suffrage and instead concentrate on protecting the Negro's legal rights, for he was sure the North would unite in favor of positive action on that matter. Also, recent developments in the South convinced him that the Negro needed adequate protection for his civil rights immediately. In November General Edward Wild, then with the Freedman's Bureau in Georgia, visited Wilson, bringing with him tales of cruel treatment that whites in the South were meting out to Negroes.[21]

[19] Wilson to Charles Sumner, Sept. 9, 1865, Sumner MSS; Pierce, *Sumner,* IV, 250.

[20] New York *Times,* Oct. 10, 25, 1865; Boston *Transcript,* Sept. 19, Oct. 17, 25, Nov. 6, 1865; Boston *Commonwealth,* Nov. 4, 1865.

[21] McKitrick, *Johnson,* 58-59; Boston *Transcript,* Nov. 15, 1865; Wilson to O. O. Howard, Nov. 20, 1865, Howard MSS.

Greatly agitated, Wilson wrote to General Howard of the Freedman's Bureau that "we have been giving up the cause of the freedman for the past five months. It is time to halt, and to face the
issues." Again he begged Seward to arrest the unfortunate tendencies
of the administration: "it seems to our people that we have been
giving up the freedmen ... to be lashed, maimed and murdered.
History records nothing more cruel than our course towards these
people." Horrified by the black codes being enacted by the reconstructed Southern governments, Wilson pleaded with the secretary of
state: "in God's name stop all this legislation!" According to Wilson,
if the administration did not act to "secure liberty, not in name only
but in substance, to the freedmen now outraged by their rebel
masters," Congress would.[22]

On December 4, 1865, Congress assembled for the first time since
the end of the war. In the months since Appomattox Andrew
Johnson had restored every Confederate state to the Union. Congress, however, proved unwilling to accept the results of the president's policy, and Wilson joined his Republican colleagues in refusing to permit the Southerners to take their seats in the nation's
legislature. For over a year congressmen debated the proper methods
and modes of reconstruction, and during that time they admitted
only one Southern state, Tennessee, to the Union.

Refusing to join in the constitutional debates over reconstruction,
Wilson instead turned to what he regarded as the important business
of Congress. On the first day of the session he introduced a bill to
abolish the black codes of the Southern states. His examination of
Freedman's Bureau records, the statements of military officers, and
letters from the South provided Wilson with a mountain of evidence
to support his contention that the codes were an outright denial of
civil liberties and immunities for the Negro. His bill was referred to

[22] Boston *Transcript,* Nov. 15, 1865; Boston *Commonwealth,* Nov. 18,
1865; Wilson to O. O. Howard, Nov. 20, 1865, Howard MSS; Wilson to William Henry Seward, Nov. 13, 20, 1865, Seward MSS. Wilson also got information that "no northern settler would be safe in the interior of Georgia,
Alabama, or Texas." Edward Atkinson to Wilson, Nov. 28, 1865, Edward
Atkinson MSS, Massachusetts Historical Society.

the Senate judiciary committee. Heartily he endorsed two bills which Lyman Trumbull reported from the committee later in the month. One enlarged and extended the operations of the Freedman's Bureau; the other, which incorporated Wilson's measure against the black codes, provided civil rights for the freedman.[23]

In defending his own bill and then Trumbull's two measures, Wilson surveyed the problems not only of protecting the freedmen but also of dealing with their former masters. His language and manner lacked any trace of vindictiveness. The war, said Wilson, had punished the Southerners enough. The rebel states were "broken, shivered, conquered, subjugated." Acknowledging that "no people since the morning of creation ever fought a braver battle than our rebel countrymen," he added that "no men have been so conquered and so punished."[24] He promised that if the South provided the Negro with "universal justice and universal liberty" he would favor "amnesty for all." He would let the rebel states fill congressional seats with their chosen leaders, "and although they might not vote with me, or love me, or love what I love, I would trust to the future, and to the healing influence of time." But he would not admit them until they had provided for the rights of all in the South, even for the "poor black boy away down in the depths of Carolina."

Wilson hoped that Congress would pass the Freedman's Bureau and civil rights bills and provide the freedman with freedom to work where and for whom he pleased, to sue in court, to own property, to educate himself and his children, and in general give him the right to walk the earth, "proud and erect in the conscious dignity of a free man." When Cowan of Pennsylvania complained that the proposed legislation discriminated against white men in favor of an inferior race, Wilson indignantly replied that he knew many Negroes "with hearts quite as good as the heart of that Senator . . . and I know some of them with brains quite as capacious and quite as well trained as his own." At any rate, said Wilson, equality of the races

[23] *Congressional Globe,* 39th Cong., 1st sess., 1865-1866, pp. 2, 39, 111, 702; Boston *Commonwealth,* Jan. 27, 1866.

[24] *Congressional Globe,* 39th Cong., 1st sess., 1865-1866, pp. 40, 112.

was not the issue: "I know that I should not be degraded by the elevation of any man or all of the men of the universe."[25]

The editors of the Boston *Transcript* praised Wilson's speeches "for the plain, straight-forward talk the hour imperatively demands" and assured their readers that they could be proud of their servant. "His oratory has greatly improved of late, and he is now one of the best debaters in the Senate." Realizing that oratory and debating skill meant nothing if Andrew Johnson refused to support congressional measures to protect the Negro, Wilson sought to maintain a conciliatory spirit toward the president. Learning that conservative Republicans and Democrats were trying to separate Johnson from the more radical wing of the party, he insisted the attempt would fail: "the president is bound to the men who elected him, by honor, by principle, and by interest." In a lengthy speech in December the senator sought to gloss over possible breaches between party and president. He was sure Johnson had "labored according to his sense of public duty" in inaugurating his reconstruction program, and he assured his colleagues that "if we enact the needed legislation to secure the equal liberties of all men and bring back the rebel states . . . it will receive the sanction and approval of the executive." Newspaper editorials praised the speech as "a Christmas gift to the friends of the administration . . . redolent of hard common sense." During January the Massachusetts senator, still hopeful of influencing Johnson's somewhat ambiguous policies, was a frequent visitor in the White House. At a dinner party late in the month he buttonholed Gideon Welles to anxiously inquire if "we were to have a break in the party."[26]

[25] Above quotes selected from Wilson's speeches of Dec. 13, 1865 (*ibid.*, 40-41), Dec. 21, 1865 (*ibid.*, 111-12), and Jan. 22, 1866 (*ibid.*, 340-46). John H. Reagan, former postmaster general of the Confederacy, claimed that Wilson promised his support for Reagan's efforts to get the South to give the Negro equal civil rights and to set up voting requirements which would permit certain Negroes to vote; in return, Wilson would oppose punishment for white rebels. See John H. Reagan, *Memoirs* (New York, 1906), 226-27, 286-96.

[26] Boston *Transcript,* Dec. 26, 1865, Jan. 23, 24, 1866; Boston *Commonwealth,* Jan. 13, 27, 1866; *Congressional Globe,* 39th Cong., 1st sess., 1865-1866, pp. 111-12; Beale, ed., *Welles Diary,* II, 405, 421-22, (Dec. 28, 1865, and Jan. 31, 1866).

On February 6, the House approved the Freedman's Bureau bill, which the Senate had already passed, and sent it on to the White House. On the nineteenth of the month, the president returned the measure with a ringing veto message indicting the Bureau for extending military jurisdiction through a section of the country no longer at war. He also demanded that Congress admit representatives from the states that he had restored to the Union. Wilson, along with his Republican colleagues, was greatly angered at Johnson's action. He criticized the president for denying Congress a role in reconstruction and accused him of demanding the immediate and unconditional admission of the rebellious states, "rebel end foremost." Still, however, Wilson hoped to postpone or avoid a final breach between Congress and the executive. Then, on March 27, Johnson vetoed the civil rights bill, and in disgust Wilson bitterly attacked the president, claiming that his veto "has made more thoughtful men and women in this country bow their heads in anxiety and sorrow . . . than did the rebel chiefs during their four years of fire and blood."[27]

Johnson's insistence that Congress accept the results of his reconstruction program prompted Republican legislators to finish plans of their own for restoring the South. Wilson and his fellow radicals hoped to establish universal manhood suffrage as one of the requirements of any congressional plan, but they knew such a policy would be very unpopular in the North. In the fall of 1866 congressional elections would be held, and Wilson, eager for new recruits for radical Republican ranks in Congress, was certain that the issue of Negro suffrage would defeat the party's nominees.[28]

On March 5 the Massachusetts senator offered his own reconstruction program in the form of a constitutional amendment which he hoped would unite the various elements of the Republican party and at the same time begin to secure for the Negro basic political rights. His program provided first for the nullification of the black codes and the elimination of discrimination in the civil rights of the citizens of any state. Then, Wilson would give the ballot to any

[27] *Congressional Globe,* 39th Cong., 1st sess., 1866, appendix, pp. 140-42, and 2452-53.

[28] Stearns, *George Luther Stearns,* 367-68.

Negro who had served in the war, or who paid taxes on real or personal property. He would also permit any black man to vote who could read the Constitution of the United States or meet any other qualification which the state itself required, provided that qualification "was not inconsistent" with the rest of the amendment.[29]

Wilson's colleague, Charles Sumner, refused to support the amendment, or any other proposal which smacked of compromising away the Negro's voting rights. Wilson was unable to interest the Senate in his proposition, and in February both he and Sumner turned to argue over another amendment presented to Congress by the Joint Committee on Reconstruction. According to the new proposal, if any state denied the vote to any of its citizens on account of race, creed, or color, those groups disfranchised would be excluded from the basis of congressional representation. Thus the Southern states could choose between Negro suffrage and reduced voting power in Congress. Sumner repudiated the amendment, which he felt was "immoral and indecent." Sumner insisted that the Thirteenth Amendment gave Congress the power to enfranchise blacks, whereas the proposed amendment would return control over suffrage to the states.

On March 7 the senior Massachusetts senator delivered a particularly vehement attack on the amendment. The following day, Wilson rose to answer his colleague. First, he avowed his own support of Negro suffrage, saying that it would be "one of the greatest crimes ever perpetrated in history" if the nation, after experiencing such a terrible civil war, would exclude "an entire race of four and a half million people" from any participation in elections. Then Wilson noted the great difficulties in the way of giving the Negro the vote. Feeling was strong throughout the nation against centralizing any more power in the federal government and robbing the states of their control over voting. Wilson denied Sumner's contention that Congress had power under the enacting clause of the Thirteenth Amendment to give the Negro the ballot. If Congress did, he might

[29] Wilson's joint resolution No. 37 can be found in the reference room of the Library of Congress, in a bound volume containing other resolutions and bills introduced into the 39th Congress, 1st session.

vote in favor of using that power, but not without great reservations. "Force suffrage by positive law upon Virginia or the Carolinas," Wilson warned, "and the Negro would go to the ballot box at the peril of his life."

The North as well as the South would resist congressional legislation enfranchising blacks. "Prejudice, party spirit, conservatism, and all that is base and mean on earth" would combine to forbid it. Consequently, said Wilson, "in the present condition of the nation we must aim at practical results, not to establish political theories." The proposed form of the Fourteenth Amendment solved the problems raised by Negro suffrage, by leaving the question of suffrage up to the states. Wilson was convinced that "after four or five years of discussion by liberal and just men" in the South, they would agree to let the black man vote without molestation. He admitted that the amendment did not go as far toward attaining complete Negro suffrage as he wished, but he saw no other choice, "at any rate for the present." Even then he feared the amendment would not get the necessary Senate support; if it lost, he would view the result with "sincere and profound regret."[30]

The issue between Sumner and Wilson found reflection in the involved Republican politics of their home state. In the Massachusetts legislature radical friends of Sumner tried to force through a resolution approving in general of his whole course in opposition to Johnson. Subsequently, conservative Republicans and some Democrats, hopeful of embarrassing Sumner, supported a resolution praising Wilson "for his wise and statesmanlike course in striving to mitigate the asperities of conflicting theories, and thereby secure the substantial and practical results which the mass of loyal people have most at heart." The House overwhelmingly approved the former resolves; the Senate also adopted them. Meanwhile the debate over the two senators' positions raged in newspapers and letters from their constituents. The conservative Boston *Transcript* found Wilson's efforts statesmanlike and approved his "eminently practical

[30] For Wilson's and Sumner's comments see *Congressional Globe*, 39th Cong., 1st sess., 1866, pp. 1254-58, 1281-82. See also New York *Times*, March 9, 1866.

views" on Negro suffrage. The paper's editors were sure the vast majority of Bay State Republicans would support him. Some correspondents criticized Sumner for his dogmatism; one was sure that "Mr. Wilson is right and you are wrong in the position you have taken." The New England Loyal Publication Society praised the junior senator for his refusal "to bring on misfortune by personal predilections of his own." On the other hand, old abolitionists, led by Frank Bird, who wrote editorials in the *Commonwealth,* lauded Sumner and attacked his colleague. Elizur Wright accused Wilson of "political McClellanism," and William P. Robinson found his position "an unnecessary confession of weakness."[31]

Despite such criticism, Wilson refused to abandon his doctrines of expediency. Sumner won a victory when the proposed constitutional amendment failed to get the necessary approval of two-thirds of the Senate, but the two senators continued to disagree over the advisability of forcing Negro voting when to do so would endanger some other legislative victory. When a bill came into the Senate to admit Colorado as a state, Sumner sought to amend it to force Coloradans to give Negroes there the vote. Wilson was anxious to get the two Colorado senators into Congress, for they had assured him they would oppose Johnson. Consequently he refused to endorse Sumner's proposal, which he thought endangered passage of the bill. He promised he would not permit any other states to come in unless they guaranteed the vote to Negroes, but nonetheless, in July he again voted against Sumner in admitting Nebraska and Tennessee without provision for Negro suffrage.[32]

[31] William S. Robinson to Charles Sumner, March 7, 1866, E. Gould to Sumner, March 10, 1866, Horatio Woodman to Sumner, March 10, 1866, Parker Pillsbury to Sumner, March 12, 1866 (which has clippings enclosed from Roxbury, Mass., *Journal*), H. L. Pierce to Sumner, March 14, 1866, H. Whitney to Sumner, March 14, 1866, C. P. Huntington to Sumner, March 20, 1866, Charles G. Davis to Sumner, March 30, 1866, all in Sumner MSS; Boston *Daily Advertiser,* March 9, 15, 1866; Boston *Transcript,* March 9, 1866; Boston *Commonwealth,* March 16, April 7, 1866; New England Loyal Publication Society, Publication No. 307, Boston Public Library.

[32] *Congressional Globe,* 39th Cong., 1st sess., 1866, pp. 1365, 1386, 1982, 2033-34, 2179-80, 4000, 4007, 4222.

Frank Bird noted that a few days before Wilson voted to admit Colorado without Negro suffrage, he had urged a group of Negroes in Washington to seek the ballot. He concluded that "Wilson should either refrain from loud speeches on antislavery platforms or else vote a little more steadily for freedom in the Senate chamber." Wendell Phillips condemned the senator's "cowardly Republicanism." Ignoring such comments, Wilson continued to search for constitutional compromises on suffrage. In March he enthusiastically applauded Stewart of Nevada when he proposed a plan that in essence was similar to Wilson's own proposal of universal suffrage and universal amnesty. When Stewart's plan failed to gain congressional approval, the Massachusetts senator promised support to Robert Dale Owen's plan to establish universal suffrage after July 4, 1876. Before that time, according to Owen, any state that discriminated against its inhabitants' voting rights should lose representation. This plan, too, was lost in the joint committee.[33]

In May the committee on reconstruction finally worked out a new proposal for a constitutional amendment and reported it to both houses. It contained a section safeguarding civil rights of all citizens from discrimination by states and promised a reduction in representation for any state that denied the ballot to any of its citizens on the basis of race or color. The proposed amendment also barred from voting until 1870 anyone "who voluntarily adhered to the late insurrection." Wilson announced that since he could not secure impartial suffrage and universal amnesty, he would vote for the amendment. He did ask for, and get, one change in the committee's proposal; the Senate struck out the disfranchising clause. Wilson opposed replacing it with anything, but agreed that if any provision punishing former Confederates had to be included, it should be one barring from federal or state office anyone who had previously taken an oath to the United States Constitution and then

[33] Boston *Commonwealth,* April 28, May 5, 29, 1866; Wendell Phillips to Charles Sumner, March 24, 1866, Sumner MSS; *Congressional Globe,* 39th Cong., 1st sess., 1866, p. 1438; Robert Dale Owen, "Political Results from the Varioloid," *Atlantic Monthly,* XXXV (June, 1875), 665.

had violated it by supporting the rebellion. Such a section was included in the final version of the amendment, which the Senate passed late in July.[34]

When Congress adjourned on July 28 talk was already in the air concerning the fall congressional elections. Administration forces were busily preparing a national convention to gather support for Johnson's stand against the congressional program of reconstruction. Wilson was sure that in the conflict between Johnson and Congress, Johnson would be defeated. Not one in one hundred Republicans, he said, stood with the president. When some of his colleagues complained that Johnson was using his control of executive patronage to develop support for his program, the senator insisted that such heavy-handed action would only excite "scorn, contempt, and indignation" against him. "The American people," said Wilson, "will not be bought or sold by government patronage."[35]

Wilson plunged into the fall campaign with a good deal of vigor. By October 27, when he delivered his last address in the canvass, he had traveled over 3,000 miles and spoken in cities as far west as Chicago. His message was much the same wherever he appeared. In Boston, Natick, and Philadelphia he told crowds that Johnson had proved to be a great disappointment. He had failed to protect the freedmen, and he had turned the Southern states over to their former rebel leaders. Wilson attacked the National Union convention that met in Philadelphia on August 14 to gather support for Johnson, calling it "a conglomeration of pardoned and unpardoned rebels, copperheads, and the flunkies of the Whig party."[36]

The senator asked his audiences to support the congressional program of reconstruction, embodied in the proposed constitutional amendment, contending that it would bring universal suffrage "if it comes at all." He refused to commit himself to the position that the

[34] Wilson, *Executive Patronage,* 8; *Congressional Globe,* 39th Cong., 1st sess., 1866, pp. 1257, 2770.

[35] Wilson, *Executive Patronage,* 3-8; *Congressional Globe,* 39th Cong., 1st sess., 1866, p. 2449.

[36] Nason and Russell, *Wilson,* 360-63; Natick *Times,* Aug. 11, 1866; Boston *Transcript,* Aug. 7, 1866.

South would be entitled to readmittance upon ratification of the amendment. Not until his last speech before the Massachusetts election did he begin to clarify his thoughts on exacting further conditions from the South. By then, anti-Johnson Republicans had already carried six Northern states, and Texas had refused to ratify the amendment. Wilson insisted that the South would have to accept the amendment or stay out of Congress; but then he stated that he was "not so sure that they will all come in in a hurry if they do it."[37]

A few weeks later the final results of the congressional election were clear. The American people had chosen to support Congress against the president and his reconstruction program; anti-administration Republicans would have a clear two-thirds majority of the next Congress. The way was clear for Wilson and his radical colleagues.

[37] Boston *Commonwealth,* Aug. 11, 1866; New York *Herald,* Sept. 4, 5, 6, 1866; New York *Times,* Sept. 6, 27, Oct. 16, 30, 1866; Boston *Transcript,* Sept. 12, 1866; Philip Foner, ed., *The Life and Writings of Frederick Douglass* (4 vols.; New York, 1950-1955), IV, 196-97; Nason and Russell, *Wilson,* 364-67.

11

Reunion Politics

When Congress convened in December, many Republicans, emboldened by election victories and noticing that three Southern states had already refused to ratify the Fourteenth Amendment, were demanding further concessions from the former Confederate states. Henry Wilson was one of many Republicans who thought the time had come to insist upon universal suffrage in the South. In justification of his position, he pointed to the severe race riots that had struck the South during the previous summer and fall. "If the eyes of the Christian and civilized world could look in upon us," he insisted, "they would see more insults, more floggings, more outrages, more maimings, more murders upon innocent and defenseless men, women and children than has marked any Christian nation of the world during the last thirty years." In order to protect the freedmen and halt such atrocities he opposed any final adjustment of reconstruction that did not "demand suffrage now."

Wilson interpreted the election results to mean that Northern voters also supported universal suffrage in the South. A senator from Delaware reminded Wilson that he had ignored the suffrage issue while campaigning in his state and denied that the election could provide any mandate for enfranchising the blacks. Wilson admitted that while speaking in states "where not much progress has been made," he had acted on "the spiritual principle of giving milk to babes." He insisted, however, that before the end of Johnson's term Negroes throughout the nation would be enfranchised.[1]

The Massachusetts senator now apologized for having voted earlier to admit both Nebraska and Colorado without Negro suffrage.[2] He also changed his position on suffrage in the District of

Columbia. He admitted that a year earlier he had advocated enfranchising only Negroes who had served in the Union army, held property, or could read and write, since then "it was all we could get." But now, he insisted, "we can demand universal suffrage," and he attacked proposals to limit suffrage through literacy requirements. The country had suffered not from ignorant voters, he claimed, but from "voters of poor character." The Negroes in the District had been "the equals of the average of the white race of the District in the observance of the laws of the nation and the laws of God" and he saw no reason to restrict their exercise of political power. If literacy requirements were permitted in the South, he maintained, only about 10 percent of the freedmen would be able to vote, particularly if Southerners administered the tests. He warned his colleagues that if they approved a literacy test in the District, opponents of the blacks "will burn their schools." With an unrestricted use of the ballot, however, the freedmen could insure that their schools would be built and maintained.[3]

In the debates over the District suffrage bill, Wilson for the first time publicly admitted that he saw political advantage in agitating for Negro suffrage. Enfranchising the freedmen would not only protect them from white terrorism and abuse; it would also protect the hegemony of the Republican party. The blacks would vote for the party of Abraham Lincoln, the party that had saved the Union, abolished slavery, promised all men equal rights, and given them the ballot. He suggested, however, that once the Negro was enfranchised, the Southern whites would seek his vote, and if the Democrats treated the Negro better than the Republicans, "then the Negro will vote Democrat and I hope he does."[4]

[1] *Congressional Globe,* 39th Cong., 2nd sess., 1866-1867, pp. 42, 43, 64, 1189; 40th Cong., 1st sess., 1867, p. 184.

[2] *Ibid.,* 39th Cong., 2nd sess., 1866-1867, pp. 190-91; Charles Sumner to Frank Bird, Dec. 22, 1866, Sumner MSS.

[3] *Congressional Globe,* 39th Cong., 2nd sess., 1866-1867, pp. 43, 64, 103-104. See also his remarks on the District suffrage bill in *ibid.,* 39th Cong., 1st sess., 1866, pp. 1255, 2770, 3433.

[4] *Ibid.,* 39th Cong., 2nd sess., 1866-1867, pp. 103-5.

The Massachusetts senator was perhaps guilty of a naive optimism, but he spoke with conviction when he said that he hoped to establish "just, humane, and equal laws, that shall recognize the rights of all classes and conditions of men." When such rights were legally established and put into execution, "the great work will be done," and Negroes, as they "grow in education and intelligence, as their rights are permanently secured," would divide like other men between two major parties.[5] He was yet to be convinced that the removal of slavery had not prepared at least some Southern whites to deal responsibly and fairly with the former slaves. For some months he had been in contact with white moderates in the South, and he hoped to encourage them to take part in the reconstruction of governments in their own states. He also believed that if these Southerners were treated with consideration, they might join the Republican party.

Such hopes help explain Wilson's course of action in the congressional debates over reconstruction, and also indicate why he had been unwilling to press for harsh treatment of former rebels at the end of the war. Always impressionable, Wilson had been strongly affected by his discussions with important Southerners like John H. Reagan of Texas and William H. Trescot of South Carolina. These men helped to convince him that there were many whites in the South ready to cooperate with Congress in reconstructing the nation on the basis of civil and political equality, provided that the Republicans did not deal harshly with them. Not wanting to repel such moderate support in the South, Wilson opposed disfranchising former Confederates, which he contended "would create more feeling and more bitterness than enfranchisement [of Negroes]."[6]

Wilson also was cool toward any suggestion of prolonging military

[5] *Ibid.,* 39th Cong., 2nd sess., 1866-1867, p. 105.

[6] On Wilson's contacts with Southern moderates see John H. Reagan, *Memoirs,* 226-27; Ambler, *Pierpont,* 286; *Congressional Globe,* 39th Cong., 2nd sess., 1866, p. 43; 40th Cong., 1st sess., 1867, pp. 145, 184; "Letter of William Henry Trescot on Reconstruction in South Carolina, 1867," in *American Historical Review,* XV (1909-1910), 574-82; Wilson letters in Hunter Dickinson Farish, "An Overlooked Personality in Southern Life," *North Carolina Historical Review,* XII (1935), 341-53.

occupation in the South. Instead, he favored a rapid restoration of the former Confederate states so that their new electorate might vote Republican in the 1868 election. In the interim before the states were restored, Wilson did hope that Congress would remove unrepentant Southern officials guilty of intimidating the freedmen and replace them with white men loyal to the country and to the principles of the Republican party. Wilson was convinced that such men could be found and refused to insist that they be forced to take an oath of past loyalty to the Constitution before they took local offices. He contended that without the cooperation of such white Southerners, congressional reconstruction would fail. Lengthy military occupation of the South would only alienate such potential Republican allies.[7]

After passing the District suffrage bill, Congress turned to examine plans for a complete reconstruction of every Southern state. On February 14 the Senate took up a House proposal that would put the states under military rule until they were properly reconstructed. Debate ran on through the night and into the morning, and still the Senate failed to reach an agreement on what the bill should contain. Finally, the Republicans called a caucus. Charles Sumner insisted that Congress require the new state constitutions in the South to provide for Negro suffrage. Wilson warmly supported his colleague. After a vigorous discussion, the Republican senators voted 17-15 to accept the suffrage requirement. Wilson gleefully expressed his "supreme satisfaction" at the result, saying that "then and there, in that small room, in that caucus, was decided the greatest pending question on the North American continent." Sumner later recalled that his colleague was so enraptured he "wished to dance with somebody." His wish for suffrage for the Southern Negro was now almost an accomplished fact.[8]

The resulting measure, as it was returned to the House, provided for military governments in the South which would be terminated as

[7] *Congressional Globe,* 39th Cong., 1st sess., 1866, pp. 3583-84, 4046; 39th Cong., 2nd sess., 1866-1867, p. 1511.

[8] Pierce, *Sumner,* IV, 313-14, 320.

soon as the occupied state had ratified the Fourteenth Amendment and given the vote to blacks. According to the Senate bill, the state could disfranchise participants in the rebellion, but it was not required. The House refused to accept the Senate version, for Thaddeus Stevens and his friends did not believe Congress should attempt a plan of reconstruction during that particular session, and they were determined to force some disfranchisement of white Southerners. Consequently, a conference committee met and drew up a compromise that forbade anyone affected by the disfranchising clause of the Fourteenth Amendment to vote during the first elections in the Southern states. Both houses voted to accept the proposal. The first reconstruction act was then passed, vetoed by Johnson, and passed over his veto.

Wilson failed in an attempt to amend the act to force states to insure that "all citizens shall equally possess the right to pursue all lawful avocations and business, to receive the equal benefits of the public schools, and to have equal protection of all the rights of citizens of the United States." He was heartily pleased with the suffrage provisions, however, and called the law "a great and grand measure, the greatest by far of the session, if not of any session we have ever had." The disfranchising clause did disturb him. He reminded the Senate that he had always favored universal amnesty and universal suffrage and admitted he had voted for the penalizing provision "with the deepest regret." As soon as the rebel states were reconstructed he promised to seek removal of the disabilities from "nearly all, if not all" persons affected by the constitutional amendment.[9]

On March 7, fearing that the white Southerners might prefer to remain under military rule rather than initiate the construction of new governments based on black suffrage, Wilson introduced a measure that Congress passed as the second reconstruction act. His bill ordered the commanding general of each military district to begin the implementation of the first reconstruction act by registering

[9] *Congressional Globe,* 39th Cong., 2nd sess., 1866-1867, pp. 1365, 1564-65, 1626-27.

voters and calling for elections to a constitutional convention. With Negro suffrage in the South assured, Wilson was eager for the readmittance of the ex-Confederate states. "The enfranchisement of seven hundred thousand freedmen . . . changes the face of affairs, makes those states friends of the country, of liberty, and of Republican policy." In addition, Wilson insisted there were "tens of thousands" of Southern whites who had been "compromised by the rebellion" but who had never supported it and were willing to cooperate with the Republican majority in Congress. By combining Negroes with loyal whites, he was sure that Mississippi, South Carolina, Louisiana, and Alabama could be carried "not only for the Union, but for candidates for Congress who will come here and vote as we vote, speak as we speak, and think as we think." And, Wilson added, "they will give their electoral votes for whoever we nominate for President in 1868. These rebel states are ours if we will accept them. Do Senators desire to repel them? Does any Senator desire to keep these states out till after the next election?"[10]

Not all of Wilson's colleagues shared his eagerness for speedy restoration. James W. Nye of Nevada, angrily declaring that "the course of legislation in this body seems to be to accommodate itself in all respects to the necessities of rebels," accused Wilson of being willing to hasten the return of ex-Confederates "if they come sandwiched between two black men." In reply, Wilson insisted that the Republican party could hardly go before the people in 1868 in face of the fact that nearly four years after the end of the war, Congress had been unable to complete restoration, "even when we have made our terms and conditions, and the men of those states were anxious to accept them."[11]

After Wilson's bill became law, he declared that the two reconstruction acts would "do wonders for peace, justice, liberty and humanity" and that the rebel states would comply with the terms

[10] Henry Wilson, *History of the Reconstruction Measures* . . . (Chicago, 1868), 386; *Congressional Globe,* 40th Cong., 1st sess., 1867, pp. 102, 113-14, 144.

[11] *Congressional Globe,* 40th Cong., 1st sess., 1867, pp. 102, 114-16, 144, 184.

and soon be represented in Congress. He urged the North to strive, "by generous words and deeds," to convince the conquered South that "we embrace in our affection the whole country and people, and that we would forgive, forget and unite." When Senator Nye asked Wilson if he had not changed his mind about the need to punish the South, the Massachusetts senator insisted that he had never harbored hatred toward any portion of his countrymen and asked that Congress bury "deeper than plummet ever sounded" all bitter memories of the late war. Now that reconstruction would achieve justice and equality, he and his constituents would "build the church, erect the school-house, send the teacher, send capital, send skill, do everything, to build up the war-worn and waste places in the rebel states."[12]

In keeping with his conciliatory statements, Wilson supported legislation to construct levees on Southern rivers, stating that the section had suffered enough from the war. He also voted for a bill to appropriate one million dollars to allow the Freedman's Bureau to give food to whites as well as blacks in the South who were in danger of starving. Some Republicans expressed concern at the expense involved, but Wilson insisted that the "humanity, elevation, development, and improvement of the people of the country are greater than saving the dollars of the people." Two years later, noting that the South suffered from lack of currency and capital, he introduced legislation seeking to increase the circulation of national bank notes in the war-blasted section.[13]

After Congress had adjourned, Wilson anxiously looked South to see if strong Republican organizations would develop there. When John Murray Forbes talked to Wilson about aiding the development of a Republican party in Virginia, the senator immediately took interest. Early in April he went to Virginia, visited some battlefields,

[12] Wilson to Mrs. Angelina Grimke Weld, April 12, 1867, Theodore Dwight Weld and Mrs. Angelina Grimke Weld MSS, Library of Congress; *Congressional Globe,* 39th Cong., 1st sess., 1866, p. 4081; 40th Cong., 1st sess., 1867, pp. 103, 114, 116, 144-46.

[13] *Congressional Globe,* 39th Cong., 1st sess., 1866, p. 4081; 40th Cong., 1st sess., 1867, pp. 41-45, 434; 41st Cong., 1st sess., 1869, pp. 8, 131, 267.

and gave several speeches to groups of Negroes and white Unionists. After three days, he returned to a special session of Congress, much pleased with his reception in the former Confederate state. He had encountered no disturbances, city officials had been attentive, and his speeches, the first he had ever delivered in the South, had been well received. North Carolinians had invited him to speak in their state, so he decided to return to the South, taking with him a reporter to record his speeches. Wilson financed the trip himself; it was an expensive journey of a month's duration that took him through Virginia, the Carolinas, Georgia, Alabama, Mississippi, and Louisiana.[14]

According to the Washington correspondent of the Richmond *Enquirer,* Wilson made his Southern tour in order to "put himself forward as the grand amalgamation candidate for the Presidency." Although the Massachusetts senator had several reasons for going, certainly a desire to ingratiate himself with potential Southern Republican leaders by speaking and advising on party organization was among his chief intentions. However, as he told the editors of the New York *Independent,* he had a message to take to the South. He wanted to convince the Southerners that they had sinned; when they realized the immensity of that sin, he believed they would repent. By discussing the reconstruction acts, by promising an early end to disfranchisement and a full restoration of political rights, he hoped to prompt their repentance and gain the support of responsible Southern whites in finishing the task of restoring the Union. He was most anxious to keep the Republican party in the South a party for both races rather than for the Negro alone.[15]

The junketing senator brought his message first to the state of Virginia. Here the Republican party was divided into two factions.

[14] William A. Croffut to John Andrew, Feb. 28, 1867, E. L. Van Lair to Andrew, April 1, 1867, Andrew MSS; Charles W. Slack to Charles Sumner, July 8, 1867, Sumner MSS; *Congressional Globe,* 40th Cong., 1st sess., 1867, p. 144; New York *Times,* April 7, 1867; Richmond *Times,* April 4, 5, 6, 1867; Boston *Daily Advertiser,* April 7, 1867.

[15] Richmond *Enquirer,* May 1, 1867; New York *Independent* quoted in Boston *Commonwealth,* June 15, 1867.

One group, supported mainly by blacks, demanded confiscation, free schools, and equitable taxation. A more conservative faction, fearing such ideas would lead to racial conflict and destroy the party, opposed them. Wilson spent three days in the state, speaking frequently to large gatherings and consulting earnestly with party leaders. He encouraged the Negroes not to be contentious but rather to exercise their new-found freedom with a "Christian spirit"; in particular, he cautioned them not to demand confiscation. Rather, he told the freedmen to save their money, work hard, avoid liquor, and buy the eighty-acre lots that Congress had provided for them. Promising whites an early end to the political disabilities imposed by the Fourteenth Amendment, he asked them to be tolerant of the Negroes and to join them in carrying out the reconstruction acts, educating the electorate, and beginning the social and economic reorganization of their state. He directed this appeal mainly to "the old Whigs, the Clay men" in Virginia by reminding them of their past antipathy to the Democratic party and warning them against cooperating with the men who had led the South to secession and defeat. They would be much wiser to join the "Union Republican party" which could promise them the kind of economic program needed to develop the industry of the state.[16]

Wilson's immediate efforts to compromise differences in the Virginia Republican party were not successful. Most of his speeches were given to audiences composed largely of Negroes, for few whites came to listen to his message of reconciliation.[17] Nonetheless, he plunged on into the lower South, bringing the same message he had brought to Virginia. He continued to slant his appeals toward the old opponents of the fire-eating Democrats—the "Henry Clay Whigs and Douglas Democrats." He hoped they would recognize their sin of

[16] Wetumpka, Ala., *The Elmore Standard*, May 22, 1867; Charleston *Mercury*, April 22, 1867; Richmond *Enquirer*, April 23, 25, 1867; New York *Tribune*, April 25, 1867; Alrutheus Ambush Taylor, *The Negro in the Reconstruction of Virginia* (Washington, D.C., 1926), 212; Hamilton James Eckenrode, *The Political History of Virginia during the Reconstruction* (Baltimore, Md., 1904), 68-70; New York *Times*, April 22, 26, 1867.

[17] New York *Times*, April 24, 1867.

having supported the Confederacy and seek redemption through assisting the Republican party, whose economic programs could resuscitate the war-torn South. He promised the white Southerner that if he were willing to abide by the new order, his property would not be confiscated, his political rights would be restored, his state would be admitted into the Union, and Northern capital would flood into his section.

Wilson's concern for the political support of moderate whites in the South was reflected in his advice to the freed Negroes. He encouraged them to support the Republican party that had recognized their manhood and given them freedom and the vote and told them to be proud of their human dignity and to bow down to no one. Yet he also warned his black audiences that party development in the South along racial lines would be detrimental to both white and black. He asked Negroes to be fair and courteous to their former masters and to cooperate with rather than punish Southern whites. "See to it that while you are pulling yourself up," he advised, "you don't pull others down." Nor could blacks expect social equality. Prejudices in both the North and South made it impossible "to legislate you into any man's parlor." Laws could safeguard civil equality, "but your own brain, heart, conscience, and life must fix your social position."[18]

The reception in the South to Wilson's speeches was somewhat varied. Usually his audiences, being largely composed of Negroes, were enthusiastically responsive. The freedmen took a great liking to the senator; an aging woman insisted in her enthusiasm that "he is Massa Linkum's son, sure." One black man, after hearing Wilson speak, assured him that "he need nebber lift his hand to do another day's work while I hab a dollar!" However, in Goldsboro, North Carolina, many whites listened with silent hostility to Wilson's speech. The senator visited but did not speak in Mobile, Alabama,

[18] Richmond *Enquirer,* May 23, 1867; Raleigh *Tri-Weekly Standard,* April 30, May 2, 4, 1867; Charleston *Mercury,* May 3, 1867; Charleston *Daily News,* May 3, 4, 6, 1867; Augusta, Ga., *Daily Press,* May 9, 1867; New Orleans *Republican,* May 16, 17, 1867; New York *Independent,* May 9, 1867; New York *Tribune,* May 1, 18, 20, 1867; New York *Times,* May 11, 1867.

where a few evenings before a white mob had threatened the life of William D. Kelley, a junketing congressman from Pennsylvania. In New Orleans someone fired a rifle into the room in which the senator spoke; the ball struck the ceiling near him. Many Southern newspapers denounced his speeches, but some, like the Raleigh *Tri-Weekly Standard*, the Charleston *Daily News*, and the New Orleans *Crescent*, defended him against attack and praised the conciliatory tone of his statements.[19]

Northern assessment of Wilson's trip was contradictory and at times impassioned. William L. Garrison noted that Wilson "was lecturing in the South successfully." Conservative newspapers that generally favored Wilson's views thought he was doing much to moderate Negro demands and ease the way to conciliation between black and white. Horace Greeley's New York *Tribune* thought Wilson a "prudent counselor" who, as a fair representative of the Republican party, was well equipped to interpret the ideals of that organization to the South.[20]

On the other hand, many Republican leaders were exceedingly critical of Wilson's speeches and ideas. Few shared the views of Gideon Welles, Johnson's chief cabinet supporter, who thought that the senator was "stirring up the blacks, irritating and insulting the whites" by making "insolent and offensive speeches." Ardent radical Republicans, like Thaddeus Stevens, were instead angry because Wilson was appearing too conciliatory and making promises concerning reconstruction that he was not entitled to make. The Pennsylvania Republican leader demanded to know "who is authorized to travel the country and peddle out amnesty? . . . to say there would be no confiscation?" One of Benjamin Wade's closest friends anxiously advised Wade: "if you have any regard for our party for the Lord's sake get Wilson of Massachusetts home," for he was raising

[19] Boston *Commonwealth*, May 11, 18, 1867; Richmond *Enquirer*, May 17, 1867; Nason, "Biographical Sketch," 266; New Orleans *Crescent* quoted in Richmond *Enquirer*, May 23, 1867; Charleston *Daily News*, May 6, 1867; Raleigh *Tri-Weekly Standard*, April 30, 1867; New York *Tribune*, May 14, 15, 1867.

[20] William Lloyd Garrison to Frank J. Garrison, April 23, 1867, Boston Public Library; New York *Tribune*, April 12, 1867.

hopes and making pledges the Republican party would not wish to redeem. Wade agreed, telling fellow radical Zachariah Chandler that "you and I know that Wilson is a —— fool." Wendell Phillips of Massachusetts was unrelenting in his criticism of Wilson. His newspaper, the *Antislavery Standard,* declared that compromising and trimming politicians like the Massachusetts senator would lose ten Negro votes in the South for every Whig vote gained for the Republican party. The Boston *Commonwealth* added its voice to the chorus of disapproval.[21]

Wilson felt the force of Thaddeus Stevens's complaint that he had no right to promise the South freedom from confiscation, and after Stevens's tirade hit the newspapers Wilson suggested in his speeches that if white Southerners refused to accept the reconstruction acts and continued to threaten the Negro's rights, they could expect confiscation and a continuation of military rule. The general tone of his remarks, however, remained conciliatory, and he was pleased with the response. In New Orleans, former Confederate General James Longstreet, who had listened to Wilson speak, was "agreeably surprised to meet such fairness and frankness" from a politician whom he had been taught to believe "harsh in his feelings toward the people of the South."[22]

The senator returned North at the end of May, in the best of health after delivering thirty-two speeches in the four weeks of his tour. The desolation still in evidence in the war-torn section had much affected him, and he was eager to convince his Republican associates to send men and money south to help unite that section with the "political, religious, educational and business interests of the nation." In December, when the second session of the Fortieth Congress convened, he told his colleagues that the Northern people

[21] Beale, ed., *Welles Diary,* III, 86-87, 89; Richmond *Enquirer,* April 30, 1867; New York *Tribune,* April 30, 1867; J. A. Brisbin to Benjamin F. Wade, April 30, 1867, with notation by Wade to Chandler, in Zachariah Chandler MSS; Boston *Commonwealth,* May 4, 25, 1867.

[22] Nason and Russell, *Wilson,* 384; Donald Bridgman Sanger and Thomas Robson Hay, *James Longstreet* (Baton Rouge, La., 1952), 332-33; Boston *Commonwealth,* June 15, 1867; Richmond *Enquirer,* May 8, 10, 1867; Raleigh *Tri-Weekly Standard,* May 9, 1867.

had no idea of "the terrible sacrifices made and losses incurred by the people of the rebel states during the rebellion." Stating that "the more I look into the condition of that section of the country I see trial and trouble and sorrow," Wilson asked his associates to do their duty by helping "those who are down, whether they are black men or white men." The former farmer's apprentice and cobbler was utterly serious when he declared: "I am always for the underdog in a fight."[23]

The senator assured prospective investors that the reconstruction acts guaranteed life and property in the South, and he appeared confident that his appeals to ex-Whigs would encourage "friends of union, equal liberty, education, diversified industries, and development of natural resources" to join the Republican party there. Encouraged by the reappearance of free speech in the former Confederacy, the senator was sure that if party organization commenced immediately, in the next four months at least eight of the Southern states would elect men sympathetic to the Republican party's principles of freedom and equality. He continued to communicate with moderate leaders in the occupied states and welcomed comment and criticism from Southern whites who he thought could aid in the process of restoring the South to regular political life in the nation. In both private letter and public pronouncement he urged the Southerners to conquer their prejudices against freedmen, accept congressional reconstruction, and join the Republican party.[24]

Since Virginia was close at hand for the senator, he worked hard to create a Republican party there to serve as a model for the rest of the South. In the middle of June former Governor John Andrew organized a joint effort of the Union Leagues of Boston, New York,

[23] *Congressional Globe,* 40th Cong., 2nd sess., 1867, pp. 205, 245-47.

[24] New York *Tribune,* May 23, 1867; Natick *Times,* May 25, 1867; William H. Crook, *Through Five Administrations* (New York, 1910), 115; Boston *Commonwealth,* June 15, July 6, 1867; New York *Times,* May 9, July 17, 1867; *Congressional Globe,* 40th Cong., 1st sess., 1867, pp. 145, 654; "Letter of William Henry Trescot on Reconstruction in South Carolina, 1867," in *American Historical Review,* XV (1909-1910), 574-82; New York *Herald,* July 2, 1867.

and Philadelphia to compromise the Republican quarrel in Virginia, a dispute "that threatened to disturb the harmony and unity of the party, not only in Virginia but throughout the South." The three clubs sent a deputation to Richmond, and Henry Wilson agreed to head the delegation from Massachusetts. As William P. Robinson noticed, the Bay State group contained mostly moderate men; however, Frank Bird, a leading Massachusetts radical, accompanied Wilson in order to "temper the somewhat too forgiving nature of the Senator." During several days in June Wilson played a leading role in reconciling the two estranged factions of the Virginia party and got them to agree on a joint call for a party convention to be held in August. He also sought government printing contracts for the Richmond *Whig,* a newspaper which supported his efforts to get a party in Virginia organized on a moderate, biracial basis.[25]

In November, Virginia elections for a constitutional convention gave a resounding victory to the radical wing of the Republican party. An anguished exponent of moderation told Wilson that without the aid of white Republicans, the constitution would be framed to appeal only to Negroes and consequently it would be defeated. In December Wilson visited the constitutional convention to warn the delegates against disfranchising former Confederates. At the same time he advised Negroes in the North Carolina constitutional convention to ignore demands for confiscation and disfranchisement. He promised whites in the state that he would vote as soon as possible to relieve them of their disabilities under the Fourteenth Amendment.[26]

Although Wilson was quite pleased with the machinery of recon-

[25] Pearson, *Andrew,* II, 319; Wilson to J. M. Edmunds, May 4, 1867, Boston Public Library; Eckenrode, *Reconstruction in Virginia,* 73; Hughes, ed., *Forbes Letters* (supp. ed.), III, 92-93, 96-97; Boston *Commonwealth,* June 15, 22, July 20, 1867; Richmond *Enquirer,* June 13, 14, 15, 1867; John H. Gilmer to Andrew Johnson, Nov. 2, 1867, RG 98, First Military District, War Department, National Archives; Wilson to Adjutant General's Office, April 23, 1867, Letters Received, Adjutant General's Office, War Department, National Archives.

[26] C. H. Lewis to Wilson, Nov. 19, 1867, Wilson MSS, Library of Congress; New York *Herald,* Dec. 12, 1867; New York *Times,* Nov. 16, Dec. 19, 1867; Boston *Commonwealth,* Dec. 28, 1867.

struction he had helped to create, he had one more goal to propose during the July session of Congress. Since the great victory in the congressional elections of 1866, he had been predicting that before the end of Johnson's administration Negroes would be enfranchised throughout the nation. To secure that result, he introduced a constitutional amendment to prohibit any state from discriminating among citizens "as to their civil or political rights" on account of race, color, or previous condition of servitude. In September he urged a convention of border-state advocates of equal rights to declare for universal suffrage. He promised the convention that his own state, Massachusetts, would support the amendment.[27]

Full of optimism, the senator left the convention for Boston in order to preside over the state Republican convention. Despite his long service in behalf of the party, it was the first time he had been accorded the honor. In his speech to the gathering he demanded "irreversible guarantees" to firmly establish the equality of all citizens of the Republic. The convention, however, refused to approve universal suffrage for the states either by act of Congress or by constitutional amendment.[28]

In the fall elections Wilson received more disappointments. Pennsylvania went Democratic, and Ohio, though going Republican by less than 3,000 votes, soundly defeated a constitutional amendment granting the vote to Negroes in that state. As Wilson told a rally in New York, the result in Ohio proved that "32,000 graves of dead blacks have not conquered the wicked prejudice of even all the members of the Republican party." Wilson's hopes and aspirations had always varied directly with election returns, and now the results of the 1867 state campaigns had crushed the optimism produced by the 1866 elections. The Republican party had revealed that it was "made up of men with the personal faults, weaknesses, and selfish

[27] *Congressional Globe,* 40th Cong., 1st sess., 1867, pp. 292, 675. Thaddeus Stevens had been worried that Wilson and other "conservatives" would not support "the doctrine of National jurisdiction over all the states in matters of the franchise." See Richard N. Current, *Old Thad Stevens* (Madison, Wis., 1942), 288. On the border state convention and Wilson's speech, see New York *Times,* Sept. 13, 1867.

[28] Boston *Commonwealth,* Aug. 10, Sept. 14, 21, 1867.

ambitions of humanity," but it had still written a great record for the country in its legislation in behalf of the poor, hated, and oppressed. If the party could win the coming presidential election in 1868, it could complete that record by enfranchising Negroes every- where; but for the moment, in recognition of the judgment of Northern voters, Wilson dropped talk of a suffrage amendment.[29]

[29] New York *Times,* Oct. 17, 1867; Natick *Times,* Oct. 19, 1867.

12

Reconciliation and Civil Rights

The elections of 1867 convinced Henry Wilson that Congress had forged ahead of the people. Most white Americans, "filled with unreasoning prejudice against a wronged and hated race," were unwilling to throw any final constitutional safeguards around the Negro's right to vote. Despite the fact that "after four years of uninterrupted progress" the Republicans had been checked in their "onward march," Wilson insisted they must not "retract, qualify, or retreat a single inch." Instead, he and his colleagues had to appeal to "heart, reason, and conscience" to convince the people of the United States "to do unto others as they would that others do unto them."[1]

The dedication of Americans to the Golden Rule would be tested in the 1868 campaign. According to Wilson, the Democrats had always been dominated by the "dark, inhuman, and unchristian spirit of slavery." Since long before the war, the whole course of the party had been directed against the best interests of the nation. Now it was building up its strength to bid once again for the highest office in the land. If the Democrats succeeded, the Republicans and the nation would be denied "the fruits of victories in the terrific struggles of the past seven years." As he told a convention of veterans in January, the election would decide whether men who carried the country safely through the war would be permitted to rule it. He urged his audience to "vote as you fought." The Republican party had to be given the chance to finish what it had begun, to protect the Negro in his legal and political rights, vindicate the authority of the nation, and restore the disloyal states to loyalty and representation. "The nation," Wilson averred, "is at the very crisis of its fate."[2]

The party could win in 1868 only if lagging members could be brought to unite behind a popular candidate in whom the nation was willing to put its trust. Wilson, along with most of his party colleagues, knew there was such a man—General Ulysses S. Grant. The Civil War had raised him above all other Union leaders as a national hero; only he could save the Republican party. After Grant became head of the Union armies in 1864, the senator and the general had become personally acquainted. They conferred frequently on matters relating to military organization and reconstruction. Quickly Wilson sensed Grant's political appeal, and as early as March 2, 1866, he suggested that the people of the country might well turn to the general to head the government as he had headed their armies. By the early summer of 1867 he was busily initiating a Grant movement in Massachusetts. During the fall campaign Wilson frequently mentioned the war hero as a logical presidential candidate, and through the following winter he wrote newspaper articles and sent letters pleading Grant's case. Consequently he established himself as a leading Grant booster not only in Massachusetts but throughout the Northeast.[3]

Wilson's support of Grant brought criticism from old antislavery men who feared that the general lacked moral commitment. They wanted a candidate with less ambiguous views and looked therefore to Chief Justice Salmon P. Chase or Benjamin Wade. A political columnist in the *Hartford Press*, recalling Wilson's earlier championing of Fremont for president in 1856, believed that the senator's "itching desire to be planning movements for *success* . . . is apt to blind his judgment." Anxiously Wilson sought to assure his

[1] New York *Times,* Oct. 17, 27, 31, 1867; *Congressional Globe,* 40th Cong., 2nd sess., 1867-1868, p. 40.

[2] New York *Times,* Jan. 22, 1868; New York *Independent,* Feb. 6, 1868.

[3] *Congressional Globe,* 39th Cong., 1st sess., 1866, appendix, p. 142; E. J. Sherman to Benjamin F. Butler, Sept. 9, 1867, Butler MSS; New York *Herald,* July 2, 1867; Boston *Daily Advertiser* (supplement), Sept. 4, 1867; Boston *Commonwealth,* Nov. 16, 1867, Jan. 4, 1868; Natick *Times,* Jan. 11, 1868; Henry Wilson to [?], March 16, 1868, Wilson MSS, Library of Congress.

radical colleagues that Grant had opposed slavery and had worked
closely with Congress to secure equal rights for the Negro. Privately
he admitted to James Redpath that he would have favored Chase, or
any dozen members of Congress, "before Grant or any other man
not experienced in public affairs." However, in order to "finish the
great work in which we have been engaged," it was necessary to win
the election in November, and only Grant promised hope of success.
Wilson assured Redpath that he "went for him on that ground
solely."[4]

Wilson had another, more personal reason for originating a Grant
movement in the Northeast. He hoped to receive the second place on
the ticket. As early as June, 1867, political observers in Massachusetts were noting Wilson's ambition for the vice-presidency. With the
death of Governor Andrew, Wilson, who seemed to be well liked not
only in Massachusetts but throughout New England, was the Bay
State's prime candidate for the place on the national ticket. On
March 12, when the Republican state convention met, the delegates
unanimously designated Grant and Wilson to head the party ticket.[5]

In February, Senator Richard Yates of Illinois recommended
Wilson to a veteran's meeting in Washington, but otherwise Wilson
lacked influential support. Even New England was not a unit for him
since Maine was anxious to back the claims of Lincoln's first
vice-president, Hannibal Hamlin. Other favorite sons, including
Benjamin Wade of Ohio, Schuyler Colfax of Indiana, and Reuben
Fenton of New York, came from "close" states; Massachusetts was
"safe" for the Republicans and consequently Wilson's claims got less
attention than those of his opponents. Even with Grant, Republicans
feared a close and hard-fought contest, and they wanted a running
mate who would strengthen the ticket.[6]

[4] "Templeton" in *Hartford Press,* quoted in Boston *Commonwealth,* July
20, 1867; Wilson to Redpath, April 3, 1868, New York Historical Society,
New York, New York.

[5] E. J. Sherman to Benjamin F. Butler, June 15, Sept. 9, 1867, Butler MSS;
Boston *Commonwealth,* Nov. 30, Dec. 28, 1867; Willard P. Phillips to Charles
Sumner, Feb. 10, 1868, Sumner MSS; Natick *Times,* March 7, 14, 1868.

[6] Boston *Commonwealth,* Feb. 22, 1868; Schuyler Colfax to "My Dear
Sir," April 28, 1868, Colfax MSS.

The Massachusetts delegation arrived in the convention city of Chicago, Illinois, on May 18, two days before the delegates officially convened. Busily they combed crowded hotel corridors, seeking more votes for Wilson. The Bay State men found that Southern delegates were especially friendly to Wilson's candidacy; the senator's Southern tour was bearing fruit.[7]

May 21 dawned clear and bright; the convention members met in high spirits. General John A. Logan of Illinois nominated Grant for president, and the delegates quickly made his choice unanimous. Then a stage curtain was drawn back to reveal a huge painting of the White House, with the Goddess of Liberty beckoning Grant toward it. Amidst wild enthusiasm, while red, white, and blue colored doves fluttered above the audience, Wilson's managers desperately tried to organize the New England states behind his candidacy for vice-president. Maine and Vermont refused to assent, however, and without the united support of his own section, the senator's chances dimmed.

After the delegates had exhausted themselves cheering for Grant, they sat down to ballot for vice-president. Wilson was nominated by a Virginian, who offered the startling argument that with Wilson as vice-president there would be no reason to assassinate Grant. After the first ballot was taken, Wilson, with 119 votes, stood third behind Wade, who led with 147. On the second ballot Wade gained 23 votes while Wilson lost 5; on the third, Wade gained 8 while Wilson lost 13 more. On the fourth ballot, Colfax forged into the lead with 226 votes, while Wilson fell to 56. During the fifth roll call, Pennsylvania switched from Wade to Colfax and decided the issue; the Indianian became Grant's running mate. Wilson's supporters were disappointed but could find solace in the fact that "he got a good vote and we feel that the candidate nominated is an immensely popular and most excellent man."[8]

[7] Boston *Commonwealth,* May 30, 1868.

[8] On the voting see Willard Smith, *Schuyler Colfax: The Changing Fortunes of a Political Idol* (Indiana Historical Collections, vol. XXXIII, Indianapolis, 1952), 280-81; W. E. Webster to Charles Sumner, May 22, 1868, Francis Bird to Sumner, May 25, 1868, Sumner MSS.

During the spring of 1868, while Wilson's friends had sought the vice-presidential nomination for him, he had been busy with his Republican colleagues in the Senate endeavoring to bring congressional reconstruction to a successful conclusion. In particular, they hoped to mark their final triumph over President Johnson by impeaching him, and then readmit the Southern states in time to cast their votes for Grant in the presidential election. In such a manner, while securing the continued ascendancy of the Republican party, Wilson and his colleagues could gain revenge upon Johnson for his determined resistance to their policies.

The road to impeachment had been a long and difficult one for congressional radicals. Never before had a United States president been impeached, and Republicans were not at all sure of the political advisability of setting such a precedent. Beginning in December, 1866, radicals in the House had on several occasions tried to vote for articles of impeachment; each attempt had failed. Wilson was keenly aware that the state of public opinion was uncertain on impeachment. As late as July 1, 1867, he declared that the country would not support such a move. Then Andrew Johnson, instead of maintaining a safe passivity, embarked on a series of actions that turned opinion against him and convinced Wilson that impeachment would be possible. On August 5 the president asked for resignation of his secretary of war, Edwin M. Stanton. Stanton for some time had been in league with congressional radicals, and they had passed a tenure-of-office act in March to prevent Johnson from removing him without the approval of the Senate. The secretary, who had earlier assured an anxious Wilson that "he would die . . . rather than leave his post," refused to tender his resignation. Consequently, President Johnson suspended him and appointed General Grant secretary *ad interim.*

Wilson immediately sent a letter to the *Nation* praising Stanton and stating that Grant had taken the office hoping to serve the country rather than Johnson. Early in September he spoke to the Massachusetts Republican convention. Noting that Johnson had removed Southern district commanders Philip H. Sheridan and

Daniel Sickles as well as Secretary Stanton, the Senator demanded that "the obstacle in the White House" be removed. William Pitt Fessenden was startled at Wilson's statements, contending his colleague had not acted "with his usual discretion." When Congress convened in December, Wilson drew up a report from his committee vindicating the suspended Stanton. He exhorted the secretary, who had barricaded himself in his office, to stand firm. On February 24, 1868, the House of Representatives voted to begin impeachment proceedings against the president.[9]

On May 16 the Senate began voting on the articles of impeachment, and at the end of the day it was clear that Johnson would survive. His opponents failed by one vote to consummate their purpose. Wilson submitted a written opinion defending his vote for impeachment. He began by noting that whenever matters of interpreting the Constitution and laws puzzled him, he had sought to find an answer which would promote the security of his country and the rights of its citizens. Consequently, he had decided that "in this great trial" he would give the benefit of the doubt to his country "rather than to its Chief Magistrate." Thus did Wilson, as the New York *Evening Post* commented, violate a fundamental principle of a free people—that an accused man be given the benefit of the doubt and be considered innocent until positively proven guilty. In pronouncing Johnson's guilt, Wilson confined himself to generalities rather than to specific articles. He emphasized the "seductive, grasping, aggressive nature of executive power" and claimed that Johnson, acting from "unworthy, if not criminal" motives had used that power to oppose the will of the people, refuse to execute congressional laws, and hamper the progress of a reconstruction program founded on justice and equality. He feared that acquittal would sanction the "monstrous powers" assumed by the president

[9] New York *Herald*, July 2, 1867; New York *Times*, Sept. 5, 1867; Henry Wilson to editor, Aug. 24, 1867, in *The Nation*, V (Sept. 12, 1867), 215-16; Boston *Commonwealth*, Sept. 14, 1867; Francis Fessenden, *Life and Public Services of William Pitt Fessenden* (2 vols.; Boston, 1907), II, 146; Henry Wilson to Edwin M. Stanton, Feb. 21, 1868, Edwin M. Stanton MSS, Library of Congress. For a discussion of the radicals and impeachment, see McKitrick, *Johnson*, 486-509, and Trefousse, *Radical Republicans*, 371-404.

and would "increase the lawlessness, disorder, and outrage now so prevalent in the states lately in rebellion."[10]

If Wilson indeed believed that "lawlessness, disorder, and outrage" prevailed in the South, such belief did not prevent him from hastening the readmission of those states in order to vote for the Republican candidate in the fall. By May, 1868, seven of them had written new constitutions and had held elections to ratify the documents and elect state and congressional officeholders under them. Congress now prepared to pass on the admittance of these states to representation. The first state to be examined, Arkansas, entered Senate debate in late May; the House had already voted to admit her. Wilson sat quietly for three days as the Senate debated the legal proprieties surrounding the formation of the state's constitution. Then, on May 30, he demanded that the Senate "cast aside this cheap legal learning that has so often burdened the debates in Congress" and proceed to the "practical consideration of the real questions involved in this and kindred measures for the restoration of the States recently in rebellion." Noting that the seven states "had elected thirty-three Representatives, twenty-eight of them Republican, and two Republican Senators," and that they were ready to elect twelve more Republicans to the upper house, he saw no reason for delay. Furthermore, said Wilson, if the seven states were restored at once they would "give more than one hundred thousand majority for General Grant." The majority of the Senate agreed with Wilson and proceeded to readmit the seven Southern states as soon as they had ratified the Fourteenth Amendment.[11]

On July 22 Congress adjourned, enabling Wilson to devote the next three months to the presidential campaign. He toured eight states and made dozens of speeches and did not return home for a rest until the eve of the election. Wilson's campaign technique consisted largely of waving the bloody shirt to discredit the Democratic party and then contrasting the obstructive and negative

[10] *Congressional Globe,* 40th Cong., 2nd sess., supplement, 1868, pp. 460-61; New York *Evening Post* quoted in Horace White, *Life of Lyman Trumbull* (New York, 1913), 314-15.

[11] *Congressional Globe,* 40th Cong., 2nd sess., 1868, pp. 2690-91.

policy of that party with the great accomplishments of the Republicans. In a speech he delivered shortly before Congress adjourned, Wilson warned that Southern and Northern Democrats, "separated for four years by the bayonets of the boys in blue," would in the election "rush together, trampling alike over the graves of three hundred and fifty thousand dead heroes and of the principles for which they fell." He told a huge mass meeting in New York that no fallen Union soldier "was sent to his account by a Republican bullet. Let the mothers, wives, and sisters of the North remember this. . . . There are over four hundred thousand heroes beneath the sod. Who sent them there? Democrats! Democrats! Democrats!" The same men now stood ready to overthrow a reconstruction program that had emancipated "a poor, friendless and hated race" and had provided members of that race with citizenship, civil rights, and the ballot.[12]

A year earlier, Wilson had predicted that Grant, if nominated, would carry thirty states and obtain a popular majority of 500,000.[13] His estimate was just four states and 200,000 too high. Although Grant's victory was not as overwhelming as the electoral count indicated, Republicans across the country could heave a sigh of relief. The Democratic threat had been met and defeated. The new occupant of the White House would be for all intents and purposes at one with Congress, and the long conflict between legislative and executive branches would at last be ended. Exhausted, Wilson retired to Natick and the comfort of his wife's attentions.

Immediately after the elections, Harriet Wilson received a letter from a friend of the family, who, although a Democrat, had high praise for Wilson's "sound judgment, great experience, and rugged honesty." He was sure that after the senator's exertions in the campaign, he would "be entitled to any portfolio he may desire among Grant's advisers." In the past friends had mentioned Wilson for the War Department, but he himself had never openly indicated a desire for the post. His friend William Schouler thought Wilson

[12] *Ibid.*, 40th Cong., 2nd sess., 1868, p. 4280; New York *Times,* July 2, Aug. 28, Sept. 18, 1868.

[13] New York *Times,* Oct. 17, 1867.

would not make a good executive officer: "he is not a man of exact knowledge and would grow weary . . . of an office in which the excitement of politics forms no element."[14]

The senator was indeed anxious for the position, and after the election he wrote Grant to ask for it. The general replied that "there is no person who would be more agreeable to me personally than yourself"; but he refused to commit himself. Throughout December and the first months of 1869, rumors continued to associate Wilson with the new cabinet. However, on March 1, shortly before Grant named his secretary of war, the Massachusetts senator, at the behest of his wife, told Grant to remove his name from consideration for the post. As Wilson told his good friend Claflin, Harriet's health had taken a turn for the worse, "and I feel it to be my duty to comply with her wishes." The concerned yet disappointed husband had to conclude to "be content and bow to the will of our Heavenly Father."[15]

In December, 1868, Wilson returned to Washington to resume his efforts to obtain a fifteenth amendment to the Constitution to guarantee Negroes the right to vote. When Democrats noted that the Republican platform of 1868 left suffrage questions for states to determine, Wilson replied that it was far better "that political organizations and public men . . . be right with the lights of today than consistent with the errors of yesterday." Heatedly he denied Democratic charges that Republicans hoped to perpetuate their political power through Negro votes. Instead, claimed Wilson, Republicans had lost more votes than they had gained by giving the Negro the ballot. His party had had to battle white passions, prejudices, misrepresentation, and misunderstanding in order to "make the humblest citizen the equal of every other citizen."[16]

[14]F. M. Granger to Mrs. Wilson, Nov. 5, 1868, Wilson MSS, Library of Congress; William Schouler to Henry L. Dawes, Nov. 15, 1868, Dawes MSS.

[15]Grant to Wilson, Nov. 24, 1868, Wilson MSS, Library of Congress; Boston *Commonwealth,* March 6, 1869; Boston *Journal,* Feb. 24, 1869; Wilson to Henry Claflin, March 1, 1869, Claflin MSS.

[16]Boston *Commonwealth,* Feb. 6, 20, 1869; *Congressional Globe,* 40th Cong., 3rd sess., 1869, p. 672, appendix, p. 154. See Lawanda and John Cox, "Negro Suffrage and Republican Politics: The Problem of Motivation in

The results of the 1868 election encouraged Wilson in his determination to gain constitutional guarantees for universal suffrage. Not only had Grant won the election; citizens in Iowa and Minnesota had by large majorities agreed to enfranchise Negroes in their own states. The senator also realized that the ratification of such an amendment by the three Southern states still under military reconstruction "could unquestionably be secured." Consequently, Wilson was prepared to demand a stronger amendment now than most of his colleagues. In February, 1869, with the example before him of white Georgians who had just expelled black representatives from the state legislature, he presented a proposal which would not only give the Negro the vote but also guarantee his right to hold office. He would also forbid states from discriminating among voters or officeholders on the grounds of nativity, property, education, or creed, as well as on the grounds of race or color. He noted that in Rhode Island naturalized citizens had to hold property to vote, in New Hampshire Catholics could not hold office, and in Massachusetts a literacy test could be required of voters.[17]

Observers both inside and outside the Senate found it hard to understand why Wilson, with his reputation "of being a practical man, seeking practical results rather than establishing theories," was so insistent upon obtaining Senate approval of such a broad amendment. For almost a week the Massachusetts senator stood firm. Even after the Senate had defeated his resolution by five votes, he and a few allies were able to keep any other recommendation from gaining the two-thirds vote that was necessary for passage.[18] The House after some debate did accept Wilson's proposal, but the Senate refused, and a conference committee then reported an amendment which simply barred states from discriminating among voters on the

Reconstruction Historiography," *Journal of Southern History,* XXXIII (1967), 303-31.

[17] Boston *Commonwealth,* Jan. 9, 1869; *Congressional Globe,* 40th Cong., 3rd sess., 1869, appendix, pp. 154, 781, 954.

[18] New York *Times,* Feb. 19, 1869; *Congressional Globe,* 40th Cong., 3rd sess., 1869, pp. 1306-7. See also William H. Gillette, *The Right to Vote: Politics and the Passage of the Fifteenth Amendment* (Baltimore, Md., 1965), 61.

basis of race or color. Reluctantly Wilson agreed to vote for the compromise, but he did so with "some degree of mortification." He refused to take responsibility for "this half-way proposition. I simply take it at this late hour as the best I can get." On February 25, 1869, Congress approved the amendment and sent it to the states for ratification.[19]

Despite his reservations about the Fifteenth Amendment, Wilson hoped it would complete the reconstruction of the nation. He assured his colleagues that when the states ratified the new amendment, "the great work, so far as legislation is concerned, will be accomplished." He hoped that with the equal rights of all citizens assured, "the negro question" would no longer occupy the politicians of the country. Instead, citizens both North and South could now cooperate in seeking social and economic progress for all sections and races.[20]

To hasten the process of sectional reconciliation, Wilson continued his efforts to remove the political disabilities of the Fourteenth Amendment from most white Southerners. He had always favored universal suffrage and universal amnesty; since he had obtained the former, he was prepared to offer the latter. He told his colleagues he did not object to letting the "natural leaders" of the South return to politics now; "on the contrary," he continued, "I am growing a little stronger in the opinion that it would be well for us to have some of them come back here." He did admit, however, that although he would not demand that a Southerner vote Republican to have his disabilities removed, "support for the ever-loyal Republican party . . . would afford to Congress and the world ample evidence of . . . genuine repentance for the errors of the past."[21]

Unfortunately for Wilson's optimistic hopes for the future, many white Southerners were not exhibiting any such repentance for

[19] *Congressional Globe,* 40th Cong., 3rd sess., 1869, pp. 1626-27.

[20] *Ibid.,* pp. 672, 1627.

[21] On Wilson's efforts to remove political disabilities, see *ibid.,* 40th Cong., 2nd sess., 1867-1868, pp. 98, 765, 2240, 2435, 2789, 3179-80; 40th Cong., 3rd sess., 1869, p. 258; 41st Cong., 1st sess., 1869, pp. 535, 545; 41st Cong., 2nd sess., 1870, p. 5369. See also 41st Cong., 2nd sess., 1870, pp. 335, 5369.

"errors of the past." News from Georgia began to reach the Massachusetts senator concerning the activities of the Ku Klux Klan, a white terroristic organization that was intimidating and murdering Negroes. On May 14, 1869, the aroused Wilson wrote to President Grant asking him to stop "these political murders."[22] Yet the senator now seemed uncertain that federal coercion alone would bring order to the South. After over a quarter-century in politics, he was convinced that policy-makers could not go far ahead of public sentiment. Southern whites, he believed, had to be persuaded by moral appeals to recognize the justice of protecting the equal rights of Negroes. Buoyed up by the fervor of a religious conversion he had experienced in the fall of 1866, Wilson was confident that the Christian churches of the country could do a great deal to educate Americans to accept their fellow men as equals.[23]

Wilson also believed that the old abolitionists could assist in the process of moral regeneration in the South. The day after he wrote Grant, Wilson attended the annual convention of the American Anti-Slavery Society. Since the society's newspaper and leaders had constantly criticized Wilson's course in Congress, William Lloyd Garrison thought the senator's visit reflected "not magnanimity, but a lack of self-respect akin to pusillanimity." He came, however, not to beg forgiveness but to tell the abolitionists that despite passage of the Fifteenth Amendment, there was still a great need "to instruct the hearts of all citizens to recognize and do justice to all classes and conditions of men." The best people to handle the responsibility, he said, were the "antislavery veterans."[24]

In June, 1869, and again in January, 1871, Wilson published a series of articles in which he continued to emphasize the role of Christianity in uniting the nation on a solid basis. The spirit of caste and prejudice that still remained despite the eradication of human slavery could only be vanquished by "moral forces and weapons."

[22] Rhodes, *History,* VI, 287-88.

[23] Nason and Russell, *Wilson,* 371; New York *Times,* May 15, 1868.

[24] New York *Antislavery Standard,* May 29, 1869; William Lloyd Garrison to Samuel May, May 15, 1869, Boston Public Library.

Perhaps recalling Alexander H. Stephens's remark that slavery was the cornerstone of the Confederacy, Wilson asserted that Christianity was the "cornerstone of our free institutions." Diffusion of its moral principles "civilizes mankind, exalts public morals, and gives efficiency to just precepts of law."

Wilson also implored Northern millionaires·to send their capital into the impoverished South, to "set in motion the wheels of industry and exorcise the demons of ignorance and secession." He urged them to pool their resources and purchase blocks of land in the South for resale in small lots, at small charges, to the landless freedmen.

In addition to the civilizing influences of capital and Christianity, Wilson believed that public education for both whites and Negroes in the South would be necessary to overcome passion and prejudice. The masses of Negroes enfranchised by the Fifteenth Amendment, along with millions of whites, lacked mental and moral training and could constitute a danger to democracy. Although Wilson hoped that churches, individuals, and philanthropic organizations would bring schools to the South, he believed the federal government had a key responsibility to assist in educating the freedmen, either through the Freedmen's Bureau or another agency.[25]

Despite Wilson's continued optimism about the progress of the nation toward justice and equality, political developments in the South were not promising. In 1869 the Republicans lost control of Tennessee and Virginia, and the continued activity of the Ku Klux Klan threatened the party's influence in other Southern states. In May, 1869, Congress passed a Force Act providing heavy penalties for anyone preventing Negroes from voting. Although Wilson voted for the bill, he did not take part in debates concerning it. He was acutely aware of the fact that Northerners were growing tired of continued debate in Congress over reconstruction measures. In light of Klan violence, he admitted that Congress had undertaken recon-

[25] New York *Independent*, June 17, July 1, 29, Dec. 16, 1869; Henry Wilson, "The New Departure," *Atlantic Monthly*, XXVII (Jan., 1871), 104-20; Boston *Commonwealth*, Dec. 11, 1869; Boston *Journal*, April 17, 1869.

struction too early and should have held the Southern states under military occupation for several more years; the country, however, would not have countenanced such a delay in restoring the Union. "We have done the best we could," said Wilson; "in spite of the violence, the great work of reconstruction goes on, and law and order, peace and justice, are making progress."[26]

Wilson's optimism was not sustained by events in the South. The Klan rode on. In the fall elections of 1870, Republicans lost control of North Carolina and Georgia. On January 18, 1871, Wilson rose to address his colleagues concerning the developments in the South. He noted that despite the liberal and generous policy of Congress toward Southern whites, violence had not stopped since the end of the Civil War. This had not surprised him, he said, for "it will take one hundred years to extirpate the evils of slavery . . . its poison is in the very blood of some of our people." The recent outrages, however, had exceeded his expectations, and he called for legislation to "support the laws and encourage the order-loving men of the South." The following day, Wilson was appointed to a committee to investigate Klan activities in North Carolina. In March, disgusted by the lengthy investigation carried on by the committee, he called for Congress to "walk up to the extreme verge of its constitutional power" and pass immediate legislation protecting Southern Negroes.[27]

In February and April Congress passed two more laws to strengthen federal regulation of Southern affairs. The measure passed in April was aimed expressly at the Klan and gave the president power to suspend *habeas corpus* and use federal troops to suppress the organization. Although Wilson gave willing support to the bills, he warned that despite such legislation, nothing would give complete protection to the freedmen. "Slavery," he said, "has wrought in the South a terrible work of demoralization" by impair-

[26] Boston *Daily Advertiser*, April 7, 14, 15, 1870; *Congressional Globe*, 41st Cong., 2nd sess., 1870, pp. 2391, 2639.

[27] *Congressional Globe*, 41st Cong., 3rd sess., 1871, pp. 570, 574; 42nd Cong., 1st sess., 1871, pp. 192, 348.

ing the dignity of humanity and cheapening human life. He repeated his conviction that "education and moral culture, aided by good laws and their faithful enforcement, and the healing influences of time, are needed to restore order to that portion of our country and give protection to our countrymen."[28]

In keeping with his concern for education in the South, in February and March Wilson introduced bills to distribute the sales of public lands for three successive years to the Southern states to aid in the establishment of public schools. For the remainder of his term in the Senate, Wilson pursued the question of financing better education in the former Confederate states. In 1873 he sought to amend an act to provide that 50 per cent of the sales of public lands should be distributed among the Southern states to support common schools. He admitted that he would have preferred to expend all the funds gathered from public land sales for such a purpose, for the South was badly in need of such assistance. He informed his colleagues that "I am among those who believe that . . . we should address ourselves especially to building up that section of the country, to get over the evils produced by a system many of us opposed."[29]

Despite Wilson's doubts about the efficacy of legislation in regulating human behavior, he realized that laws and their effective enforcement were necessary to create a framework in which the forces of Christianity and education might foster respect for all races and classes of men. In the winter of 1871-1872, he strongly supported Charles Sumner's attempts to pass a civil rights bill to free Negroes from any social discriminations which had the sanction of law. In Massachusetts he had battled against Jim Crowism in the public schools and in public transportation. During the war he had supported efforts to remove such legal discriminations in the District

[28]*Ibid.*, 42nd Cong., 1st sess., 1871, appendix, pp. 254-57; 42nd Cong., 2nd sess., 1871, p. 248.

[29]*Ibid.*, 41st Cong., 3rd sess., 1871, p. 1460; 42nd Cong., 1st sess., 1871, p. 68; 42nd Cong., 2nd sess., 1872, pp. 452, 606; 42nd Cong., 3rd sess., 1873, pp. 563, 1710.

of Columbia, and in February, 1865, he had sought sweeping legislation that would forbid any discrimination anywhere in the country
among passengers on public rail or water transportation. Also he had
supported Sumner's attempts to amend the reconstruction acts to
provide for mixed schools in the South.[30]

In February, 1871, while arguing for the elimination of segre-
gated schools in Washington, Wilson clarified his position on equal
rights: "The only thing for us to do is to go right steadily forward
and insist . . . that in all matters of public nature there shall be a
perfect equality of rights and privileges." School segregation, he said,
was designed "to gratify the pride of the race that assumes to be the
dominant, the superior race." The resulting systematized discrimination degraded "the rights, the interest, the sensibilities of the colored
man." He admitted that school integration would be difficult to
carry out, but he saw in it "a mode and manner of educating
people . . . to the high plane of republican and Christian principle, so
that they will look down on no class of their fellow men because of
race or color." When Democratic senators claimed the Negro was
doomed to be excluded from "the society of the respectable,"
Wilson rose to declare bitterly that because society, "frivolity, and
fashion" put their ban on the black man, it was no reason to deny
him equal rights. It seemed that the old indignation of Jeremiah
Jones Colbath at class distinctions had burst through his calm
exterior. "The poorer he is," said the former farmer's apprentice,
"the greater our obligation; the more society averts his face from
him, the more God bids us to stand by, shield and protect him."[31]

In December, 1871, when Charles Sumner sought to amend a
proposed amnesty bill in order to end segregation in public schools,
transportation, juries, theaters, inns, cemeteries, and churches,

[30] *Ibid.*, 38th Cong., 2nd sess., 1865, p. 795; 39th Cong., 2nd sess., 1867,
p. 1365; Wilson, *Slave Power*, III, 510-11; Alfred H. Kelly, "The Congressional
Controversy over School Segregation, 1867-1875," *American Historical
Review*, LXIV (April, 1959), 539, 540, 542.

[31] *Congressional Globe*, 41st Cong., 3rd sess., 1871, p. 1061. See also
Boston *Commonwealth*, Feb. 20, 1869.

Wilson unhesitatingly supported his colleague's effort. Whatever divergencies of opinion existed in the country on the question of racial equality, one thing was clear to him: "there should be no distinction recognized by the law of the land." He hoped that "this talk about superiority of race, about these distinctions in this Christian and democratic land, should pass away forever." In May, 1872, while Sumner was absent from the Senate, his colleagues, after first removing provisions for integrating schools and juries, passed his civil rights measure. Wilson resisted the alterations but voted then to pass the resulting bill. When Sumner returned to the Senate, however, Wilson supported his unsuccessful efforts to recover the exscinded clauses. Even in its emasculated form, the civil rights bill did not pass both houses until 1875, after Sumner had died.[32]

Wilson also voted willingly for the amnesty bill passed by Congress in 1872; it freed most Southerners from the political disabilities imposed upon them by the Fourteenth Amendment. While supporting Sumner's civil rights proposal, Wilson was critical of his attempt to unite it with the amnesty bill, fearing the tactic would endanger passage of both measures. Sumner contemptuously accused his colleague of being more concerned with amnesty than with civil rights.[33] For Wilson, however, it was quite logical to support both proposals. He had never advocated denying whites the opportunities he wished to extend to Negroes, and he was still hopeful that limiting the punishment accorded to the former Confederates would make them more amenable to accepting the equalitarian policies of Congress.

During debates on the civil rights bill, Wilson announced that "this measure in its length and breadth covers the unsettled questions; if we pass it we will not have to legislate again."[34] Since Grant's election he had grown increasingly aware of Northern

[32] Kelly, "Congressional Controversy," 550; *Congressional Globe,* 41st Cong., 3rd sess., 1871, p. 1061; 42nd Cong., 2nd sess., 1872, pp. 819-20, 897, 3253, 3254.

[33] Charles Sumner to E. L. Pierce, Dec. 27, 1871, Sumner MSS.

[34] *Congressional Globe,* 42nd Cong., 2nd sess., 1872, p. 819.

disenchantment with reconstruction, and he had begun to seek new issues for the Republican party to champion. He had begun to draw up proposals for a "New Departure" for his party, which were designed to draw the attention of his fellow Republicans to issues that had been shunted aside by reconstruction legislation. In particular, he hoped the party would consider legislation to restrict the power of business, reform the civil service, enfranchise women, encourage temperance, and ease the lot of working men.

13

The New Departure

By 1870 many of the old Republican radicals who had led their party and the nation toward the abolition of slavery and equality for Negroes believed the life and meaning was ebbing out of their organization. With their reconstruction goals well-nigh accomplished, many agreed with Ben Butler, who contended that the Republican party possessed no "peculiarity of doctrine for its future aspirations .... Its record is of the past alone." George W. Julian found that many regarded the party "as a spent political force."[1] Henry Wilson was particularly concerned lest the differences between Republican and Democratic parties be obliterated, and he struggled to make his party relevant to the changing needs of the country.[2]

Although slavery had been destroyed, Wilson believed that other national problems just as imposing demanded some solution. In articles in the *Independent* and *Atlantic Monthly* in 1869 and 1871 he took aim at a new menace, which he defined as "the power of wealth, individual and associated, concentrated and diffused." This power of wealth, once wielded by the Southern planter, was now in the hands of railroad entrepreneurs, corporation managers, and bank presidents. At the very moment when self-government was meeting its most severe test presented by a huge uneducated electorate, these capitalists were bidding to control the nation, and those who before the war had prostrated themselves before the Slave Power were now succumbing to the "money power." Wilson was worried that Americans, in hot pursuit of wealth, were forgetting the interests of their fellow man. Technical and material advances were costing the workers their respectability, their personal independence, and their general equality. Corporation owners abused their competitors and customers and corrupted legislators. The Erie Railroad ring and the gold-cornering schemes of speculators all revealed "selfishness, recklessness, and an utter disregard for the claims of morality and common decency."[3]

Identifying the menace posed by the "money power" was much simpler than suggesting policies to control it. Wilson knew that agitation of economic questions could endanger party unity and alienate important Republican businessmen. Yet he could not ignore questions concerning tariffs, banking, currency, and the national debt. In the summer of 1867 archprotectionist Henry Carey of Philadelphia wrote a series of letters to Wilson in which he warned that New England's support of free trade and specie resumption was endangering the iron, coal, and steel producers of the country. If the Massachusetts representatives continued to support low tariffs, Pennsylvania, according to Carey, would have to reassess the political ties binding her to the Bay State. Wilson assured Carey of his concern for the "vast iron and coal interests of your great state." In 1872, with a presidential election in the offing, he voted for higher duties on iron; having done so, he told Carey he hoped that "the election in November may reveal that the Republican party . . . still retains the confidence of the people."[4]

Wilson faced even greater problems in resolving regional and class conflicts over federal currency policy. During the war the government had created two new currencies: legal tender notes, or green-

[1] Butler and Julian quoted in W. R. Brock, *An American Crisis: Congress and Reconstruction, 1865-1867* (New York, 1963), 281. See also Trefousse, *Radical Republicans*, 443-47.

[2] Boston *Commonwealth*, May 13, 1871; *Congressional Globe*, 41st Cong., 3rd sess., 1871, p. 574.

[3] Henry Wilson, "The New Departure," 107-12; New York *Independent*, June 10, 1869.

[4] Henry C. Carey, *Reconstruction: Industrial, Financial, and Political: Letters to Henry Wilson* (Philadelphia, 1867), *passim;* Wilson to Carey, June 7, Sept. 21, 1869, June 10, 1872, Carey to Wilson, June 14, Sept. 25, 1867, Carey MSS; *Congressional Globe*, 42nd Cong., 2nd sess., 1872, pp. 3905-6. See also Stanley Coben, "Northeastern Business and Radical Reconstruction: A Re-Examination," *Mississippi Valley Historical Review*, XLVI (June, 1959), 67-90.

backs, issued by the treasury, and bank notes issued by a new system of national banks. Although Wilson voted to support both programs, he was critical of the new banks. He recalled how over the past thirty years people had lost "hundreds of millions" through bank failures and fluctuations of bank note values. Contemptuously he spoke of the "brokers, jobbers, and money changers" who used their financial power against the best interests of the American people. In 1864 he advocated that the national bank system be abolished and the bank notes replaced by "a safe and uniform national currency" made up of government-issued greenbacks.[5]

At the end of the war, many Middle State industrialists and Western farmers, fearing deflation, agitated to keep the greenbacks in circulation. The government, however, in accordance with the wishes of bankers and capitalists in the Northeast who feared inflation, began retiring them. Wilson, bowing to the wishes of his constituents, supported this policy until early in 1868, when a presidential election was in the offing. The trough of a business depression had been reached the previous December, and in elections in Ohio Democrats had demonstrated the popular appeal of calling for an end to greenback contraction. Consequently, in January, despite the complaints of Boston entrepreneurs who did not want the currency question reopened, Wilson asked that the treasury stop retiring greenbacks. Congress eventually passed a bill to prohibit further currency reduction.[6]

Wilson remained opposed to the note-issuing power of banks.

[5] *Congressional Globe,* 37th Cong., 2nd sess., 1862, p. 788; 37th Cong., 3rd sess., 1863, p. 881; 38th Cong., 1st sess., 1864, p. 1870. For a thorough discussion of the currency issue in post-Civil War America, see Irwin Unger, *The Greenback Era: A Social and Political History of American Finance, 1865-1879* (Princeton, N. J., 1965).

[6] *Congressional Globe,* 39th Cong., 2nd sess., 1867, p. 835; 40th Cong., 2nd sess., 1868, pp. 523-25; Edward Atkinson to Charles Sumner, Feb. 19, April 21, 27, 1868, Sumner MSS. Robert P. Sharkey, in his *Money, Class, and Party: An Economic Study of Civil War and Reconstruction* (Baltimore, Md., 1959), 280 n, has noted the difficulty of classifying Wilson's views on currency. He clearly belongs in Sharkey's category of radicals whose votes on financial matters were determined by largely political considerations. His personal views, which were antibank and progreenback, would place him with Sharkey's "ultra-Radicals."

Recognizing the power of bankers and financiers, however, he never insisted on his views. Instead he sought other ways to control the "money power." He tried, and failed, to limit by statute the interest national banks charged on loans. He also attacked a bill to raise interest rates in the District of Columbia from 6 to 8 percent, charging that "the whole legislation of the country recently adopted of this character has been in favor of capital." In 1869 he advocated federal supervision of gold sales in order to stop gold speculation.[7] Wilson also turned a critical eye toward railroads. Eager to exert the power of government over the "giant corporations," he advocated a general incorporation law which would allow the national government to supervise the financial activities of the roads. He also opposed granting any further financial aid to Western railroad schemes.[8]

If Wilson thought that the Republican party ought to adopt a more critical attitude toward corporations and their powers, he also believed that the party should be more sympathetic to the needs of the laboring classes. His own background gave him sympathy for the individual who had to make up in muscle what he lacked in capital. As a state legislator he had shown some concern for the interests of workers, and he had attacked slavery as a degradation of all labor. Post-Civil War agitation in Massachusetts for an eight-hour work day stimulated Wilson's latent sensitivity to working class issues. Although the movement to shorten the work day transcended the state, it found its most ardent champions there.[9]

Wilson first faced the issue of the shorter work day in March, 1867, when, after admitting some hesitation about considering such matters while reconstruction was uncompleted, he supported a bill establishing an eight-hour day for government workers. After Congress had enacted the bill, he bitterly protested that executive officials were reducing the workers' pay. Angrily he informed Secre-

[7] New York *Independent,* Oct. 14, 1869; *Congressional Globe,* 41st Cong., 1st sess., 1869, p. 366; 41st Cong., 2nd sess., 1870, p. 1392.

[8] Boston *Journal,* Feb. 6, 9, 1869; *Congressional Globe,* 41st Cong., 3rd sess., 1871, pp. 990-91.

[9] Ware, *Public Opinion,* 184-87; Sharkey, *Money, Class, and Party,* 199-206.

tary of War John Rawlins, the chief violator, that Congress had no intention of approving his actions. The senator then led a committee of workmen to confer with President Grant about the matter. Grant issued an order forbidding reduction of pay, and government workers in the shipyards of Massachusetts deluged their senator with resolutions of thanks.[10]

Wilson's support of an eight-hour day was consistent with his earlier concern for reforms in the interest of the working classes, especially if they were not too radical. He had no real understanding, however, of the growing labor movement that was emerging in reaction to consolidations of corporations and trusts, and he sought to avoid drawing sharp distinctions between labor and capital. Wilson's views reflected his experience with a shoemaking industry that had been conducted on the basis of small, locally owned shop operations. Since he had left the business, however, it had been transformed by the emergence of large factory systems with masses of unskilled workers supervised by managerial classes and financed by large aggregations of capital. He did criticize large corporations which tended to obliterate personal relationships between worker and employer, but he still believed that there need be no friction when "the worker of today can become the capitalist of tomorrow." In response to continued labor unrest, however, he recommended the establishment of a government commission to commence a full investigation of the laboring interests of the country.[11]

[10] *Congressional Globe,* 40th Cong., 1st sess., 1867, p. 413; 40th Cong., 2nd sess., 1868, p. 2804, 3425; 41st Cong., 1st sess., 1869, pp. 468, 721-22; 41st Cong., 2nd sess., 1869-1870, p. 152; Boston *Journal,* Jan. 20, April 12, 13, 24, 26, 29, May 3, 20, July 9, 1869; New York *Times,* April 26, 1869.

[11] Boston *Daily Advertiser,* May 16, 1870; Boston *Journal,* Jan. 20, 29, 1869, Nov. 18, 1871; Henry Wilson, *Father Mathew, the Temperance Apostle* (New York, 1873); *Congressional Globe,* 42nd Cong., 2nd sess., 1872, pp. 2844, 4016-19.

W. R. Brock has contended that the radicals "did not think of themselves as agents of the masters of capital but of the small businessman, the active farmer, and of the enterprising working man." (Brock, *American Crisis,* 224). He cites Wilson, correctly, I believe, as an example of his generalization. Yet as David Montgomery, in his book *Beyond Equality: Labor and the Radical Republicans, 1862-1872* (New York, 1967) has observed, the radicals' equalitarian doctrines did not satisfy the demands of the labor movement for

Wilson's sensitivity to labor issues increased as 1871, the date for his reelection to the Senate, came closer. In December, 1869, he asked Congress to prohibit the importation of contract labor from abroad. He called such a practice "a scheme of soulless corporations" to acquire cheap labor through a "modern slave trade" and thereby degrade American workers. The bill sat forgotten in committee until June, 1870, when it was revived not by Wilson but by California senators anxious to stop the importation of Chinese coolies. Thus the measure acquired racial connotations. Simultaneously with the introduction of the bill, Wilson learned that shoe manufacturers in his own state had brought in Chinese workers to break a strike. Angrily he condemned "the conspiracy of capital" responsible for "bringing degraded labor here" to compete with native workers.[12]

Wilson's views of contract labor were consistent with his earlier attacks on slavery; he contended that both systems degraded the native white worker. Many of his constituents, however, interpreted his reference to "degraded labor" as a racial slur against the Chinese people, and believed that Wilson opposed any migration of Orientals to the United States. They accused him of courting favor among the white workers by appealing to their baser prejudices. When Wilson protested that his whole career, which had been devoted to "the equal rights of all men, of every clime and race," provided ample refutation of such charges, those who remembered his flirtation with the Know Nothings refused to listen. In July, Wilson made the situation worse by refusing to support Charles Sumner's efforts to amend a bill to eliminate fraud in elections. The proposed amendment removed the word "white" from the country's naturalization laws, and Republican senators from the West Coast feared that mass naturalization of Chinese immigrants would result. Wilson contended that Sumner's rider would defeat the bill, which he thought should

freedom from economic oppression. Certainly Wilson's interest in labor issues did not go beyond advocating the eight-hour day.

[12] *Congressional Globe,* 41st Cong., 2nd sess., 1869-1870, pp. 86, 1389, 4755, 5046; Boston *Daily Advertiser,* June 16, 17, 20, 22, 1870; Boston *Commonwealth,* July 2, 9, 1870.

pass without hindrance. His old friend William P. Robinson, who was then writing a column for the *Springfield Republican,* remained unconvinced by Wilson's explanation; he charged the senator with giving way "to his native disposition to manage and compromise" in order to pacify Republicans in the western states. Robinson concluded that by his recent actions Wilson had forsaken any right to be reelected.[13]

There were others in Massachusetts eager to take advantage of Wilson's predicament in order to seize his Senate seat. Friends of A. H. Bullock still hoped to elevate their man to the Senate, and partisans of Congressman Benjamin F. Butler sought to give him the coveted post. Republicans in western Massachusetts, angry at the way in which their eastern brethren had monopolized the highest offices, hoped to gain the senatorship for Congressman Henry L. Dawes of Pittsfield. Fortunately for Wilson, however, the several contenders for the post divided his opposition. Also, many in Massachusetts feared Butler's heretical inflationary theories, and the party leaders preferred the incumbent. During the interim between the fall elections and the convening of the Massachusetts legislature, much was said, and little done, about putting forth a rival for Wilson's seat. The leading men mentioned, Dawes, Butler, and Secretary of the Treasury George Boutwell, refused to have their names used.[14]

Consequently, despite a lack of enthusiasm for Wilson, the

[13] Boston *Daily Advertiser,* June 25, 1870; *Congressional Globe,* 41st Cong., 2nd sess., 1870, pp. 5122-24, 5161-62, 5627-29; *Springfield Republican* quoted in Boston *Commonwealth,* July 23, Aug. 6, 1870; E. L. Pierce to Charles Sumner, July 3, 1870, W. S. Robinson to Sumner, July 12, 1870, F. W. Bird to Sumner, July 7, 1870, Sumner MSS.

[14] Natick *Bulletin,* July 16, Oct. 29, 1870; Boston *Commonwealth,* Nov. 19, 1870; Boston *Journal,* Sept. 16, Oct. 17, 1870; Boston *Post,* Sept. 15, 1870; William Schouler to Henry L. Dawes, May 9, Oct. 24, 1870, A. Richardson to Dawes, June 28, 1870, Samuel Bowles to Dawes, June 29, 1870, F. B. Sanborn to Dawes, July 1, Aug. 6, 1870, Gardiner G. Hubbard to Dawes, July 24, Aug. 5, 14, 1870, Julius Rockwell to Dawes, Aug. 25, 1870, Dawes MSS; Edward Winslow to Sumner, July 8, 1870, J. Dupree to Sumner, July 10, 1870, Lewis B. Marsh to Sumner, July 6, 1870, Francis F. Emery to Sumner, July 9, 1870, John Murray Forbes to Sumner, July 9, 1870, Sumner MSS; Henry Wilson to Butler, Sept. 19, 1870, Butler MSS.

Republican caucus, meeting in January, 1871, agreed to nominate him again. The Republicans who attended were critical of his constant tendency to compromise. Yet they felt kindly toward the old antislavery warrior and recognized he had contributed to the welfare of the Negro and the nation. Frank Bird, who knew Wilson well, bemoaned the fact that "most men are satisfied to compromise what they must; Wilson goes about with a notice on his head signifying his willingness to meet everybody half-way, or two-thirds way, if needful." Nonetheless, Bird concluded, although "chances are that the next thing he does will be foolish, a large portion out of a hundred will be sensible, or at least well-intentioned." Then the legislature proceeded to reelect the senator, and he returned to Washington with the well-wishes of his friends. Had he completed his new term, Henry Wilson would have served his state as senator for more years than anyone except his colleague Sumner.[15]

Back in Washington, Wilson continued his efforts to define a new departure for the Republican party by presenting a bill to institute civil service reform. Since the end of the Civil War pressure had been building up for reforming the method by which government offices were distributed. Begun at first by a small group of dedicated Eastern reformers, the movement by 1869 had spread across the country and had the support of many newspapers and businessmen's organizations.[16] Civil service advocates, who wanted to replace executive patronage with an independent commission which would administer competitive examinations to candidates for office, were sure that President Grant would assist them in their program. Unfortunately, he soon disillusioned them with his tendency to favor friends and political hacks in appointments to office. By the fall of 1870 civil service advocates posed a real threat to the stability

[15] Boston *Journal,* Nov. 4, 8, 15, 1870, Jan. 14, 17, 18, 1871; Bird quoted in Boston *Commonwealth,* Jan. 28, 1871; F. W. Bird to Charles Sumner, Jan. 11, 1871, Sumner MSS; J. W. Egan to Wilson, Jan. 30, 1871, Neal Dow to Wilson, Jan. 18, 1871, Richard Busteed to Wilson, Feb. 9, 1871, Wilson MSS, Library of Congress.

[16] For a discussion of the progress of civil service reform, see Ari Hoogenboom, *Outlawing the Spoils* (Urbana, Ill., 1961).

of the Grant regime and the security of the Republican party. Demand for reform was especially great in Wilson's home state. Consequently in January, 1871, he proposed creating boards of examiners in each executive department to review applications and approve appointments to office. He also sought to prohibit the levying of political assessments on government employees and to forbid their engaging in political activity.[17]

Although Wilson had taken an opportune moment to champion civil service reform, he had been interested in the idea since 1835, when he had argued before the Natick debating society in favor of reducing executive patronage. In later years he had blamed the president's powers of appointment for forcing Texas into the Union and putting slavery in Kansas. He had also bitterly condemned President Johnson for using his appointive powers to increase support for his reconstruction policies. By 1871, however, Wilson supported civil service reform in order to protect the integrity of his party. He was uncomfortably aware of a smoldering revolt within the Republican organization, and at least one ostensible cause of the discontent was festering grievances over the distribution of offices. Making appointments on an impartial rather than partisan basis would, he hoped, reduce party dissension.[18] Although Wilson's bill was not enacted, Congress did authorize Grant to appoint a civil service commission, and the president complied.

In the process of defining a new departure for the Republican party Wilson turned to other questions besides labor and corporate legislation and civil service reform. In 1870 he observed that "political reconstruction is substantially complete; the moral must now occupy our hearts and hands . . . is not the 'whiskey question' the next in order?" The senator had already driven whiskey out of his

[17] *Congressional Globe*, 41st Cong., 3rd sess., 1871, pp. 37, 594; for Wilson's remarks on other bills, see *ibid.*, pp. 669-70. See also Hoogenboom, *Outlawing the Spoils*, 55, 71-89.

[18] Minutes of the Young Men's Debating Society, Dec. 30, 1835, in Morse Institute; Nason and Russell, *Wilson*, 68, 164; *Congressional Globe*, 40th Cong., 2nd sess., 1868, supplement, pp. 460-61; 41st Cong., 3rd sess., 1871, p. 670.

own vicinity; in 1866 he had obtained a law to bar the sale of liquor in the Capitol, and the following year, to the discomfiture of many of his colleagues, he had prohibited the consumption of alcohol in the building. He also organized a Congressional Temperance Society, became its president, and persuaded several of his colleagues to "conquer the vitiated appetites of their fallen nature" by pledging total abstinence. Yet he found in the antiliquor campaign the same problems that he had met in devising laws to combat racial prejudice: "no legislation is of much value which is far in advance of public sentiment." Nonetheless, a few months before he left the Senate to assume the vice-presidency Wilson proposed the creation of a federal commission to "consider restrictive and prohibitive legislation for the suppression of intemperance."[19]

Women's rights as well as temperance claimed Wilson's attention. By 1868 a movement in Massachusetts to give women the vote had gathered some strength. Suffragettes worked hard to get Republican endorsement of the idea, and in 1870 they missed by only a few votes of getting the reform into the state party platform. As early as 1853 Henry Wilson had publicly supported female suffrage. In December, 1866, however, when the issue came up in concrete form in an attempt to amend the District suffrage bill to allow women to vote as well as Negroes, Wilson failed to support it. He refused to endanger Negro suffrage, "which is now an imperative necessity," by connecting it with female voting. Two years later, admitting that he was ashamed for having voted against suffrage for both sexes, he introduced a bill in the Senate to make women in the District of Columbia eligible for voting and holding office. He also recom-

[19] *Congressional Globe,* 38th Cong., special session, 1865, p. 1425; 39th Cong., 1st sess., 1866, p. 1877; 40th Cong., 1st sess., 1867, pp. 13, 30-32, 92; 42nd Cong., 3rd sess., 1873, p. 464; Natick *Times,* Feb. 23, March 2, April 20, 1867; Boston *Journal,* May 19, 1869, Dec. 18, 1871; George F. Clark, *History of the Temperance Reform in Massachusetts, 1813-1883* (Boston, 1888), 256, 259; Henry Wilson, *The Relations of Churches and Ministers to the Temperance Cause* (Boston, 1870); Wilson, *Father Mathew;* Natick *Bulletin,* May 17, 1873; New York *Independent,* March 24, 1870; Boston *Daily Advertiser,* Jan. 17, 1870; Richard Yates to Henry Wilson, Feb. 4, 1867, Wilson MSS, Library of Congress.

mended giving female government clerks equal pay with men, advocated allowing women in the territories to vote and hold office, and even considered a sixteenth amendment to the Constitution to permit the ladies to vote in all states of the Union.[20]

There were few humanitarian causes that escaped Wilson's eye. After Grant's election the senator urged a more humane Indian policy, stating that "we who have emancipated one race and given it the rights of citizenship, will now enter upon the policy of taking care of and preserving and civilizing the small remnant of the Indian tribes on this continent." He demanded an investigation of the government's conduct of Indian affairs and asked that Congress redress the grievances of tribes deprived of land promised them by government treaty.[21] In 1870 and again in 1872 he sought legislation to strengthen the government's efforts to suppress the African slave trade and to prohibit Americans from deporting and enslaving natives of the South Sea Islands.[22] He demonstrated great concern about Spanish treatment of native Cubans and publicly sympathized with the insurgent movements on the island.[23] In 1870 Wilson also introduced resolutions in Congress seeking to provide for better observance of Sunday in the military and naval academies and to abolish the sport of prize-fighting.[24]

[20] Ware, *Political Opinion,* 187-89; Ida H. Harper, *The Life and Work of Susan B. Anthony* (3 vols.; Indianapolis, 1898-1908), I, 317-18, 377, 418; Elizabeth Cady Stanton, *et al.,* eds., *History of Woman Suffrage* (3 vols.; Rochester, N. Y., 1887), II, 390, III, 267; *Official Report of the Debates,* I, 101; Boston *Journal,* Jan. 8, 15, March 3, 1869, Jan. 17, April 21, 1870, Jan. 13, 1871; *Congressional Globe,* 39th Cong., 2nd sess., 1866, pp. 63-64, 84; 40th Cong., 3rd sess., 1868, p. 61; 42nd Cong., 2nd sess., 1872, 452.

[21] Boston *Journal,* March 16, 1870; *Congressional Globe,* 41st Cong., 2nd sess., 1870, pp. 1753, 1857, 1921, 1924, 2154.

[22] *Congressional Globe,* 39th Cong., 1st sess., 1866, p. 4298; 41st Cong., 2nd sess., 1870, pp. 1624, 1728; 42nd Cong., 2nd sess., 1872, p. 582.

[23] Boston *Daily Advertiser,* March 10, 1870. Shortly after becoming vice-president, Wilson accepted the office of president of the Cuban League, an organization sympathetic to Cuban independence. When the Spanish ambassador complained about the matter to Secretary of State Hamilton Fish, Wilson resigned. See New York *Times,* Sept. 21, Nov. 18, 22, 1873; Polo do Barnabe to Fish, Aug. 22, Sept. 8, 1873, and Wilson to Fish, Aug. 30, 1873, Fish MSS, Library of Congress.

[24] *Congressional Globe,* 41st Cong., 2nd sess., 1870, p. 1609.

By the time of the election of 1872, then, Henry Wilson, who had sensed the country's growing disinterest in the older issues of civil war and reconstruction, had managed to redefine the program of his party and pronounce his views on a number of subjects. Taken all together, his recommendations outlined a varied pattern of federal intervention. He had endorsed federal aid to education, federal legislation on hours of labor, a federal labor relations commission, federal chartering and regulation of corporations, controls on speculation and stock marketing, civil service reform, federal legislation for equal rights for women and for protection of Indians, and even national prohibition of liquor. Although he was personally interested in these reforms, he never sought to develop a coherent and consistent program and sometimes manipulated the issues for their political advantage. Above all, he hoped by agitating new reforms to maintain the strength of the Republican party, which he had always traced to "its ideas, or rather to the fact that it has been a party of ideas" lifted above the "mere scramble for place and power." As long as the Republicans appealed to "the higher principles of thought and feeling, a love of country, a sense of justice, and regard for human rights," they would continue to merit the support of the voters.[25]

[25] Wilson, "The New Departure," 117-18.

14

A Career Draws to a Close

Henry Wilson had little success in convincing his Republican colleagues to undertake any new programs of social and economic reform. The pressures of civil war and reconstruction had brought him to the apex of his career as an effective politician; during that time he had played an important role in securing the ascendancy of equality over privilege, as well as in establishing the Republican party in power. In 1872 Republican voters would make him vice-president of the United States, but the gesture was in gratitude for past services rather than in anticipation of future contributions. After 1870 Wilson's influence in the party waned, as younger men interested in protecting corporations and raising tariffs replaced the older generation of antislavery leaders.

As Wilson's dwindling personal influence left him more and more in political solitude, he found himself without a family upon which to rely. In the fall of 1859 his father, Winthrop Colbath, had fallen seriously ill and had died the following February. On August 7, 1866, Wilson's mother Abigail followed her husband to the grave. The Colbaths, who had moved to Natick in 1848, had lived with one of Wilson's brothers, George Colbath. Wilson, who was busy with his incessant political campaigns, apparently made little effort to maintain close ties with his family. He did provide jobs for at least two of his four brothers; George became a customs collector in Boston, while Samuel Colbath served as doorkeeper of the United States Senate.[1]

Wilson did not have much more time for his wife and son; his political activities kept him away from home for weeks on end. In October, 1865, when the Wilsons celebrated their twenty-fifth wedding anniversary, the senator had to interrupt a campaign tour to be with his wife on the occasion. Harriet Wilson did manage to encourage her husband to participate actively in the affairs of the local Congregational church, and Wilson established close association with the several men who served the congregation. Much to his wife's dismay, however, he had never become a member of the church. In the fall after Abigail Colbath's death, an itinerant evangelist, Henry Durant, visited Natick, and Harriet coaxed her husband into listening to him. When Durant finished his sermon, he asked for converts to rise and speak. To everyone's surprise, Senator Wilson was the first to stand. In humble tones he confessed: "I have never felt so needy in my whole life as I do this morning. I need Jesus Christ, and I would like to join the church."[2]

Wilson soon stood in dire need of the faith he had avowed in the fall of 1866. On Christmas day of the same year, he and Harriet learned that their son, Henry Hamilton, then serving on the Texas frontier as a lieutenant in the regular army, had died of a stomach hemorrhage.[3] The young man was barely twenty years old. The grieving senator told Amos Lawrence: "I try to bear this terrible blow but the heart is desolate . . . I so loved my dear boy, hoped so much that it seems to be more than I can bear to part with him forever." Wilson could only ask God to "help me feel that He had done right in taking what He gave."[4] The grief-stricken father's suffering was compounded by remorse. Now that the boy was gone, Wilson could find little in the past twenty years to assure him of his success as a father. From the time Henry Hamilton was born, he had

[1] Nason, "Biographical Sketch," 261; Natick *Bulletin,* Feb. 14, 1902; Natick *Times,* Aug. 11, 1866.

[2] Frank M. Bishop, comp., *300th Anniversary of the First Congregational Church, Natick, Massachusetts, 1651-1951* (Boston, 1951), 17; Natick *Times,* Sept. 22, 28, Oct. 13, 20, Nov. 3, 1867; Boston *Commonwealth,* Oct. 20, 1866; Natick *Bulletin,* Dec. 3, 1875, April 15, May 6, 1892.

[3] On cause of Henry Hamilton's death see Natick *Times,* Jan. 12, 1867.

[4] Wilson to Lawrence, Jan. 2, 1867, Lawrence MSS. For letters of condolence see Wilson MSS, Library of Congress, Dec., 1866, through Jan., 1867.

been his mother's charge. When the boy was old enough, his parents sent him off to boarding school while they were in Washington. When Harriet returned home at the end of the session, her husband went off campaigning. In 1861 Wilson estimated he had traveled over 80,000 miles since he had become senator. Jeremiah Jones Colbath had suffered because his father was too lazy; Henry Hamilton Wilson suffered because his father was too active.

In 1861, apparently hopeful that military school would give his son the training and attention he needed, Wilson sent the young fellow off to cadet school in Worcester. In September of the following year he obtained an appointment at the Naval Academy for Henry Hamilton; the sixteen-year-old boy remained there for one year and then left to enroll in the Union army. Under his father's close supervision, he went to New York City to help recruit a regiment of Negro infantry. In May, 1864, he obtained a commission as first lieutenant in the regiment. Less than a year later, Henry Hamilton went to Beaufort, South Carolina, to help recruit the 104th Regiment of Colored Troops; then the boy, not yet nineteen, became lieutenant colonel in command. When the 104th was mustered out early in 1866, Henry Hamilton Wilson joined the regular army, got an appointment as second lieutenant in the 6th U. S. Cavalry, and was sent to Austin, Texas. It was there that he died.[5]

From start to finish the young man's military career had been a source of anguish, worry, and financial embarrassment for his father. The lad was simply too young and undisciplined to take the responsibility of leading troops. While serving in South Carolina he permitted discipline and order in the 104th regiment to collapse. When the adjutant general tried to revoke his commission, Senator Wilson

[5] For a brief resume of Henry Hamilton Wilson's military career, see Francis Bernard Heitman, *Historical Register and Dictionary of the United States Army, 1789-1903* (2 vols.; Washington, D.C., 1903), I, 1046. For examples of Wilson's frequent use of personal influence in his son's behalf, see Wilson to General Benjamin F. Butler, Aug. 5, 1864, Butler MSS; Major General Edward Ferrero to Wilson, [1864], Wilson MSS, Library of Congress; Wilson to Headquarters, Oct. 28, 1865, Office of the Secretary of War, War Department, National Archives; Wilson to Bureau of Colored Troops, Sept. 15, 1865, Adjutant General's Office, War Department, National Archives.

intervened to stop the proceedings. Then certain officers and men in Wilson's regiment brought charges against him for "conduct unbecoming an officer and a gentleman." According to witnesses Wilson had cursed a subordinate and had been "so much intoxicated that he was incapable of performing his duties." His father's puritanical habits and teachings had clearly had no effect upon the young son. The charges were forwarded to the headquarters of the Port Royal district, where they were buried. In March, 1866, Wilson was only too glad to leave the regiment and the state. Before moving on to Texas, however, he went to Washington to get some assistance from his father. He had run up a bill with merchants in Beaufort for the sum of $613.20 and the adjutant general was threatening to withhold his pay. In total Henry Hamilton's debts exceeded $1,000.[6]

Thus Henry Wilson paid the price for failing to guide his son in the proper manner. If the cost in dollars was high, the cost in terms of family pride was higher. Jeremiah Jones Colbath had never had a father who shared his problems or tendered him aid in any way; he could not provide for his son what he himself had never experienced. Burdened with grief and remorse, Wilson had his son's body sent to Washington, and on January 7, 1867, he boarded a train in the capital to join a military escort carrying the remains on to Massachusetts. On the afternoon of January 9 businesses in Natick closed, and the citizenry crowded into the Congregational church to attend Henry Hamilton's funeral. A few of Wilson's close friends then accompanied him as he followed his son's body out to the cemetery, where the late afternoon sun had failed to melt the snow that covered the wintry landscape. The large and expensive monument that Wilson later provided for the new grave was an empty attempt

[6] For detailed information on Henry Hamilton Wilson's military career I have consulted his service file and also pertinent records in the Commission Branch, both in the Adjutant General's Office, War Department, National Archives. I also found useful information in the Bureau of Colored Troops, Adjutant General's Office. Henry Hamilton Wilson's commissions can be found in the Natick Historical Society Museum; here also are receipts and notes concerning various debts accumulated by young Wilson that his father scrupulously honored.

to provide for his son in death the attention he should have received in life.[7]

Now only his wife remained. Their recent bereavement brought the two closer together, and Wilson began to spend more time at home between sessions of Congress. In the summer of 1867 they planned a trip to Europe, but Harriet became too sick to make the trip. In 1868 she began to show signs of recovery, but in March of the following year the disease, apparently cancer, again incapacitated her. By December Harriet was well enough to accompany her husband to Washington, but early in May, 1870, she was forced to return home. On May 12 her husband, anxious and overwrought, asked leave from his Senate duties and hurried after her. The following days were filled with agony for Wilson as well as his wife. As Harriet lay in bed, too weak to move, her husband sat close by, not daring even to remove his clothes or sleep lest he be absent when she needed him.[8]

On May 27 Lydia Maria Child wrote Mrs. Wilson to suggest she try some spring water her husband had been using—but Harriet never read the letter. On May 28, at the age of forty-six, she died without a murmur. Her husband sat by her side, helpless to halt her passing. So Henry Wilson lost his dedicated wife, a woman "without an enemy, so patient and enduring, too frail to bloom in this world." Friends who expressed their sympathy to the bereaved husband would all stress Harriet's patience, humility, tenderness, delicacy, gentleness, and generosity. She had been a woman who gave her husband quiet yet firm support and confidence, who was more than willing to sit in the shadow and let him play the public role. In life he seemed perhaps unneedful of her; in death he would miss her sorely.[9]

[7] Natick *Times,* Jan. 12, 1867. The monument Wilson placed at his son's grave "was one of the most elegant ever made in Massachusetts." *Ibid.,* June 13, 1868.

[8] Henry Wilson to Henry Claflin, March 1, 1869, Claflin MSS; *Congressional Globe,* 41st Cong., 2nd sess., 1870, p. 3388; Wilson to Samuel Hunt, May 20, 1870, Brown University Library; Wilson to Charles Sumner, May 23, 1870, Sumner MSS.

[9] Lydia Maria Child to Mrs. Wilson, May 27, 1870, Houghton Library,

The funeral was held in the Congregational church, where for thirty years Harriet had been a steady and devoted member. A large crowd gathered in the sanctuary. Some of her husband's good friends, including Governor William Claflin, attended. The casket, in keeping with the spirit of the deceased, was simply covered, and the services were brief and solemn. Pallbearers included Claflin, William Schouler, Frank Bird, and Edward Walcott, all close friends of the family. For the fourth time in a decade, Henry Wilson followed a funeral cortege out to Dell Park Cemetery; for the fourth time he saw a loved one buried forever. This last loss was the greatest.[10]

In an attempt to assuage his grief, Wilson devoted himself to a project he had begun some years before; the writing of a history of the rise and fall of the Slave Power in America. Wilson had begun his new avocation out of a fear that the contributions and achievements of his generation of antislavery leaders would soon be forgotten by a fickle and ungrateful America. Particularly after Grant's election, when he began to sense that his own political influence was waning, Wilson sought to preserve the antislavery record in print. He also hoped to realize some financial gain from the publication of his efforts. After his wife's death, his writing became more and more an escape from reality, as he sought to lose his sense of loneliness by reviving past accomplishments.

Virtually from the day Wilson entered politics, he had been concerned about how later historians would view the great events of his day and how they would treat his role as a participant in those events. Early in his career he reached the conclusion that "the world cares little for our lives and will soon forget us and what we say or do." After reading William H. Prescott's *Conquest of Mexico,* he told a friend that Prescott "had raised a monument that will carry his name when the granite on Bunker Hill shall moulder and mingle with

Harvard University. Quoted comment on Mrs. Wilson is from Laura Eggleston to Henry Wilson, June 8, 1870; see also F. Eames to Wilson, June 30, 1870, both in Wilson MSS, Library of Congress; Elias Nason to Wilson, June 10, 1870, Henry E. Huntington Library and Art Gallery; reminiscences of Adelaide Waldron in Natick *Bulletin,* April 15, 1892; Boston *Journal,* May 30, 1870.

[10] Boston *Journal,* June 1, 1870.

the dust." Henry Wilson wanted a monument in his own honor, a history of the antislavery movement that would vindicate the "true men" who had resisted the aggressions of the Slave Power.[11]

To insure that his own services to the antislavery cause would not be forgotten, Wilson took close interest in the preparation of sketches of his career that appeared in various publications. Carefully he saved newspaper articles about himself to provide to prospective biographers. On one occasion he even sent money to a writer who planned to publish a history of Massachusetts containing information on Wilson's life and service. In the spring of 1864, when Wilson learned that the secretary of the American Anti-Slavery Society was drawing up the society's annual report, he anxiously inquired if the report would reveal his efforts to abolish slavery and the black codes in the District of Columbia.[12]

The best way for Wilson to obtain adequate coverage in historical accounts of the day was to write his own books. Before the Civil War ended, he published a history of the antislavery measures passed by the preceding two Congresses. The volume, which chronicled congressional debates on all legislation concerning slavery, gave its author a disproportionate share of the space. He received many letters complimenting his literary efforts; Harriet Martineau thought the volume made "the progress of your antislavery legislation clear to persons who are sadly in need of such knowledge."[13]

Encouraged by such favorable response to his writings, over the next four years Wilson published a history of the military legislation of the Civil War Congresses, and also a chronicle of the reconstruc-

[11] Wilson to William Schouler, Dec. 17, 1843, Schouler MSS; Wilson to George Sumner, Dec. 19, 1858, Houghton Library, Harvard University; Wilson to Joshua Giddings, Sept. 15, 1858, Giddings MSS; Wilson to Reverend Elias Nason, Nov. 20, 1872, Morse Institute; Pierce, *Sumner,* IV, 562n.

[12] Wilson to Robert Carter, Aug. 17, 1862, Houghton Library, Harvard University; Wilson to Elias Nason, Sept. 19, 24, Dec. 10, 1865, Morse Institute; Wilson to William Lloyd Garrison, April 14, 1864, Samuel May to C. C. Burleigh, Nov. 3, 1867, Boston Public Library.

[13] Henry Wilson, *A History of Anti-Slavery Measures, passim.* See letters to Wilson from Harriet Martineau, Gerrit Smith, Neal Dow, Benson J. Lossing, and others in Wilson MSS, Library of Congress, covering dates from Dec., 1864, to Nov., 1865.

tion measures passed through 1867. Wilson, whose own letters betrayed his incorrigible grammar and spelling, had help from his old friends, the clergymen Nason and Hunt, in preparing the three volumes. The pattern of all three books was much the same; he gave a good deal of attention to his own speeches and gleaned his material largely from the *Congressional Globe*.[14]

As soon as Wilson had finished his history of the reconstruction measures, he began to collect material for a far vaster three-volume narrative that would elaborate in a detailed fashion upon the rise and fall of his longtime enemy, the Slave Power. He worked hard on his writing and gathered information from a wide variety of sources. He sent letters to veterans of the antislavery battles asking for their personal reminiscences and perused newspaper files and the records of state and national legislatures.[15]

Early in 1870 he began publishing in the New York *Independent* material later used in his history. John Greenleaf Whittier found the

[14] Wilson, "Military Measures," and *History of Reconstruction Measures;* Wilson to Elias Nason, Sept. 28, 1865, Morse Institute. In 1870 Wilson embarked upon another publishing venture, when he prepared an article for the *Atlantic Monthly* discussing the behavior of Edwin M. Stanton while he served in Buchanan's prewar cabinet. In dealing with Stanton's controversial role, Wilson seized the opportunity to denounce Buchanan and his cabinet for surrendering the government's right of self-preservation during the secession crisis. The article drew an angry reply from Jeremiah Black, who had been Buchanan's attorney general. The whole dispute was printed: Henry Wilson and Jeremiah Black, *A Contribution to History. Edwin M. Stanton: His Character and Public Services on the Eve of the Rebellion* (Easton, Pa., 1871). See also William N. Brigance, *Jeremiah Sullivan Black* (Philadelphia, 1934), 242-46.

[15] Wilson to William Henry Seward, May 23, 1870, May 4, 1872, Seward MSS; Wilson to Eli Thayer, Oct. 18, 23, 1869, Sept. 23, Oct. 10, 1873, Eli Thayer MSS, Brown University Library; Wilson to Theodore Dwight Weld, June 11, 1870, Houghton Library, Harvard University; Wilson to James A. Briggs, Oct. 6, 1870, J. M. McKim to Wilson, Sept. 30, 1873, Wilson MSS, Library of Congress; Wilson to Daniel Ullmann, Sept. 23, 1873, New York Historical Society; Wilson to Theodore Dwight Weld, Aug. 30, 1869, William L. Clements Library, Ann Arbor, Mich.; Wilson to James R. Doolittle, May 12, 1873, quoted in Duane Mowry, "The Corner Stone Resolution," *Journal* of the Illinois State Historical Society, III (1910-1912), 88; Wilson to William L. Garrison, Aug. 9, 1869, Aug. 29, 1870, Boston Public Library; Wilson to Gerrit Smith, Dec. 18, 1868, July 23, 1869, Aug. 27, Sept. 19, 1870, Oct. 14, Nov. 4, 1871, Smith MSS.

newspaper series constituted "a valuable and readable history of the great struggle in which the author has borne so honorable a part." Gerrit Smith believed that Wilson had written the articles "thoroughly, accurately, and handsomely." Wilson's announced goal was to write an "impartial" history of the Slave Power; however his objectivity was extended only to participants in the struggle against that Power and its human instruments. He had had personal disagreements with Wendell Phillips, William Lloyd Garrison, Eli Thayer, and many other abolitionists, over the means which they chose to use in combating slavery, but in chronicling the history of their common efforts, he tended to gloss over past antagonisms. Nonetheless, Garrison and Samuel May were quite upset at Wilson's articles dealing with their wing of the antislavery movement. Wilson had described the Garrisonians as being somewhat misguided in their antipolitical attitude, and weak in numbers. The old antislavery editor reminded the senator that had he and his friends "been driven from the field," then "neither a Giddings nor a Sumner, neither a Wilson nor a Julian, would have been seen as political representatives of the movement in Congress."[16]

In the spring of 1872 James R. Osgood and Company of Boston published Wilson's first volume and two years later released the second. The works were well received. William Lloyd Garrison, despite his earlier strictures, found the first volume "fair and comprehensive"; John Greenleaf Whittier called it "very conscientious . . . a truthful and impartial contribution." The reviewer in the Boston *Traveller* was convinced that Wilson had through his writing added the title of "scholar and historian to those of politician and statesman." The author's friend and critic, Frank Bird of the Boston *Commonwealth,* called the volume "a monument to antislavery workers of a generation." He praised Wilson heartily for his ability and impartiality. After reading the second volume, abolitionist

[16] John G. Whittier to Charles Sumner, March, 1870, quoted in Samuel T. Pickard, *Life and Letters of John Greenleaf Whittier* (2 vols.; Boston, 1894), II, 563; Gerrit Smith to Wilson, Feb. 14, 1871, Wilson MSS, Library of Congress; May to Garrison, Jan. 20, 24, 1872, Garrison to May, Jan. 23, 27, 1872, Garrison to Wilson, May 2, 1872, Boston Public Library.

Parker Pillsbury, previously an outspoken opponent of Wilson, thanked him for his "too generous consideration of my humble services in our common cause, as indicated by your truly grand and noble [book]."[17]

The definition and analysis of the Slave Power which Wilson used in his history he had developed over a lifetime of speech-making. First he distinguished between slavery and the Slave Power. The former was a system of holding men in bondage for financial gain. It was also based in a desire to gratify "the most intense spirit of personal pride, a love of class distinctions, and the lust of dominion." The slaveowners, who eventually held four million people as property, in their eagerness to extend and perpetuate slavery, developed great political influence in the nation. It was this influence which Wilson chose to designate as "the Slave Power." He attributed the plans and plots of the Slave Power to an ill-defined conspiracy: "it was as if somewhere some imperious autocrat or secret conclave held court or council in which slavery's every interest, necessity, and demand were considered or cared for." This conspiracy was directed "against the forms and spirit of the laws and the Constitution, against the justice, liberty, faith, honor, humanity and religion of the nation, for purposes of personal ambition and sectional domination."[18]

Painstakingly Wilson developed his thesis that the Slave Power, locked in an irrepressible conflict with the forces of liberty and justice, marched from victory to victory until it was rebuffed by the

[17] See reviews in Wilson MSS, Library of Congress; Boston *Commonwealth,* April 6, 1872; John Jay to Wilson, Aug. 11, 1872, Parker Pillsbury to Wilson, July 2, 1874, in Wilson MSS, Library of Congress; John A. Dix to Wilson, April 12, 1873, New York Historical Society. Eli Thayer approvingly cited Wilson for his "correct idea of the decisive work of the Emigrant Aid Company" in his *A History of the Kansas Crusade* (New York, 1899), 72. On the other hand, George Julian was disappointed to see Wilson's history "disfigured by his elaborate efforts to whitewash [the Know-Nothing movement] into respectability." Julian, *Political Recollections* (Chicago, 1884), 143.

[18] New York *Times,* Dec. 17, 1860; Wilson, *Democratic Leaders for Disunion; Aggressions of the Slave Power* (Washington, D.C., 1860); *Letter of Henry Wilson to Honorable Caleb Cushing;* Wilson, *Slave Power,* I, 2, 528; II, 188-89.

election of Abraham Lincoln in 1860. He attributed much of the success of the Slave Power to the fact that although it represented a slaveholding minority, the slaveowners were tightly organized, determined, and inflexible. Wielding the political influence they had gained from the constitutional provision enabling them to count three-fifths of their slaves in apportioning representation in Congress, they were able to extort concessions from politicians. Since the masters of several million slaves also possessed great economic power, they were able to wrest concessions from Northern commercial interests eager to conciliate the South. The underlying cause of Slave Power dominance, however, Wilson ascribed to "the inadequate conception by the people of the high and comprehensive duties of self-government." Busy on their farms, in their workshops, stores, and factories, the masses of people had little time to give to political matters and to fulfilling the duties of citizenship. Thus they failed to realize that "human rights are indissolubly linked with human responsibilities; that freedom is not a glittering bauble which constitutions can confer, but a prize that is to be won and kept in the presence of active and ever-watchful foes."[19]

Wilson also realized that the same forces of racial prejudice, love of power, and basic intolerance that upheld slavery in the South were present in the North as well. "Though the tree of slavery was planted on Southern soil, its branches overshadowed, as its roots penetrated, the whole land, shedding its blighting influences on Northern as well as Southern hearts."[20] With anti-Negro feelings present in the North, the Slave Power could find many allies. Ultimately, wrote Wilson, the political representatives of slavery could fall back on sarcasm, insolence, and abuse in overwhelming their opponents in Congress; and if that failed, outright violence, which Wilson contended was at the very heart of slavery, could be used. Thus Wilson's colleague Charles Sumner collapsed under the cane of a minion of the Slave Power, and abolitionist editor Elijah P. Lovejoy was shot to death. Usually, however, the Southerners

[19] Wilson, *Slave Power*, I, 650.
[20] *Ibid.*, 238.

stopped short of such extremes. According to Wilson, if they found Northerners stiffening their resistance to the Slave Power's demands, they would threaten to dissolve the Union, and "Union savers" like Daniel Webster and Henry Clay would rush to make concessions.

Against the tremendous influence of the Slave Power, Wilson posed a small but dedicated band of abolitionists. They represented to him the forces of right, of justice, of Christian morality and humanity. Unfortunately, they, along with the rest of the North, failed to comprehend the magnitude of the problem they were attacking. They were too optimistic about their ability to eradicate slavery; they did not "comprehend how firmly it was imbedded in the very foundation of the civil, industrial, social, and ecclesiastical institutions of the country, or estimate aright the tenacity of its hold on life."[21] What finally defeated the Slave Power was not the moral light provided by the abolitionists, but the physical power provided by Union armies in the Civil War. "The sword of steel and not the sword of truth" brought ultimate victory for the forces of democracy and humanity.[22]

Thus Wilson was led to seek an explanation for the reason why the Slave Power risked all in a desperate attempt at secession and Civil War. After examining the evidence, Wilson was led to conclude that only the interference of Divine Providence could explain the suicidal course the Slave Power embarked upon.[23] The turning point came in 1844, when the Slave Power successfully conspired to add Texas, a slaveholding state, to the Union. This in turn precipitated the Mexican War, which the South utilized in order to further expand slave territory.

This series of events for the first time alarmed large numbers of Northerners about the aggressions of the Slave Power, and began the process of dissolving both the Whig and Democratic parties, which the Southerners depended upon to manipulate Northern voters. Invigorated by its victories, the Slave Power sought to make slavery

[21] *Ibid.*, 171.
[22] *Ibid.*, 369.
[23] *Ibid.*

national, by repealing the Missouri Compromise and getting the Supreme Court to issue the Dred Scott decision. By so overreaching itself, the Slave Power precipitated the emergence of the Republican party, which had no Southern wing to throttle its antislavery views. By 1860, the Slave Power was aggressive enough to demand that the Democratic party accept a strongly proslavery platform and thus destroyed the party and its chances for victory in the presidential campaign. Driven to desperation, the slaveholders embarked upon the suicidal course of seceding from the Union, thus setting the stage for Civil War and emancipation of the slaves.

15

Wilson's Last Years

In the summer of 1871, at the suggestion of his physician, Wilson turned away from writing and politics in order to take the first extended vacation of his life. Early in June he left Boston to sail for England. Visiting foreign lands revived his spirits. Eagerly he explored London, Berlin, and Vienna. His experiences and thoughts clearly reflected his own particular concerns. Thus, in London he "mingled considerably with the politicians" and attended church "quite constantly." He made repeated temperance speeches in England, but in Germany, according to rumor, after observing the Germans enjoy beer on Sundays his strict ideas on observance of the Sabbath and on total abstinence began to weaken. When he visited gambling dens, however, his puritan spirit revolted. He noted with astonishment that "this is a strange way of living yet persons of high standing spend weeks here." In Ireland he was struck by the stark comparison between "the wretched cabins of the people . . . and the vast landed estates of the few." He came away convinced that "if I were a resident of that land, I would be a most radical reformer, if not a revolutionist."[1]

Despite the stimulation of new sights and new associations, Wilson grew homesick. He was eager to resume writing, and he also wanted to return to the feuds and squabbles of the Republican party, to see if he could promote another bid for the vice-presidential nomination. Consequently, in September he cut short his European trip and returned to the United States.[2]

No sooner had Wilson arrived in Boston than he found himself unwillingly dragged into a party dispute in Massachusetts that centered on the audacious Benjamin F. Butler, who hoped to be the Republican candidate for governor in 1871. The congressman had raised a great deal of consternation among hard-money Bay Staters by his espousal of inflationary schemes; he also busily hawked the reforms of an eight-hour day, woman suffrage, and prohibition. Far off in Europe, Wilson, who sympathized with Butler's ideas, believed he probably would get the nomination. Upon his return in September, however, he began to deplore the tremendous furor Butler had stirred up in the party by his inflammatory speeches. Wilson feared tangling with the powerful Butler, but he feared even more for the unity for his party and therefore agreed to join Sumner in a public statement condemning Butler's campaign tactics and opposing his nomination.[3]

Butler, whose anger at Wilson increased after he failed to receive the nomination, entered into an acrimonious correspondence with the senator. Greatly alarmed at rumors that Butler was working to defeat his bid for the vice-presidential nomination in 1872, Wilson struggled to heal over the personal breach; by the following spring Butler calmed down and withdrew his opposition to Wilson's candidacy.[4]

Wilson had blunted one threat to his ambitions only to find that a much larger movement than that originated by Butler threatened to split not simply the state party but the national Republican organization. Since President Grant had taken office a growing number of Republicans had become disaffected with his administration. Civil service reformers objected to his appointments; important politi-

[1] Nason, "Biographical Sketch," 266-67; Boston *Commonwealth,* June 10, Aug. 12, 19, Sept. 30, 1871; Wilson to Henry Claflin, July 20, 1871, Claflin MSS; Natick *Bulletin,* July 22, 1871.

[2] Wilson to Henry Claflin, July 20, 1871, Claflin MSS; Natick *Bulletin,* Sept. 9, 1871.

[3] Butler to Wilson, Sept. 16, 1871, Wilson MSS, Library of Congress; Butler to Wilson, Oct. 29, 1871, Wilson to Butler, Sept. 18, Oct. 7, 1871, Butler MSS; Pierce, *Sumner,* IV, 494-95; Hoar, *Autobiography,* I, 217; Boston *Daily Journal,* Sept. 19, 20, 26, 1871.

[4] Lowell *Courier,* Dec. 28, 1871; Wilson to Butler, Feb. 13, 1872, Butler MSS; Boston *Commonwealth,* March 23, 1872.

cians, ignored when the patronage was dispensed, were primed for revenge; free-traders objected to Republican protectionism; many party members were disillusioned with reconstruction and were dismayed by Grant's Southern policy; and finally, evidences of corruption in the administration frightened many away from the president. By 1872 a formidable movement was on foot to form a "Liberal Republican" party to nominate another man.

For some time Wilson had been aware of the growing opposition to Grant, and he had frequently tried to mitigate some of the discontent by praising the few positive achievements of the administration.[5] In his anxiety to pacify the Republican malcontents, his biggest job was to soothe his own colleague, Charles Sumner. By 1871 a serious breach had developed between the president and Sumner. Grant had obtained a treaty annexing the Caribbean island of Santo Domingo, and Sumner, chairman of the Senate Committee on Foreign Affairs, had persistently resisted the scheme.

Although Wilson did not approve of the annexation, he supported it in the interest of party unity. The Senate, however, defeated the treaty. Relations between Grant and Sumner steadily grew worse, and in March, 1871, administration supporters voted in the Senate Republican caucus to remove the Massachusetts senator from the chairmanship of his committee. Wilson, who had been urging Grant to be "charitable and forgiving," protested hotly against the maneuver, but to no avail. E. L. Pierce reported that Wilson was so disgusted with Grant that he angrily "applied a term to the President which it is not worth while to perpetuate." Wilson also expressed irritation with his colleague Sumner, who refused to moderate his attacks upon the president.[6]

[5] Boston *Commonwealth*, May 22, 1869; Natick *Bulletin*, Oct. 15, 1870.

[6] Boston *Daily Advertiser*, March 18, 1870, March 16, 18, 1872; Boston *Journal*, July 16, 1870, Feb. 21, March 18, 1872; *Congressional Globe*, 42nd Cong., 1st sess., 1871, pp. 35, 42-43, 52; Pierce, *Sumner*, IV, 454, 471-75, 497, 521; Natick *Bulletin*, Feb. 7, 1902; McClure, *Recollections*, 290-91; Sumner to Wilson, June 2, 1871, Wilson MSS, Library of Congress; Wilson to Sumner, June 6, 1871, March 17, 1872, Sumner to Wilson, March 18, 1872, Sumner to E. L. Pierce, Dec. 27, 1871, Henry C. Bowen to Sumner, Feb. 24, 1872, Sumner MSS; Wilson to E. L. Pierce, June 11, 1872, Houghton Library, Harvard University.

While Wilson was busy trying to conciliate Sumner, the move-ment to make him Grant's running mate in 1872 gathered strength. Wilson said nothing about his own ambitions, but as early as 1870 his friends were busy in his behalf. The senator's years of campaign-ing throughout the eastern half of the country had won him a good deal of support in various states. In December, 1871, the Washington correspondent of the Boston *Commonwealth* noted that since Wilson was a firm advocate of Grant's reelection and also "more generally acceptable to anti-Grant Republicans than anyone else" he would make an excellent compromise candidate for the vice-presidency. He added that he knew of no one "towards whom the masses of the country feel more kindly, or in whose integrity and fidelity they have deeper faith." Wilson felt no embarrassment about seeking Schuyler Colfax's position, since the Indianan had declared he would not run again, but early in 1872 Colfax withdrew that decision. Wilson was then forced to make a statement. He admitted his surprise at the vice-president's change of mind and stated that he was tempted to withdraw; however, "by advice of some of the best Republicans in the nation" he·consented to remain a candidate for the position.[7]

In April the Massachusetts Republican convention selected Wilson for vice-president. He was more than gratified with the support of his own state, for it was absolutely essential to his success, but he noted that some of his friends and associates, like Bird, Edward Atkinson, Robinson, and Elizur Wright, had turned away from the convention to give their support to the growing Liberal Republican movement. On April 17, when Wilson addressed an immense gather-ing in the Cooper Institute in New York, he pleaded with those discontented with the party's course to remain in it instead of opposing it through a third party organization.[8]

The bolting Republicans ignored Wilson's remarks. On May 1, they met at Cincinnati and nominated Horace Greeley of the New

[7] Boston *Commonwealth,* Dec. 30, 1871; New York *Times,* Feb. 16, 1872.

[8] Boston *Journal,* March 15, April 10, 11, 18, 1872; New York *Times,* April 18, 1872; Ware, *Political Opinion,* 173; Edward Atkinson to Sumner, April 13, 1872, Sumner MSS; Wilson, *Stand by the Republican Colors.*

York *Tribune* to run against Grant. Wilson ridiculed the splinter party. He was sure that it would not "secure one electoral vote or obtain a popular vote of a hundred and fifty thousand." Yet he was clearly upset at the defection from the Republican party of many men with whom he had maintained long and close political associations. He became even more disturbed when the Democrats also nominated Greeley. For the moment, however, his chief concern was winning a place on the Republican ticket with Grant, and it promised to be a difficult task.[9]

Although Wilson's friends issued periodic and confident statements about his chances, giving him at least seventeen states by the time of the convention, only three state conventions instructed their delegates to vote for him. Eleven were pledged to Colfax. Wilson, however, had a good deal of support among unpledged delegations. In a contest where public opinion had not clearly designated a selection, newspaper editors and correspondents were important, and they almost unanimously supported the Massachusetts senator. The journalists disliked Colfax, who had kept his distance from them. On the other hand, the talkative Wilson leaked news to the men of the press so often that they fondly characterized him as "the official reporter of the executive sessions of the Senate." Colfax later commented that in the weeks before the convention, Wilson invited newspapermen in "nearly every evening, asking them to telegraph that he was gaining steadily." According to Colfax, the journalists complied, "so urgent were his appeals and so much had he set his heart on it."[10]

The Massachusetts delegation was filled with dedicated men ready to expend every effort for their candidate, and Wilson's wealthy friend, Congressman James Buffington, sent large amounts of money to finance his campaign expenses. Doubtless conventioners were influenced by the fact that adding Wilson to the national ticket would offset the probable defection of his contentious but well-

[9] Boston *Journal*, May 6, 1872.

[10] *Ibid.*, March 28, May 9, 15, 30, 1872; Boston *Commonwealth*, May 27, 1871; New York *Independent*, Dec. 9, 1875; Natick *Bulletin*, Feb. 7, 1902; Smith, *Colfax*, 358-59.

known colleague, Sumner. If these factors were not enough to win the nomination for the former shoemaker, President U. S. Grant's known preference for him over Schuyler Colfax made the outcome almost inevitable.[11]

Despite these factors, on the eve of the convention, the Boston *Journal* gave Wilson only a thirty-vote lead over Colfax. Colfax men were quite active in Philadelphia working for their candidate, but Wilson's adherents were just as busy. During the night of June 4, while bonfires roared and bands pushed for space in crowded streets, Wilson men got assurances from the vastly important Pennsylvania delegation. On the other hand, Colfax's supporters won the equally important state of New York. For every state the former camp claimed, the latter's supporters found another. By June 6, when balloting began rumors flooded the convention to the effect that the South had given its support to Colfax. Wilson men refused to panic, for they had strong assurances from the Carolinas, Georgia, Mississippi, and several border states. In the great convention hall, surrounded by a colorful variety of flags, streamers, and decorations, delegates quickly renominated Grant and then moved on to the vice-presidency. Wilson was nominated first; a former mayor of Philadelphia, Morton McMichael, made the first nominating speech. Wilson's adherents loosed their demonstration and then paused to hear veteran abolitionist Gerrit Smith, who had frequently disagreed with Wilson in the past, second the nomination. Finally a Negro from Georgia told the convention why he supported the Massachusetts senator.

As the speeches rolled on, and as the name of Colfax was presented, an impatient convention began demanding the roll call. The balloting proceeded apace, and it soon became apparent that neither candidate would receive the needed total of 370 votes. Wilson was closest with 364; Colfax was 40 votes behind him. Virginia, which had cast its 22 votes for a favorite son, then rewarded the man who

[11] Poore, *Reminiscences,* II, 286; White, *Trumbull,* 393-94; N. P. Banks to wife, June 7, 1872, Nathaniel Banks MSS, Library of Congress; Smith, *Colfax,* 343-55.

had worked so diligently for the party in that state. The delegation's chairman rose to change its votes to Wilson. With that, Ohio followed and quickly the convention made the nomination unanimous.[12]

Thus the Republican party rewarded Henry Wilson for his long service to the organization. His appeal to the ordinary voter, his long association with antislavery, and his somewhat prolabor legislative stance all combined to strengthen Grant's candidacy. George Boutwell found Wilson's selection "a just tribute" to his "faithful and eminent services to the Republican party." George B. Loring attributed Wilson's victory to the fact that "you had worked so hard for the cause of freedom and human equality. Your reputation was a strong weapon."[13]

For Henry Wilson it was the pinnacle of his career. But in his moment of success, he had no one to share his joys, and despite his elation at the tribute, he thought of his lost wife and son and sent flowers to their graves. With the aid of his old friend, Samuel Hunt, he then drafted a letter of acceptance to the Republican convention. In the missive, he set forth many of the proposals he had earlier presented in speeches and articles. The Republican party, he thought, should enforce the new constitutional amendments, grant amnesty to the white Southerners, reduce the national debt and interest rates, resume specie payments, encourage American commerce, and follow a humane Indian policy. He called upon the party to move ahead to deal with new social problems presented by "the labor question" and the demands of women for full equality. The government, he hoped, would reform its civil service and give the national domain to people rather than railroads. Perhaps recalling the furor he himself raised over Chinese immigrants in 1870, Wilson demanded the "continued encouragement and protection of voluntary immigration" and protection of the rights of "adopted

[12] Boston *Journal*, June 4, 5, 6, 7, 1872; New York *Times*, June 5, 6, 7, 1872.

[13] George Boutwell to Wilson, June 7, 1872, Wilson MSS, Library of Congress; George B. Loring to Wilson, June 11, 1872, Houghton Library, Harvard University.

citizens." Finally, Wilson reviewed his own efforts for the party and gratefully accepted the nomination.[14]

Back in Natick, Wilson's fellow townsmen prepared a grand reception. Wilson gratefully thanked his friends: "to a public man who has been so long in the public service, who has little else in this world, the kind words of political friends and personal acquaintances are ever grateful." He recalled the many instances in which the people of Natick had given him their respect and devotion, and again looking into the past, he thanked them for their kindness to his departed wife. He had forgotten all past animosities and in this hour of triumph he could truly thank God that "there is not a man or woman in my country that I cannot meet and offer the hand of friendship to."[15]

Among the first to offer the hand of friendship to Wilson was his long-time colleague and friend, Charles Sumner. Although Sumner's own mail was full of criticism of Wilson's course, the senior senator refused to break personal relations with him. Wilson, however, was upset at the fact that Sumner, portraying himself as "the special advocate of Negro rights," advised freedmen to vote for Horace Greeley rather than for Grant and Wilson. Since William Lloyd Garrison supported Grant, Wilson got some assistance from him in disputing Sumner's claim to be the only man concerned with the Negro's interests. Garrison publicly reminded Sumner that "in nothing of courage and vigilance, of zeal and fidelity in securing rights for the colored race have you outstripped your colleague." The old abolitionist editor noted that long before Sumner had revealed his antislavery beliefs, Wilson was "actively engaged" in the movement. The crusading journalist concluded that "the nomination of one so openly pronounced on all the leading reformatory movements of the age as Henry Wilson is a crushing blow to the hollow charge that the Republican party is without a mission and given over to corruption."[16]

[14] Boston *Journal*, June 14, 1872; New York *Times*, June 14, 1872.
[15] Natick *Bulletin*, Feb. 16, 1906; New York *Times*, June 22, 1872.
[16] Boston *Journal*, June 8, 1872; William Lloyd Garrison to Charles

During the campaign Wilson had to defend his name against charges of bigotry arising from his earlier alliance with the Know-Nothings. The candidate answered the charge that he had "hoped dirty foreigners would never vote for him" with his accurate observation that he was "one of those men who believes in getting all the votes he can, and of asking no questions."[17] Wilson had no sooner disposed of the charges of nativism, than he faced an even more dangerous accusation. Early in September, the New York *Sun* revealed that in 1868 several leading Republican congressmen, including Senator Henry Wilson, had received stock from the managers of a construction firm, the Credit Mobilier, engaged in building a transcontinental railroad. Since the railroad could be affected by congressional legislation, an outcry immediately resulted at the palpable conflict of interest involved. Wilson was panicked by the revelation. He had indeed purchased some of the stock for his wife, but only after he had queried the salesman, Oakes Ames, congressman from Massachusetts, about the chance of having to vote on any legislation affecting the railroad. Ames assured him no legislation was in the offing, so Wilson completed the transaction; however, within a few months he got worried and cancelled the deal. Ames returned the money and Wilson gave up the stock.

After four years, Wilson considered the matter closed, but now the *Sun's* charges, presented in the heat of an election campaign, prompted him to authorize an immediate denial of the charges. He went so far as to maintain he had never owned a single share of Credit Mobilier stock. Literally, his claim was correct, since Harriet had been legal possessor, but his statement was misleading. Fortunately for Wilson's election hopes, the public accepted his innocence, for his long public record had already proved his incorrupti-

Sumner, Aug. 3, 1872, quoted in *Letters of William Lloyd Garrison, Wendell Phillips, and James G. Blaine* ... (Concord, Mass., 1872), 5-8; Wilson to Garrison, Oct. 16, 1872, Boston Public Library.

[17] New York *Times,* Aug. 1, 31, Sept. 2, 7, 10, 1872; Wilson to Schouler, July 31, 1872, Schouler to Wilson, July 30, 31, 1872, William Schouler MSS; Wilson to "my dear sir," Sept. 3, 1872, Rutherford B. Hayes Library; Schuyler Colfax to Wilson, Aug. 19, 1872, Henry E. Huntington Library and Art Gallery.

bility. Thus the whole affair failed to damage Wilson's chances, and the following spring, a congressional investigatory committee cleared him of all charges. A Senate committee did contend that his statement during the campaign lacked frankness.[18]

Wilson weathered other stresses of the campaign without much difficulty. He did come near physical exhaustion by the middle of October, for unlike most nominees for high national office, Wilson, an inveterate campaigner, had immediately taken to the hustings. When he returned to Natick on October 12 to rest briefly, he had made 96 speeches and traveled 10,000 miles.[19] His optimism about the outcome of the campaign was confirmed on election day; Greeley carried only six states. After striving hard for several years for the nomination, and then exhausting himself campaigning, the results seemed almost anticlimactic for the Massachusetts senator. He had indeed come a long way from that miserable shack in New Hampshire. The one-time cobbler was now vice-president-elect of the United States. He had had to cover the last miles of that trip alone, however, and in this final hour of triumph, despite the hearty congratulations of his friends, he sorely missed his wife and son.[20]

On February 8, Wilson formally relinquished his Senate seat to prepare to assume his new duties the following month. He assumed the vice-presidency without a dollar in his pocket; he had to borrow one hundred dollars from Sumner to purchase a suit of clothes for his inauguration. Although he had never before allowed pecuniary matters to burden him, now, as he approached his sixty-first birthday, he began to worry about his financial status.[21] Anticipating

[18] New York *Independent*, Feb. 6, March 20, 1873; New York *Times*, Sept. 16, 1872; Hoar, *Reminiscences*, I, 318-19; *Senate Report No. 519*, 42nd Cong., 3rd sess., 1873, vol. III, ii, v, 14-15, 32-33; W. P. Phillips to Wilson, Feb. 21, 1873, Wilson MSS, Library of Congress; T. M. Pomeroy to Henry L. Dawes, Jan. 30, 1873, Dawes MSS; *House Report No. 77*, 42nd Cong., 3rd sess., 1873, vol. II, 186-90.

[19] Natick *Bulletin*, Oct. 19, 1872. Republicans throughout the country wanted Wilson to speak in their localities. See the W. E. Chandler MSS, Library of Congress, especially Aug. through Oct., 1872.

[20] Natick *Bulletin*, Nov. 23, 1872.

[21] Natick *Bulletin*, Oct. 19, 1906; New York *Tribune*, Jan. 6, 1874; New York *Independent*, Nov. 25, 1875. There are a variety of worthless stocks in

additional income from the sales of his unfinished history, he began
to devote as much as sixteen hours a day to writing. His physical
condition had been poor for the last two years, and he told Sumner
he half-expected his health to fail him, but he did not lessen his
exertions. On May 19, 1873, Wilson was struck by paralysis. He lost
control of the muscles of his face. Doctors immediately forced him
to cease work, and administration officials concealed the event from
the public. Reluctantly he went to Massachusetts to spend the
summer with his friends, the Claflins. Mrs. Claflin assured Sumner
that while she was doing all she could for the vice president, his
chafing at forced inactivity was preventing full recovery: "You know
he was never still five minutes, and it is more difficult for him than
for most persons to sit quietly and dream away the time . . . Mr.
Wilson wonders what will become of his *book,* and what will become
of a thousand things, and how the world can move on without
him."[22]

Wilson began to undergo a series of painful treatments in hopes of
finding a cure. Mrs. Claflin struggled to keep him from the hands of
"charlatans and quacks." She found it "pathetic to see him wander-
ing from place to place in search of rest." By the end of the summer
his face had resumed a normal appearance, but his speech was still
somewhat halting. In December the vice-president went to Washington, but he was forced to refuse public engagements. As he told one
petitioner, *"it would risk my life."* Late in January, 1874, he was
forced to retire to Massachusetts once again.[23]

Although Wilson managed to return to the Senate again for a

the Wilson materials in the Natick Historical Society Museum. A few weeks
before Wilson died, he told a friend he would gladly sell all his property for
$8,000. Cowdin, *Tribute to Henry Wilson,* 13.

[22] Boston *Commonwealth,* March 25, 1871; Wilson to Sumner, May 27,
1873, F. W. Bird to Sumner, June 19, 1873, George S. Boutwell to Sumner,
June 20, 1873, Mary B. Claflin to Sumner, June 3, 30, 1873, Sumner MSS;
New York *Times,* July 3, 29, Aug. 1, 1873.

[23] Mary B. Claflin, *Under the Old Elms* (Boston, 1895), 42-43; Wilson to
Eli Thayer, Oct. 10, 1873, Thayer MSS; C. A. Phelps to Sumner, Oct. 23,
1873, Sumner MSS; Wilson to Mrs. Anthony, Dec. 9, 1873, and Wilson to
Prof. Joseph Henry, Jan. 24, 1874, in Henry E. Huntington Library and Art
Gallery.

short while in April and May, he spent most of the year resting, visiting friends, and working on his history. He also found time to give political advice to President Grant. Hoping to heal over the party breach of 1872, he appealed to Grant to strengthen his administration by wise appointments. Wilson had already made overtures to Charles Francis Adams, a leading Liberal Republican, concerning the possibility of Adams's taking a position in the Grant administration. In 1872 he had also approached his old opponent, Robert Winthrop, about accepting a foreign mission, but Winthrop had refused to consider it.[24]

Although Wilson's discussions with such men had some political motivation, his aims were largely personal. As the years passed, he became more and more concerned about maintaining his personal and political associations. His family was gone; and although he carried with him photographs of his wife and son, they could not supply him with companionship. He clung desperately to mementos of the past. He grieved much over the theft of a watch presented to him in 1852 by members of the state legislature. In searching for some form of personal security, he sought, rather successfully, to overcome antipathies and prejudices engendered by past political differences, so that he might be surrounded by friends wishing him well. Winthrop, who had not forgotten that Wilson had arrested his Senate career two decades previously, admitted that "he means kindly by me . . . I have acquired a sort of liking for him." Adams was also pleased by Wilson's advances and declared that the vice-president had "a good and kindly disposition and generally sound principles."[25]

Wilson was particularly eager to patch up relationships with his old antislavery colleagues who had joined the Liberal Republicans in 1872. The deaths of some of his old associates disturbed him greatly

[24] Barnes, *Memoir of Weed,* 520; Wilson to Winthrop, May 9, 1872, Winthrop MSS, Massachusetts Historical Society; Winthrop to [?], Oct. 29, 1872, quoted in Winthrop, *Memoir,* 280-81; C. F. Adams Diary, Nov. 26, 1872; New York *Times,* April 28, 1874; New York *Tribune,* May 7, 1875.

[25] Cowdin, *Tribute to Henry Wilson,* 15; New York *Times,* March 2, 1873; Winthrop, *Memoir,* 281; C. F. Adams Diary, Sept. 2, 1873.

and led him to redouble his efforts to "bind together the men who stood side by side in the dark days of 1848."

Early in March, 1874, Wilson was resting quietly in Natick when word came to him that Charles Sumner lay dying in Washington. Despite his doctor's advice, the convalescing vice-president boarded the next train, determined to reach his colleague's side. In Boston friends persuaded him not to journey further. Within a few hours the senior Massachusetts senator died. The grief-stricken Wilson pronounced him "the greatest man in the Senate in my time." Sumner had died before he had completed editing a collection of his speeches and writings, and Wilson became even more concerned lest death overtake him too before he had finished his history. But now, as he turned back to his writing table, he did so with a heavy heart.[26]

Despite continued fears of his friends that the persistent effort would kill him, the vice-president, with the aid of his old compatriot, Samuel Hunt, wrote chapter after chapter. His second volume appeared early in 1874, and in May Wilson reported that the third and final volume was nearing completion. In the fall Dartmouth College, Daniel Webster's alma mater, awarded Wilson an LL.D; and his health seemed to prosper with his personal success. In December he returned to Washington, ready to resume his duties as vice-president.[27]

During the following year, most of Wilson's important political activity was carried on outside the Capitol. To be sure, while he presided over the Senate some dramatic moments did occur. In March, 1875, he had to swear in a new senator from Tennessee: Andrew Johnson. On that day, before a crowded chamber and gallery, the former president, square and sturdy, walked up to Wilson, who had once pronounced him "a violator of the Constitu-

[26] Bird, *A Biographical Sketch*, 2-3, 79; Robinson, ed., *Warrington*, 139, 146; Wilson to Willard P. Phillips, Feb. 19, 1873, Wilson to E. L. Pierce, June 11, 1872, Houghton Library, Harvard University; Pierce, *Sumner*, IV, 607; Boston *Journal*, March 12, 16, 17, 1874.

[27] New York *Tribune*, May 6, Nov. 10, 1874; *New England Historical and Genealogical Register*, XXXIII (1879), 257.

tion, a violator of the laws, and a violator of his oath," and offered him his hand. As Wilson complied with the gesture, a thunder of applause came from the onlookers.[28]

Wilson's restless ambition had not been satisfied by his elevation to the vice-presidency. Despite his frail condition and the absence of significant political support, he was prepared to bid now for the highest office in the land. To succeed in that goal, he decided he would have to dissociate himself from President Grant and his policies. Wilson had always been a reluctant Grant supporter and had for some time been convinced that the president's policies were destroying the party. Grant had ignored Wilson's advice about conciliating the Liberal Republicans, and the vice-president found himself with almost no influence in the president's circle. Consequently, it was not hard for him to criticize the chief executive. He told an Ohio congressman that Grant was "the millstone around the neck of the party that would sink it." Before Congress met in 1874, he urged Grant publicly not to listen to third-term suggestions. According to newspaper accounts, the president was so outraged at Wilson he refused to see him at the White House.[29]

Wilson was particularly concerned about Grant's policies, because the Republican party had sustained severe losses in the fall elections of 1874. For the first time since the Civil War, Democrats had won control of the House of Representatives. They also elected the governor of Massachusetts. The vice-president had always taken election defeats as personal blows, and he was clearly upset at these recent Republican losses. When asked for his evaluation of the reasons for the election results, Wilson blamed Grant's apparent desire for reelection in 1876, stating that he would oppose the election of any man to a third term, "were he the best who ever lived." He also believed that workers thrown out of jobs by the

[28] David Miller Dewitt, *The Impeachment and Trial of Andrew Johnson* (New York, 1903), 624; William H. Crook, *Through Five Administrations* (New York, 1910), 150.

[29] Merriam, *Bowles,* II, 273; New York *Times,* Nov. 11, 12, 1874; Theodore Clarke Smith, *The Life and Letters of James Abram Garfield* (2 vols.; New Haven, Conn., 1925), I, 520; New York *Tribune,* April 16, 1875.

panic and ensuing depression that began in 1873 had voted against the Republican party. He told Wendell Phillips that the Republicans had permitted their opponents to "start the greenback cry" and thus win key states like Pennsylvania, where people blamed contraction of the currency for their economic troubles.[30]

The 1874 elections confirmed Wilson's belief that in order to win in 1876, the Republicans would have to win back the Liberals who had abandoned it in 1872. In January, 1875, the vice-president used the columns of a leading Liberal journal, the *Springfield Republican,* to urge Republicans to "throw the doors wide open for the return of those who voted for Mr. Greeley." Wilson realized that to bring the dissidents back to the party, he would have to recognize their criticisms of Grant's programs. In particular, he knew the Liberals, along with many other Northerners, were becoming more and more critical of Grant's support of Negro and carpetbag governments in the South; they wanted restoration of home rule there.

The vice-president reviewed the results of radical reconstruction with mixed feelings. He insisted that the national Republican party should not be blamed for the misdeeds of individual carpetbaggers in the South. He admitted that their mistakes hurt the Republican party that had helped put them in power, but in light of Southern brutalities toward the freedmen, he denied that the party's policies and programs had been ill-advised. In private, he agreed with Wendell Phillips, who contended that the Southern states should have been held as territories and governed by federal officials until a "different mood" could have been detected among Southern whites. Wilson told Phillips, however, that such a program would have been politically impossible.[31]

Wilson was concerned lest Democratic victories in 1874 encourage the white South to launch a "counter-revolution." He urged the old abolitionists to use their influence to protect the blacks. Yet he

[30] New York *Tribune,* Nov. 10, 1874; Wendell Phillips, "The Outlook," *North American Review,* CXXVII (1878), 102.

[31] Article in *Springfield Republican* quoted in New York *Tribune,* Jan. 19, 1875, and in Boston *Morning Journal,* same date; Phillips quoted in *North American Review,* CXXVIII (1879), 261.

still believed that equalitarian legislation could be enforced only by "weapons of moral warfare." He continued to hope that by championing a "broad, wise, and magnanimous policy" toward the South, ex-Whigs could be separated from the ranks of white extremists. Upon the success of such an effort, said Wilson, depended "peace in the South, the blotting out of divisions on the line of race, the advancement of real reconstruction, permanent Southern prosperity, and the success of the Republican party." Wilson drew encouragement from Liberal Republicans who were pressing for the same kind of program. When a good friend and Liberal Republican urged him to visit the South and examine the situation for himself, the vice-president decided to go.[32]

Early in May, Wilson left on a six-week Southern tour. Ostensibly, the trip was for relaxation and to give him a chance to visit the place of his son's death. Although he denied rumors that his trip was "to advertise himself" for the presidency, he managed to make twenty-nine speeches and attend many receptions and dinners. Cities in his path offered Wilson a cordial welcome; elected officials, ex-Confederate officers and generals, and former state governors feted him. The vice-president of the country might well expect such treatment, but the effect upon the impressionable Wilson was to convince him that the policy he had already begun to advocate was the right one. Receiving apparent acceptance and respect from the remnants of an aristocracy he had once denounced seemed to erode the sense of social discrimination he always carried with him. To be wined and dined by Southerners only encouraged his efforts to erase the last barriers to sectional harmony.[33]

Wilson returned home prepared to speak authoritatively about Southern affairs. He assured the people of the North that he had

[32] Wilson to Garrison, Dec. 17, 1874, Boston Public Library; *Centennial Anniversary of the Pennsylvania Society for Promoting the Abolition of Slavery* (Philadelphia, 1875), 7-8, 35-37; New York *Independent,* Jan. 14, 1875; Cassius Clay to Wilson, March 17, 1871, and John Cochrane to Wilson, Feb. 28, 1875, Wilson MSS, Library of Congress.

[33] On Wilson's Southern trip, see New York *Independent,* May 13, 1875; New York *Times,* June 6, 1875; and Boston *Journal,* May 3-June 2, especially May 3, 6, 8, 10, 17; Wilson to Mrs. Claflin, June 10, 1875, Claflin MSS.

found a good deal of progress in race relations in most sections of the old Confederacy. He renewed his plea that Republicans seek the support of the "three hundred thousand white conservatives" in the South who had never supported the Democrats. He was sure that if he had his full health he could win them over in ninety days. "I know these men," he insisted. "I have talked with them down there, and know how they feel." To attract them to the Republican fold, Wilson suggested the same policy that future President Rutherford B. Hayes would apply in 1877: appoint a Southern ex-Whig to the cabinet and offer the business-minded conservatives of the South economic assistance.[34]

Wilson's opinions favoring liberal treatment of Republican dissidents and Southern whites received much favorable attention. Frequently Wilson granted interviews to newspapermen and worked hard to gain a reputation as a man who could heal the wounds in both the Republican party and the nation.[35] Thurlow Weed visited Wilson in the fall and found "his whole heart was enlisted" in becoming president. In October, however, his doctor finally convinced him to lay aside his ambition in order to preserve his health.[36]

The conflict between Wilson's weakened body and his thriving ambition might have produced the paralytic attack which struck him later in the month. His speech was again affected. He managed to say: "I have received my mortal blow; but I greatly desire to remain a few years longer to finish my work." He desperately yearned to complete his book, which he hoped would "live when I am in my

[34] New York *Tribune*, June 5, 28, 1875; New York *Times*, June 5, 1875; Boston *Journal*, June 7, 25, 28, July 2, 1875; New York *Independent*, July 1, 1875. On Wilson's hopes to attract Southern Whigs by offering one of them a cabinet post, see New York *Times*, Nov. 28, 1875; Natick *Bulletin*, Dec. 17, 1875.

[35] *Springfield Republican* quoted in New York *Herald*, Jan. 24, 1875; New York *Times*, Jan. 18, 19, 20, 1875; New York *Independent*, Jan. 28, July 1, 29, 1875; Boston *Morning Journal*, Jan. 20, 23, June 5, 1875. For clippings from some dozen newspapers referring to Wilson's letter, see New York *Herald*, Jan. 24, 1875.

[36] Boston *Morning Journal*, May 20, 21, Sept. 1, Oct. 5, Nov. 25, 1875; Hoar, *Reminiscences*, I, 218; C. F. Adams Diary, Oct. 5, 1875.

grave."[37] Perhaps that great desire explained his rapid recovery, for he left for Washington early in November. On November 10, he was struck with yet another severe paralytic shock. Doctors put him to bed in the vice-president's room in the Capitol. For the moment his health appeared to rally; by November 18, he was able to sleep without medication and could receive visitors. On November 20, he talked to a reporter from the New York *Times* about the attentions he had received from President and Mrs. Grant, which called the reporter's attention to the fact that Wilson had no family to minister to him. His best friends, the Claflins, were touring Europe, and by the time Mrs. Claflin heard of Wilson's condition and had written to him, he was gone.[38]

Perhaps Wilson's death was hastened by his bare, plain room in the Capitol. It seemed as though in order to die he had returned to the scene of his greatest accomplishments. On November 21 he was greatly distressed to learn of the death of Senator Orris Ferry of Connecticut and remarked that "that makes eighty-three dead with whom I have sat in the Senate." Wilson spent a restless night. Shortly after seven o'clock the following morning, with only a nurse in attendance, he died. His brother, Samuel H. Colbath, the door-keeper of the Senate, did not arrive until eight.[39]

The country grieved Wilson's passing. In January, William P. Robinson commented that "the popular feeling of sorrow for General Wilson's decease lasts longer than such feeling generally does for eminent men. He was so universally known, that this is not a matter of surprise." Some of his former political opponents, like Richard Henry Dana, could find no words of praise for Wilson even

[37] New York *Independent,* Oct. 14, 1875; Natick *Bulletin,* April 22, 1892; Wilson to Mrs. Claflin, Aug. 9, 1875, Claflin MSS.

[38] The Boston *Morning Journal* has complete accounts of Wilson's illness and his progress through the month of November; New York *Times,* Nov. 23, 1875; Mrs. Claflin to Henry Wilson, Nov. 21, 1875, Claflin MSS.

[39] Natick *Bulletin,* Oct. 26, 1906; April 5, 1912; Boston *Morning Journal,* Nov. 23, 1875; New York *Independent,* Dec. 23, 1875. The physician who performed an autopsy on Wilson concluded that he died from a brain disease that affected nerves, respiration, and circulation. See William A. Hammond, "On the Cause of Vice-President Wilson's Death," *Boston Medical and Surgical Journal,* Dec. 16, 1875, pp. 1-14.

at his death; but many more agreed with Charles Francis Adams, who admitted that despite his earlier antipathy for Wilson, "I did feel a revival of kindly feeling which makes me now regret his departure." Cities and towns in Massachusetts passed a flood of respectful resolutions, the national armed forces made their motions of respect, and the Union Leagues of New York and Philadelphia adopted eulogistic resolves. The *Army and Navy Journal* observed that the army had lost a friend to whom it was more indebted than to any other man "in the legislative branch of government." Even in the South people observed his death with a variety of formalities.[40]

Many journalists were struck by the death of one of the last antislavery Republicans. Although editors quarreled about the quality of Wilson's statesmanship, most agreed that his legislative abilities, his perception of popular sentiment, and his devotion to the antislavery cause and the Negro had been unparalleled. They praised him for his triumph over obstacles of poor education, poverty, and insignificant family connections. To them he was an excellent example of the success available to the common man. Commentators praised his integrity and honesty and noted that he died without the wealth that many another politician had acquired. Forgotten now were Wilson's moments of weakness, his proneness to compromise, his vaulting ambition, and his frequent tendency to subordinate principles to politics. Instead, observers recalled his service to his state and his country, and his concern for the welfare of all classes, rich or poor, black or white.[41]

After Wilson was buried, the development he most feared while he was alive took place. He was forgotten. Several months before his death he had predicted that "no statue will keep my form or face for friends to sometimes recall my name." His aged mother-in-law erected a large stone in her own memory at the cemetery five years before she died, but she was content to place a small marker at the

[40] Robinson, ed., *Warrington,* 400-401; Shapiro, *Dana,* 184; C. F. Adams Diary, Nov. 22, 1875; Natick *Bulletin,* Nov. 26, 1875; *Army and Navy Journal,* Nov. 27, 1875, p. 253.

[41] New York *Times,* Nov. 23, 1875; Boston *Morning Journal,* quoting various newspapers on Wilson, Nov. 24, 27, 1875.

grave of her son-in-law. In the vice-president's room in Washington friends placed a tablet honoring Wilson, and others took up a collection to put his portrait in Boston's Faneuil Hall. A group of officers established a fund for a marker honoring "Henry Wilson, the Soldier's Friend," which was stationed on the grounds of the Soldier's Home in Washington. However, periodic attempts through the next half-century in Natick to raise funds for a monument at Wilson's grave failed. The town was also reluctant to listen to friends who requested Natick to observe Wilson's birthday.[42]

Wilson had always hoped that if his memory was not perpetuated in bronze or stone, he would be remembered for his contributions to history. Yet within two years of his death, when a group of old Massachusetts Free-Soilers held a reunion, one of Wilson's friends noted that "the prominent speakers, Charles Francis Adams, Amos Tuck, E. Rockwood Hoar and the others made only the merest allusion to Henry Wilson, and a stranger to the facts would have gone from the dinner with the impression that he, the foremost man in the movement . . . was little more than a small dog limping along after the wagon which carried the band." It seemed as if Wilson's associates, who had once been jealous of his prominence in the movement, were now ignoring his contributions.[43]

Wilson's greatest concern, his three-volume history, was finished the year after his death by his friend, Samuel Hunt. The tone of most of the third volume reflected Wilson's conviction that ultimately, given the effect of time and Christian teaching, the legislative standards of justice and equality established by the reconstruction Congresses could be achieved. The last two hundred pages of the

[42] Wilson to Mrs. Claflin, Aug. 9, 1875, Claflin MSS; Natick *Bulletin,* Dec. 3, 1875, Sept. 2, 1881, Feb. 14, 1902; "Report of Librarian," American Antiquarian Society *Proceedings,* XV (1902-03), 178-79; undated circular, entitled "To the Friends of Henry Wilson," in Rutherford B. Hayes Library, concerning subscription of funds to pay for portrait in Faneuil Hall; on the monument on grounds of Soldier's Home, see materials of "executive committee of Henry Wilson Monument Association," dated Sept. 30, 1878, in the Quartermaster General's consolidated File, War Department, National Archives.

[43] J. B. Mann, recalling the reunion in 1877, quoted in Natick *Bulletin,* March 17, 1899.

third volume, on the other hand, reflected a rather basic pessimism about the future of the country under the reconstruction amendments. These were the pages Reverend Samuel Hunt finished after Wilson died, and they revealed the opinions of the minister rather than the senator. Hunt discussed the fact that in 1875, ten years after the end of the war, violence, oppression, and prejudice still held sway in the South. The continuing outrages against Negroes resulted from "causes that lie too deep to be reached by law—from a disease for which there is as yet no adequate remedy."[44] For Hunt, the conclusion was inescapable. "The history of slavery and the Slave Power has been but the history of human nature . . . and though the one has been destroyed and the other dethroned, the cause, the disease, still remains." In the future as well as in the past, wrote Hunt, there will "rankle and burn in the human heart the same passions, the same love of 'power and pelf'; . . . there will be those who 'fear not God nor regard man,' . . . who will join hand in hand to oppress the poor and circumvent the good."[45]

It was unfortunate that Wilson was unable to write his own conclusion to his massive history, for it was a monument to a life time of constant struggling and labor. Each volume revealed a prodigious amount of research and investigation, and despite Wilson's obvious biases, many of his conclusions and characterizations were drawn with restraint and fairness. Certainly he grossly exaggerated the evidence of a Slave Power conspiracy, yet many of his contemporaries shared his conviction that it existed. In light of Wilson's desire that his contributions to the demise of the Slave Power be remembered, it is not surprising that his name appears quite frequently in the pages of his history. Yet if the record gave Wilson too much attention, it still stands as a fitting and impressive reply to those who would deprecate his efforts or forget his contributions to freeing the slave and making him a citizen. For, despite Wilson's frailties as an individual, his contributions to the war effort, his party, and his country were great.

[44] Wilson, *Slave Power,* III, 696.
[45] *Ibid.,* III, 723-24.

16

Wilson in Retrospect

Throughout Henry Wilson's rather complex career, one thought, which he repeated again and again to the point of dulling the ears of his listeners, supplied a thread of continuity to his political perambulations and gave meaning to his life. "The same influences that go to keep down the rights of the poor black man," he constantly reiterated, "bear down and oppress the poor white laboring man." In that statement Wilson conveyed a conviction that many others in his generation shared. Some, like Abraham Lincoln, could express the thought in more compelling terms, but none believed more deeply in its truth. Driven by a sense of the misfortunes of his own early life and isolated from the centers of power and privilege within Massachusetts, Wilson intuitively sympathized with the underprivileged and downtrodden.

Wilson was eager to strike a blow against slavery and for freedom, but he was also searching for a way to make his mark in the world. As soon as possible he devoted his life to politics, for he found that seeking, obtaining, and maintaining public office helped to ease an insatiable ambition. He craved recognition and respect and lived in constant fear that his accomplishments would not be duly appreciated. Political activity also gave Wilson a sense of personal worth and supplied him with a role, an identity, that he could have developed in no other way. He obtained a great pleasure from arranging bargains and compromises, upsetting and rearranging coalitions, and fancied himself as adept in creating, strengthening, and operating the machinery of political parties. He enjoyed being a politician for the excitement and sense of power that it provided him.

Yet Henry Wilson never came to regard election to political office, and the victories of his political party, as ends in themselves. Political power to him provided the means whereby he could implement moral principles. He never accepted Garrison's assertion that political activity corrupted moral ideals. Instead, through legislation he strove to secure the liberty and equality of the downtrodden and thereby to assure the rights and dignity of all men. The impressive body of egalitarian legislation that Wilson helped to produce in Boston and Washington bears testimony to the strength of his conviction.

In devoting himself to a lifetime in politics, Wilson willingly accepted its limitations. He would not have quarreled with the observation made by John F. Kennedy, who served Massachusetts in the Senate one hundred years after Wilson: "Politics and legislation are not matters for inflexible principles or unattainable ideals."[1] Ambitious for higher office and eager for party success, Wilson was acutely sensitive to the vagaries of public opinion and accepted the legislative philosophy that half a loaf was better than none. Although as a Conscience Whig, Free-Soiler, and coalitionist, Wilson challenged the power of the economic and social elite of Massachusetts, he was able to come to terms with men like Amos Lawrence after the Republican party was formed and he thought it needed their assistance. As long as he was free to pursue humanitarian causes, Wilson showed little interest in economic legislation, except to serve the material interests of his state. Such a policy enabled him to maintain the support of Massachusetts capitalists and strengthen his hold on his Senate seat.

While Wilson sought to satisfy the needs of Boston industrialists, he also maintained his close ties with Bay State abolitionists, who exerted a constant pressure upon him to steer close to the principles which they held in common. Without such pressure Wilson probably would have succumbed much more easily to political expediency. He

---

[1] John F. Kennedy, *Profiles in Courage* (New York, 1955), 4.

was eager to strengthen the national Republican party and maintain its hold on the government in Washington, and as every election approached he was prone to muffle ideas that might endanger popular support. Such machinations irritated and even infuriated his supporters, but none of them ever doubted the durability of his convictions. Even one of his bitterest critics, Charles Francis Adams, admitted that Wilson's moral sense kept him from becoming a demagogue.[2]

Given Wilson's penchant for seeking the middle way, it is hard to classify him as a radical in politics. He does exemplify quite clearly the constructive relationship between moral absolutists like Garrison, who disdained politics, and the politicians who helped to approximate the absolutes.[3] Henry Wilson never denied Garrison's assertion that abolitionist agitators had helped to create the attitudes that elected politicians like him to office. In return, Wilson, while alternately showing hurt and anger at the criticisms the abolitionists showered upon him, sought manfully to realize their aims through legislation. One perceptive observer, although prone to exaggerate, thus compared Wendell Phillips and Wilson: "Phillips is the Sheridan of the reform Army, who beats up the enemy, draws his fire, and unmasks him; Wilson is the Thomas of that Army, who collects the troops, organizes, brings up supplies, and is *ready* before he will order the attack."[4]

Wilson does belong to the group of Civil War radicals in Congress who demanded an immediate and outright emancipation of slaves as a total, absolute, and final solution to the problem of bondage in the United States.[5] At times in his career, Wilson appeared to be more

[2] Adams quoted in Boston *Morning Journal*, Nov. 29, 1875.

[3] Two recent studies of abolitionists have emphasized the manner in which the moral agitators influenced the direction of politics: Louis B. Filler, *The Crusade Against Slavery, 1830-1860* (New York, 1960) and James M. McPherson, *The Struggle for Equality* (Princeton, N. J., 1964).

[4] Jesse H. Jones, quoted in Natick *Bulletin*, Nov. 5, 1870. Jones was a Congregational minister in Natick.

[5] For a useful characterization of the radicals, see T. Harry Williams, "Lincoln and the Radicals: An Essay in Civil War History and Historiography," in Grady McWhiney, ed., *Grant, Lee, Lincoln and the Radicals*

concerned with destroying the power of the arrogant and domineering white Southern planter class than he was about rescuing the Negro whom the planter enslaved. He talked little of slavery, but he spoke much of the Slave Power. He thought in terms of generalities and abstractions and referred to the system of oppression rather than to individual oppressors or victims. Consequently, he bore no hatred or malice toward slaveholders as individuals, and once slavery was destroyed, he was more anxious to elevate the condition of the freedmen than eager to humiliate their former owners. He parted with some of his radical associates in Congress in his willingness to appropriate money to compensate slaveholders for their loss and thus ease the process of emancipation. Although at times he indulged in passionate outbursts against the South, he never demonstrated the vindictiveness of men like Benjamin Wade, Thaddeus Stevens, and Zachariah Chandler toward the rebels.

It is also difficult to define Wilson's approach to problems of reconstruction as radical. His contemporaries called him a radical, and Wilson regarded himself as one, for championing Negro suffrage as well as civil rights. Yet his course on the voting issue was tortuous. He was prepared to accept any number of compromises short of full and complete manhood suffrage and only moved on to the Fifteenth Amendment when political circumstances seemed to warrant it. In keeping with his lack of vindictiveness toward the South, he refused to join those who demanded severe punishment for leading Confederates. He resisted disfranchisement of white Southerners and worked to remove such political disabilities as rapidly as possible. He lent no support to Stevens's scheme of confiscating plantations and redistributing the land to freedmen. His position on that matter reflected his characteristic indifference to the significance of the economic organization of society and also stemmed from his conviction that political opinion in the North would never sustain such a project.

(Evanston, Ill., 1964), 100-101. Using the distinctions provided by Hans L. Trefousse, one might classify Wilson as a "practical radical," one who was sensitive to the political possibilities in any given situation and was ready to compromise in order to approximate his goals. See Trefousse, *Radicals,* 339.

Wilson's intense preoccupation with what programs the people would or would not support kept him from advocating any prolonged military occupation of the South and encouraged him to seek the early readmission of the ex-Confederate states to the Union. Wade, Chandler, and Stevens all disapproved of Wilson's leniency toward the South, and Charles Sumner took issue with his colleague's compromising approach to questions of suffrage. All these men were considered radicals by their contemporaries, and the term has similarly been applied to them by later observers. Their disagreements with Wilson were many and varied.

Although Wilson voted for strong federal intervention in the South to protect Negroes exercising the vote, he could never accept the position of some of his colleagues: that the states should cease to function as important political units. Wilson once heard his friend Sumner speak on the need for completely subordinating the states to the central government in order that the freed Negroes could be more fully protected; he left the auditorium muttering that "the states are something, still."[6] His constitutional conservatism stemmed from his own struggle during the Civil War to protect from federal encroachment the prerogatives of the governor of Massachusetts in raising troops, and also from his sensitivity to the fact that the principle of states' rights drew much support from the North as well as the South.

Rather than abolishing states, the reconstruction program that the Massachusetts senator sought to defend rested on a minimum of federal intervention in the South. Wilson clearly wanted to insure the Negro's equal rights before the law and present him with at least limited opportunity to exercise the suffrage. Once these principles were established in law, he hoped that individuals could be encouraged through appeals to conscience and morality to respect them. If peace, justice, and racial harmony were to come to the South, he believed, Southern whites would have to play a major role in the process. After Wilson's death in 1875, John R. Lynch, a black congressman from Mississippi, praised the Massachusetts politician's

[6] Pierce, *Sumner,* IV, 335n.

efforts to discourage formation of parties in the South along racial lines. According to Lynch, had Wilson's views on reconstruction prevailed, the South would have been prosperous and flourishing, rather than riven by race antagonism and violence.[7]

Probably Wilson's lenient attitude toward the South, his desire for Southern white support for reconstruction, and his unwillingness to endorse prolonged military occupation left him an easy mark for white Southerners hopeful of convincing him that they were ready to assume responsibility for maintaining order and establishing justice in their own states. Thus at an early date he lent support to the kind of settlement of sectional issues implemented by President Rutherford B. Hayes in 1877. He did not live to see such a policy of reconciliation fail as completely as radical reconstruction to bring racial harmony and equality to the South and to the nation.

Wilson's vacillation between a reliance on moral suasion and governmental coercion, his efforts to bring about far-reaching social change without challenging the existing political, economic, and constitutional system, and his alternating mood of pessimism and optimism about the future of race relations within the United States reflected the struggle of the whole nation to reach a satisfactory solution to the problems created by slavery and the Civil War.[8] Wilson and his fellow Republicans were members of the first generation of Americans to probe the dimensions of racial injustice which the nation was still unable to resolve one hundred years later. Many white Americans opposed Wilson's efforts or viewed them with doubt and skepticism, but the Negroes who in 1875 accompanied his body from Washington to Boston testified to the strength of his conscience and the significance of his accomplishments. Frederick Douglass, noting that for the first time in American history Negroes served as pallbearers for a vice-president, considered Wilson to be

[7] Lynch quoted in *Memorial Addresses,* 130-31.

[8] Most abolitionists were also uncertain as to whether to depend upon coercion or moral suasion to change patterns of race relations in America. See James M. McPherson, "Grant or Greeley? The Abolitionist Dilemma in the Election of 1872," *American Historical Review,* LXXI (Oct., 1965), and "Coercion or Conciliation? Abolitionists Debate President Hayes' Southern Policy," *New England Quarterly,* XXXIX (Dec., 1966).

"among the foremost friends of the colored race in this country." Robert Purvis, another leading Negro abolitionist and civil rights advocate, declared that "we are more indebted to [Henry Wilson and Charles Sumner] than to any men in the national councils for all that now enables the colored race to feel that they have a country to love, and a flag which they can conscientiously honor and defend."[9]

[9] Douglass quotation is from Frederick Douglass, *Life and Times of Frederick Douglass* (Collier Book edition; New York, 1962), 418-19; Purvis quoted in *Centennial Anniversary*, 29.

Bibliography

Although Henry Wilson was an active correspondent, not many of his letters have survived. The Wilson materials in Natick, Massachusetts, are disappointingly small, and the collection of papers in the Library of Congress contains less than one hundred items, consisting chiefly of incoming correspondence. Fortunately I was able to locate a number of Wilson's letters scattered in other depositories from California to Maine. The greatest number of manuscripts are in various collections in the Massachusetts Historical Society and in the Sumner papers in the Houghton Library at Harvard University. Most of these letters deal with political matters; a few useful Wilson manuscripts of a more personal nature are available in the papers of William Claflin and William Lloyd Garrison.

Much manuscript material exists for tracing Wilson's pre-Civil War career, but it must be used with care. The diary of Charles Francis Adams is indispensable; however Adams viewed Wilson's political activity with considerable distaste. The same can be said for John G. Palfrey and Edward Everett, whose papers are also quite useful. William Schouler, Charles Sumner, and Theodore Parker looked more favorably upon Wilson, and their papers help to balance the impressions given by Palfrey and Adams.

Manuscript sources are thinner for Wilson's career after his election to the Senate. The papers of Amos Lawrence and John Andrew provide some useful material, but the chief manuscript source for this stage of Wilson's career is the voluminous correspondence of Charles Sumner. His papers are particularly useful in offering an impression of how some of Wilson's constituents viewed him. In Congress Wilson rarely missed a roll call and expressed himself on almost every measure that came before the Senate; this activity is documented in the *Congressional Globe*. The files of the Adjutant General's Office, War Department, contain a number of Wilson's queries and criticisms concerning the administration of the conscription law that he helped to write. Wilson's letters in the records of the

Freedman's Bureau and in the Seward and Howard collections reveal the extent of his concern for the former slaves during the War and Reconstruction periods.

Several newspapers are also very helpful in tracing Wilson's public career. His own newspaper, the *Emancipator and Republican,* is indispensable in covering the years 1848-1850, which were a critical period for Wilson. Wilson recognized the importance of journalists in building his image, and he cultivated friendships with editors and reporters. Included among his friends were publishers or editors of such newspapers as the Boston *Atlas,* the Boston *Commonwealth,* the Boston *Evening Telegraph,* and the New York *Independent.* All of these papers carried considerable information about Wilson's activities. During the period 1863-1875, the *Commonwealth,* which spoke for the radical wing of the Republican party, remained rather critical of Wilson's moderation. The more conservative Boston *Advertiser* was also cool towards Wilson and did not support his reelections to the Senate. The Boston *Transcript's* editors were much more favorably disposed towards him. One journalist friend and critic of Wilson, William S. Robinson, contributed many perceptive observations about him to the New York *Tribune* and *Springfield Republican.* Some of his columns can be found in a book edited by his wife, entitled *Warrington Pen-Portraits.* Finally, the files of the Natick *Citizen* and Natick *Bulletin* provide a large number of personal reminiscences about Wilson by people who knew him well.

Wilson's own writings, particularly his *History of the Rise and Fall of the Slave Power in America,* are the source of dependable information about his views and activities. Biographies of Wilson written by J. B. Mann and by Elias Nason and Thomas Russell contain information not obtainable elsewhere. Both books are quite uncritical of their subject, but both are useful works by men who were well acquainted with Wilson. Another friend and occasional critic of Wilson, Edward L. Pierce, included a substantial amount of material relating to Wilson in his four-volume *Memoir and Letters of Charles Sumner.*

A number of scholarly monographs and biographies illuminate

various aspects of Wilson's career. David Donald's second volume of his biography of Sumner appeared too late to be utilized, but the first volume is a useful source for material about Wilson. Frank Otto Gatell's biography of John Gorham Palfrey, Martin Duberman's of Charles Francis Adams, Fred Harvey Harrington's of Nathaniel Banks, Harold Schwartz's of Samuel Gridley Howe, Samuel Shapiro's of Richard Henry Dana, Jr., and Kinley J. Brauer's *Cotton versus Conscience*—all are valuable for following Wilson's career in state politics. Henry G. Pearson's two volume biography of John A. Andrew is also extremely helpful. In tracing Wilson's relationship to the conscription bill, Fred Shannon's *Organization and Administration of the Union Army* is useful. The works of Eric McKitrick and John and Lawanda Cox are of great assistance in providing insight into the struggle between Congress and President Johnson over Reconstruction, and W. R. Brock's study of the same subject offers a number of excellent perceptions of the radical wing of the Republican party.

The following bibliography does not constitute a comprehensive list of all materials used in the writing of this book. Sources which I have utilized only once or twice are cited in full in the footnotes.

A. *Manuscript Collections*

Boston Public Library, Rare Book Room, Boston, Mass. Antislavery collection, including William Lloyd Garrison MSS; Samuel J. May, Jr., MSS; and miscellaneous MSS.

Bowdoin College Library, Brunswick, Me. O. O. Howard MSS.

Brown University Library, Providence, R. I. Eli Thayer MSS, and miscellaneous MSS.

Henry E. Huntington Library and Art Gallery, San Marino, Cal. Miscellaneous MSS.

Historical Society of Pennsylvania, Philadelphia. Henry Carey MSS; Salmon P. Chase MSS; and miscellaneous MSS.

Kansas State Historical Society, Topeka. Charles Robinson MSS.

Library of Congress, Washington, D. C. Benjamin F. Butler MSS;
Zachariah Chandler MSS; Salmon P. Chase MSS; Schuyler
Colfax MSS; Henry L. Dawes MSS; Hamilton Fish MSS;
Giddings-Julian MSS; Robert Todd Lincoln MSS; Henry
Wilson MSS.

Massachusetts Historical Society, Boston. John A. Andrew MSS;
Richard Henry Dana, Jr., MSS; Edward Everett MSS; Samuel
Gridley Howe MSS; Amos A. Lawrence MSS; Horace Mann
MSS; Marcus Morton MSS; Theodore Parker MSS; William
Schouler MSS.

Morse Institute, Natick, Mass. Miscellaneous Wilson MSS.

Natick Historical Society Museum, South Natick, Mass. Miscellaneous Wilson MSS.

New York Historical Society, New York, N. Y. Miscellaneous
MSS.

Ohio Historical Society, Columbus. Joshua Giddings MSS.

Rutherford B. Hayes Library, Fremont, Ohio. William Claflin
MSS, and miscellaneous MSS.

State Historical Society of Wisconsin, Madison. Microfilm copy of
the Adams Family MSS.

University of Kansas, The Kenneth Spencer Research Library,
Lawrence. Miscellaneous MSS.

University of Rochester Library, Rochester, N.Y. William Henry
Seward MSS.

University of Syracuse, The George Arents Research Library,
Syracuse, N. Y. Gerrit Smith MSS.

Yale University Library, New Haven, Conn. Samuel Bowles MSS,
and miscellaneous MSS.

B. *War Department Manuscripts in the National Archives, Washington, D. C.*

Adjutant General's Office.

Adjutant General's Office, Bureau for Colored Troops.

Office of the Provost Marshal.

Office of the Secretary of War.

Headquarters of the Army.

Bureau of Refugees, Freedmen, and Abandoned Lands.

C. *Public Documents*

Massachusetts:

House Journal, 1841-1850. Manuscript in Massachusetts State Library, Boston.

House *Legislative Documents, 1841, 1842, 1846, 1850.*

Official Report of the Debates and Proceedings in the State Convention Assembled May 4, 1853, to Revise and Amend the Constitution of the Commonwealth of Massachusetts. 2 vols. Boston, Mass.

Senate Journal. 1844-1852. Manuscript in Massachusetts State Library, Boston.

Senate *Legislative Documents, 1845.*

United States: Congress

Congressional Globe. 1855-1873.

House Report No. 182. 34th Cong., 1st sess. 1856. Vol. 1.

House Report No. 77. 42nd Cong., 3rd sess. 1873. Vol. 2.

Senate Report No. 278. 36 Cong., 3rd sess. 1859.

Senate Report No. 519. 42nd Cong., 3rd sess. 1873. Vol. 3.

War of the Rebellion . . . Official Records of the Union and Confederate Armies. 128 vols. Washington, D. C., 1880-1901.

D. *Newspapers*

Boston *Atlas,* 1840-1855.

Boston *Bee,* 1855.

Boston *Commonwealth,* 1850-1854, 1862-1875.

Boston *Courier,* 1844, 1860.

Boston *Daily Advertiser,* 1860-1861, 1866-1867, 1870-1872.

(Boston) *Emancipator and Republican,* 1848-1850.

Boston *Evening Telegraph,* 1854-1856.

(Boston) *Liberator,* 1841-1846.

Boston *Post,* 1845, 1855, 1870.

Boston *Transcript,* 1855-1856, 1864-1866.

Boston *Traveller,* 1852.

Lowell *Daily Courier,* 1845-1846.

Natick *Bulletin,* 1870-1912.

Natick *Citizen,* 1869-1884.

Natick *Observer,* 1856-1861.

Natick *Times,* 1865-1868.

New York *Herald,* 1855, 1864-1867.

New York *Independent,* 1867-1875.

New York *Times,* 1856-1875.

New York *Tribune,* 1848, 1855-1867, 1875.

E. *Published Works of Henry Wilson*

Address to Constituents. Boston, 1853.

Aggressions of the Slave Power. Washington, D. C., 1860.

A Contribution to History. Edwin M. Stanton: His Character and Public Services on the Eve of the Rebellion. With Jeremiah S. Black. Easton, Pa., 1871.

The Death of Slavery Is the Life of the Nation. Washington, D.C., 1864.

Democratic Leaders for Disunion. New York, 1860.

The Draft. n. p., 1863.

Executive Patronage. Washington, D. C., 1866.

Father Mathew, the Temperance Apostle. New York, 1873.

History of the Antislavery Measures of . . . Congress. Boston, 1864.

History of the Reconstruction Measures of . . . Congress. Chicago, 1868.

History of the Rise and Fall of the Slave Power in America. 3 vols. Boston, 1872-1877.

How Ought Working Men to Vote in the Coming Election? Boston, 1860.

Letter of Henry Wilson to the Honorable Caleb Cushing. Washington, D. C., 1860.

"Military Measures of Congress." In Frank Moore, ed., *The Rebellion Record,* X, 1-88. New York, 1867.

"The New Departure." *Atlantic Monthly,* XXVII (January, 1871), 104-120.

Position of John Bell and His Supporters. Boston, 1860.

The Relations of Churches and Ministers to the Temperance Cause. Boston, 1870.

Stand by the Republican Colors. n. p., 1872.

F. *Unpublished Theses and Dissertations*

Anderson, Godfrey T. "The Slavery Issue in Massachusetts Politics from the Compromise of 1850 to the Outbreak of the Civil War." Ph.D. dissertation, University of Chicago, 1944.

Bean, William G. "The Transformation of Parties in Massachusetts . . . from 1848 to 1860." Ph.D. dissertation, Harvard University, 1922.

Kenney, Carol Jean. "An Analysis of Political Alignments in Massachusetts as Revealed in the Constitutional Convention of 1853." M.A. thesis, Smith College, 1951.

Loubert, J. Daniel. "The Orientation of Henry Wilson, 1812-1856." Ph.D. dissertation, Boston University, 1956.

G. *Published Books and Articles*

Ambler, Charles H. *Francis H. Pierpont.* Chapel Hill, N. C., 1937.

Bacon, Oliver N. *History of Natick*. Boston, 1856.

Barnes, Thurlow Weed. *Memoir of Thurlow Weed*. Boston, 1884.

Beale, Howard K., ed. *The Diary of Gideon Welles*. 3 vols. New York, 1960.

Bean, W. G. "Puritan Versus Celt, 1850-1860." *New England Quarterly*, VII (1934), 70-89.

Bird, Francis William: A Biographical Sketch. [By his children.] Boston, 1897.

Blaine, James G. *Twenty Years of Congress*. 2 vols. Norwich, Conn., 1884.

Boutwell, George S. *Reminiscences of Sixty Years in Public Affairs*. 2 vols. New York, 1902.

Bowen, James L. *Massachusetts in the War, 1861-1865*. Springfield, Mass., 1889.

Brauer, Kinley J. *Cotton Versus Conscience: Massachusetts Whig Politics and Southwestern Expansionism, 1843-1848*. Lexington, Ky., 1967.

Brock, W. R. *An American Crisis: Congress and Reconstruction, 1865-1867*. New York, 1963.

Brooks, Noah. *Washington in Lincoln's Time*. New York, 1895.

Centennial Anniversary of the Pennsylvania Society for Promoting the Abolition of Slavery. Philadelphia, 1875.

Chase, Salmon P. "Diary and Correspondence of Salmon P. Chase." *Annual Report* of the American Historical Association, 1902. 2 vols. Washington, D. C., 1903.

Congdon, Charles T. *Reminiscences of a Journalist*. Boston, 1880.

Cowdin, E. C. *A Tribute to the Memory of Henry Wilson*. New York, 1875.

Cox, Lawanda, and John H. Cox. *Politics, Principles, and Preju-dice, 1865-1866: Dilemma of Reconstruction America.* Glen-coe, Ill., 1963.

Darling, Arthur B. *Political Changes in Massachusetts, 1824-1848.* New Haven, Conn., 1925.

Dennett, Tyler, ed. *Lincoln and the Civil War in the Diaries and Letters of John Hay.* New York, 1939.

Donald, David. *Charles Sumner and the Coming of the Civil War.* New York, 1960.

Duberman, Martin. *Charles Francis Adams, 1807-1886.* Boston, 1961.

Eckenrode, Hamilton J. *The Political History of Virginia During the Reconstruction.* Baltimore, Md., 1904.

Forney, John W. *Anecdotes of Public Men.* 2 vols. New York, 1873.

Garrison, Wendell Phillips, and Frances Jackson Garrison. *William Lloyd Garrison, 1805-1877.* 4 vols. New York, 1889.

Gatell, Frank Otto. *John Gorham Palfrey.* Cambridge, Mass., 1963.

Gurowski, Adam. *Diary.* 3 vols. Boston, 1862-1866.

Handlin, Oscar. *Boston's Immigrants.* Rev. ed. Cambridge, Mass., 1959.

Harrington, Fred Harvey. *Fighting Politician: Major General N. P. Banks.* Philadelphia, 1948.

Haynes, George H. "Know-Nothing Legislature." *Annual Report* of the American Historical Association, 1896. Vol. I. Washing-ton, D. C., 1897. 175-87.

Hazard, Blanche E. *The Organization of the Boot and Shoe*

Industry in Massachusetts Before 1875. Cambridge, Mass., 1921.

Headley, P. C. *Massachusetts in the Rebellion.* Boston, 1866.

Hesseltine, William B. *Lincoln and the War Governors.* New York, 1948.

Hoar, George F. *Autobiography of Seventy Years.* 2 vols. New York, 1903.

Hoogenboom, Ari. *Outlawing the Spoils.* Urbana, Ill., 1961.

Howard, O. O. *Autobiography of Oliver Otis Howard.* 2 vols. New York, 1907.

Hughes, Sarah Forbes, ed. *Letters of John Murray Forbes.* Supp. ed. 3 vols. Boston, 1905.

Kelly, Alfred H. "The Congressional Controversy Over School Segregation, 1867-1875." *American Historical Review,* LXIV (April, 1959), 537-64.

Lawrence, William. *A Life of Amos A. Lawrence.* Boston, 1889.

Mann, J. B. *Life of Henry Wilson.* Boston, 1872.

Marshall, Jessie Ames, ed. *Private and Official Correspondence of General Benjamin F. Butler During the Period of the Civil War.* 5 vols. Norwood, Mass. 1917.

McClure, A. K. *Recollections of Half a Century.* Salem, Mass. 1902.

McKay, Ernest A. "Henry Wilson and the Coalition of 1851." *New England Quarterly,* XXXVI (1963), 338-58.

———. "Henry Wilson: Unprincipled Know-Nothing." *Mid-America,* XLVI (1964), 29-37.

McKitrick, Eric L. *Andrew Johnson and Reconstruction.* Chicago, 1960.

Memorial Addresses on the Life and Character of Henry Wilson. Washington, D. C., 1876.

Merriam, George S. *Life and Times of Samuel Bowles.* 2 vols., New York, 1885.

Montgomery, David. *Beyond Equality: Labor and the Radical Republicans, 1862-1872.* New York, 1967.

Nason, Elias. "Biographical Sketch of Henry Wilson." *New England Historical and Genealogical Register,* XXXII (1878), 261-268.

Nason, Elias, and Thomas Russell. *Life and Public Services of Henry Wilson.* Boston, 1876.

Parker, John L. *Henry Wilson's Regiment: History of the Twenty-Second Massachusetts Infantry.* Boston, 1887.

Pearson, Henry G. *The Life of John A. Andrew.* 2 vols. Boston, 1904.

Pierce, Edward L. *Memoir and Letters of Charles Sumner.* 4 vols. Boston, 1877-1894.

Poore, Ben: Perley. *Perley's Reminiscences of Sixty Years in the National Metropolis.* 2 vols. Philadelphia, 1886.

Proceedings of the State Disunion Convention Held at Worcester, Massachusetts, January 15, 1857. Boston, 1857.

Quarles, Benjamin. *The Negro in the Civil War.* Boston, 1953.

Reagan, John H. *Memoirs.* New York, 1906.

Rhodes, James Ford. *History of the United States, 1850-1877.* 9 vols. New York, 1920-1928.

Riddle, Albert Gallatin. *Recollections of War Times.* New York, 1895.

Robinson, Mrs. W. S., ed. *Warrington Pen-Portraits.* Boston, 1877.

Schafer, Joseph, trans. and ed. *Intimate Letters of Carl Schurz, 1841-1869.* Madison, Wis., 1928.

Schouler, William. *A History of Massachusetts in the Civil War.* 2 vols. Boston, 1868.

Schwartz, Harold. *Samuel Gridley Howe.* Cambridge, Mass., 1956.

Shannon, Fred A. *The Organization and Administration of the Union Army, 1861-1865.* 2 vols. Cleveland, Ohio, 1928.

Sharkey, Robert P. *Money, Class, and Party: An Economic Study of Civil War and Reconstruction.* Baltimore, Md., 1959.

Sellery, George Clark. *Lincoln's Suspension of Habeas Corpus as Viewed by Congress,* Bulletin of the University of Wisconsin History Series, vol. 1, no. 2. Madison, Wis., 1907.

Seward, Frederick W. *Seward at Washington.* 2 vols. New York, 1891.

Shapiro, Samuel. "The Conservative Dilemma: The Massachusetts Constitutional Convention of 1853." *New England Quarterly,* XXXIII (June, 1960), 207-24.

———. *Richard Henry Dana, Jr.* East Lansing, Mich., 1961.

Smith, Willard. *Schuyler Colfax: The Changing Fortunes of a Political Idol.* Indiana Historical Collections, vol. XXXIII. Indianapolis, 1952.

Sparks, David S., ed. *Inside Lincoln's Army: The Diary of Marsena Rudolph Patrick.* New York, 1964.

Stearns, Frank P. *The Life and Public Services of George Luther Stearns.* Philadelphia, 1907.

Trefousse, Hans L. *The Radical Republicans.* New York, 1969.

Ware, Edith Allen. *Political Opinion in Massachusetts During the Civil War and Reconstruction.* New York, 1916.

White, Horace. *Life of Lyman Trumbull.* New York, 1913.

Williams, T. Harry. *Lincoln and the Radicals.* Madison, Wis., 1960.

Winthrop, Robert C., Jr. *A Memoir of Robert C. Winthrop.* Boston, 1897.

Index

Abolitionists: in Natick, 10; in Middlesex County, 12; oppose racial discrimination, 22; oppose Texas annexation, 25; hold disunion convention, 89. *See also* American Anti-Slavery Society; Garrison, William Lloyd; Phillips, Wendell

Adams, Charles Francis: as Conscience Whig, 24; likes Wilson's speech, 27; as Free Soil candidate for vice president, 34; resists party discipline, 35; opposes coalition, 39-40; opposes Webster, 41; assesses Wilson, 44, 48, 53, 66, 83, 262; opposes proposed state constitution, 53-54; shuns new Republican party, 56; and antislavery fusion movement, 76; as Liberal Republican, 250; regrets Wilson's death, 257; mentioned, 42, 67, 258

Adams, John Quincy, 26, 28, 31

Allen, Charles: as Conscience Whig, 24; bolts Whig convention, 32-33; condemns Wilson, 59; mentioned, 35

Alley, John, 42, 81

American Anti-Slavery Society: membership in 1836, 10; thirtieth anniversary of, 148-49; annual convention in 1869, 207; annual report of, 232. *See also* Abolitionists

American party. *See* Know-Nothing party

Ames, Oakes, 247

Andrew, John: at Republican national convention, 106; during secession crisis, 111-12, 113; guards executive prerogatives, 128; has difficulties with draft, 129, 130, 134-35, 140-41; urges use of black troops, 135-36; maintains silence on slavery, 143; urges emancipation of slaves, 146; hinders Wilson's reelection, 154; seeks cabinet post, 154; aids Virginia Republicans, 192; death of, 198; mentioned, 115, 126

Anthony, Susan B., 145

Appleton, Nathan, 20, 28, 33

Ashmun, George, 106

Atkinson, Edward, 242

Bailey, Gamaliel, 54

Banks, Nathaniel: supports coalition, 38; joins Know-Nothing party, 57; urges nomination of Fremont, 84-86; elected governor, 98-99; mentioned, 41, 82

Beach, Thomas P., 11

Beauregard, P. G. T., 117

Bell, John, 107

Bird, Francis W.: assesses Wilson, 56, 89, 154, 221; criticizes Wilson's position on suffrage, 176, 177; praises Wilson's history of Slave Power, 234; as Liberal Republican, 242; mentioned, 193, 231

Black, Jeremiah S., 233*n*

Blair, Montgomery, 148, 150, 152

Boston *Advertiser,* 153

Boston *Atlas,* 32, 62, 63, 83

Boston *Chronicle,* 61-62

Boston *Commonwealth,* 43, 53, 147, 176, 191

Boston *Know-Nothing and American Crusader,* 61

Boston *Post,* 25, 62, 67

Boston *Republican,* 36, 44

Boston *Transcript,* 153, 172, 175

Bounty system, 135. *See also* Conscription Act of 1863

Boutwell, George S.: supports coalition, 38; elected governor, 41, 45; in Massachusetts constitutional convention, 50-51; mentioned, 220, 245

Bowles, Samuel: criticizes Wilson, 59; reports on Know-Nothing convention, 73-75; praises Wilson, 75, 105

Brewer, J. N., 32

Brooks, Preston, 80, 82

Brown, John, 100-103

Buchanan, James, 87, 93

Buffington, James, 243

Bullock, A. H., 154, 220
Burlingame, Anson, 57, 59, 60, 68
Burns, Anthony 57
Burnside, Ambrose, 116
Butler, Andrew, 80, 81, 84, 85
Butler, Benjamin: runs for Congress, 49; and Wilson's Senate seat, 154, 220; on future of Republican party, 214; as gubernatorial candidate, 240

Calhoun, John, 13
Cameron, Simon, 114, 121
Carey, Henry, 98, 215
Cass, Lewis, 33, 47
Chandler, Zachariah, 125, 191, 263, 264
Chase, Salmon P.: on Wilson's election to Senate, 68; possible Republican nominee in 1860, 105-6; and presidential nomination in 1864, 150-51; mentioned, 71, 78, 110, 197
Child, David Lee, 104
Child, Lydia Maria, 10, 104, 230
Civil service reform, 221-22
Claflin, William, 204, 231
Claflin, Mrs. William, 249, 256
Clay, Clement C., 163
Clay, Henry, 23, 237
Clifford, John A., 141
Coalition (of Free-Soilers and Democrats): planned and organized, 37-38; program, 38-39, 49-50; attacked by Free-Soilers, 39, 42; controls Massachusetts, 41, 45; elects Sumner to Senate, 42-43; weakens, 46, 49; organizes Massachusetts constitutional convention, 49-52; collapses, 54. See also Democratic party (Massachusetts); Free Soil party (Massachusetts)
Colbath, Abigail Witham: marries Winthrop Colbath, 2; character of, 3; death of, 226, 227; mentioned, 1, 4
Colbath, George (Wilson's great-great-grandfather), 1
Colbath, George (Wilson's brother), 226
Colbath, James, 1

Colbath, Jeremiah Jones. See Wilson, Henry
Colbath, Samuel, 226, 256
Colbath, Winthrop, Jr.: born in New Hampshire, 1; personal characteristics of, 1-2; marries Abigail Witham, 2; shows sensitivity about family background, 64; death of, 226; mentioned, 1, 3, 29
Colfax, Schuyler: and vice-presidential nomination in 1868, 198, 199; in 1872, 242-44
Commutation: in Conscription Act, 132; Wilson defends, 132-33; Stanton and Fry oppose, 133; criticized and repealed, 139-40. See also Conscription Act of 1863
Concord Academy, New Hampshire, 9, 11
Conscience Whigs: origins and membership of, 24; oppose Mexican war, 27-28; seek control of Whig party, 28, 31; oppose Taylor nomination, 31-33; bolt Whig party, 32-33; help form Free Soil party, 33-34. See also Whig party (Massachusetts)
Conscription Act of 1863: demand for, 130; introduced and passed, 130-32; opposition to, 132; impact on Massachusetts, 133. See also Bounty system; Commutation
Constitutional Union party, 107
Coolidge, Deacon, 8, 17
Cowan, Edgar, 171
Credit Mobilier scandal, 247-48
Crittenden, John J., 112-13
Cushing, Caleb, 42, 54, 109

Dana, Richard Henry, Jr.: opposes coalition, 40; in Massachusetts constitutional convention, 50; assesses Wilson, 51, 53, 66, 67, 256-57; attacks nativists, 77
Davis, Garrett, 123
Davis, Jefferson, 110, 162, 163
Davis, John, 16, 20
Dawes, Henry L., 220
Dayton, William L., 85
Democratic party (Massachusetts): program of, 16, 20-21; weakened

by divisions, 34; forms coalition with Free-Soilers, 37-41; resists Sumner's election to Senate, 42-43. *See also* Coalition; Free Soil party (Massachusetts)

Democratic party (U. S.): splits over slavery, 105; nominates McClellan in 1864, 151-52; nominates Greeley in 1872, 243; wins control of House of Representatives, 252

Douglas, Stephen A.: introduces Kansas-Nebraska Act, 55; opposes Lecompton Constitution, 94; assesses Wilson, 95; and secession crisis, 113; mentioned, 80

Douglass, Frederick, 265-66

Durant, Henry, 227

Dwight, Timothy, 3

Early, Jubal, 151

Eastman, Mrs. Nehemiah, 4

Elections: of 1840, 16-18; of 1848, 34; of 1852, 46, 49; of 1856, 87; of 1860, 107-9; of 1863, 148; of 1864, 150-52; of 1866, 178-79; of 1867, 194; of 1868, 203; of 1872, 248; of 1874, 252

Ellis, Vespasian, 70, 71

Everett, Edward: a leading Massachusetts Whig, 20; resigns from Senate, 55; assesses Wilson, 64, 71; mentioned, 69.

Fenton, Reuben, 198

Ferry, Orris, 256

Fessenden, William Pitt, 201

Fifteenth Amendment, 205-6

Fish, Hamilton, 118*n*

Forbes, John Murray, 135, 138, 186

Fourteenth Amendment: first formulation of, 174-75; final form of, 177-78; an issue in 1866 campaign, 178-79; Southern states reject, 179, 180; and disqualification section of, 184; removal of disabilities under, 206

Freedman's Bureau, 160, 170, 171, 173

Free Soil party (Massachusetts): organized, 33-34, 35-36; forms coalition with Democrats, 37-41;

members disagree over coalition, 39, 42; coalition begins to disintegrate, 49; members attack proposed constitution, 53-54; many members shun Republican party, 56; some members enter Know-Nothing party, 57-58; attempts to reorganize, 61; reunion in 1877 of, 258. *See also* Coalition; Democratic party (Massachusetts)

Free Soil party (U. S.), 33-34, 47

Fremont, John C.: nominated for president in 1856, 84-85; loses election of 1856, 86-87; emancipates slaves in Missouri, 146; seeks presidency in 1864, 152

Fry, James: critical of commutation, 133, 138-39; and administration of draft, 134-35; revises Massachusetts draft quota, 141

Gardner, Henry: elected governor by Know-Nothings, 59, 60, 77; and Wilson's election to Senate, 62; at Know-Nothing national convention, 73; mentioned, 86

Garrison, William Lloyd: praises Wilson's antislavery leadership, 23, 25, 26, 75, 149; charges Wilson with political cowardice, 89, 207; approves of Wilson's Southern trip, 190; disputes accuracy of Wilson's history, 234; supports Grant and Wilson in 1872, 246; critical of political process, 261, 262; mentioned, 100, 155

Giddings, Joshua Reed, 31, 80

Grant, Ulysses S.: as Republican presidential candidate, 197-99; as interim secretary of war, 200; elected president, 203; Wilson seeks cabinet post under, 203-4; and eight-hour day, 218; and civil service reform, 221, 222; Republican disaffection with, 240-41; renominated for president in 1872, 244; advised on appointments by Wilson, 250; mentioned, 151, 155, 256

Greeley, Horace, 94, 242, 246, 248

Greenhow, Rose O'Neal, 117-18

Grimes, James W., 122
Gurowski, Adam, 115
Gwin, William, 91

Hale, John P., 47
Hamlin, Hannibal, 125, 198
Hammond, James H., 90-91, 105
Hay, John, 150
Hayes, Martin Luther, 6
Hayes, Rutherford B., 255, 265
Herndon, William, 107
Herring, George M., 23
Higginson, Stephen, 43, 66
Hoar, E. Rockwood: as Conscience
  Whig, 24; opposes proposed state
  constitution, 53-54; recommends
  honorary degree for Wilson, 155;
  mentioned, 35, 39, 66, 258
Hoar, George F., 65
Howard, O. O., 159, 166, 170
Howe, Samuel Gridley: and John
  Brown, 101-3; assesses Wilson, 66,
  95, 124n
Hunt, Samuel: Wilson's amanuensis,
  23, 233, 245, 251; amazed at
  Wilson's ambition, 46; finishes
  Wilson's history of Slave Power,
  258-59; mentioned, 82

Johnson, A. B., 91
Johnson, Andrew: war-time career
  of, 165; and reconstruction program, 166; and Henry Wilson,
  167-69, 172; opposes Congress,
  173; tests reconstruction plan in
  1866 campaign, 178-79; impeachment of, 200-201; uses patronage
  power, 222; elected U. S. Senator,
  251-52
Johnson, William F., 85
Joint Committee on Conduct of the
  War, 125
Jones, Jeremiah, 1
Jordan, Thomas, 118n
Julian, George W., 214, 235n

Kansas: conflict over control of, 78;
  free-state men in, 92-93; approves
  Lecompton Constitution, 93-96;
  John Brown in, 101
Kansas-Nebraska Act, 55, 57, 69

Kelley, William D., 190
Kennedy, John F., 261
Knight, William, 4-5
Know-Nothing party (Massachusetts): organization of, 56-57;
  dominates the state, 57, 60; Free-
  Soilers in, 57-58, 61, 68; follows
  antislavery course, 75-76; refuses
  to join antislavery fusion movement, 76-77; last remnants of,
  absorbed into Republican party, 99
Know-Nothing party (U. S.): national
  convention of, 72-74; northern
  members support Fremont, 84-85
Kossuth, Louis, 46-47
Ku Klux Klan, 207, 208-9

Lawrence, Abbott: a leading Whig,
  20; promotes Taylor for president,
  31; mentioned, 28, 32, 33
Lawrence, Amos A.; anticipates
  Wilson's election to Senate, 63;
  impressed by Wilson's ability, 64;
  works with Wilson on Kansas affairs, 92-93; advises Wilson on
  economic legislation, 96, 97-98;
  favors compromise with South,
  111; sets up recruiting system, 135;
  recommends honorary degree for
  Wilson, 155; mentioned, 33, 100,
  227, 261
Lecompton Constitution. See Kansas
Lee, Robert E., 155
Liberal Republicans, 240-41, 242-43
Liberty party, 16, 26
Lincoln, Abraham: nominated for
  president, 106; elected president,
  108; and Fort Sumter, 114; pros-
  ecutes war, 122; calls for more
  troops, 128; and emancipation
  proclamation, 135, 145, 146,
  147-48; authorizes use of Negro
  troops, 136; opposes commutation,
  138; renominated in 1864, 150-51;
  wins second term, 152; supports
  Thirteenth Amendment, 152, 155;
  assassinated, 156; reconstruction
  plans of, 165; mentioned, 107,
  137, 144, 236, 260
Lincoln, Ezra, 76
Lincoln, Levi, 20, 41

Logan, John A., 199
Longstreet, James, 191
Loring, George B., 245
Lovejoy, Elijah P., 236
Lynch, John R., 264-65

McClellan, George B., 118, 124, 125-26
McDowell, Irwin, 115-16
McLean, John, 23
McMichael, Morton, 244
Mallory, Robert, 162
Mann, Horace: an educational reformer, 9; elected to Congress, 31; receives Free Soil gubernatorial nomination, 48-49; mentioned, 50
Mann, Jonathan B., 15, 17, 35, 108
Martineau, Harriet, 232
Massachusetts constitutional convention, 49-54
May, Samuel, 234
Mexican war, 28
Moore, Erasmus D., 8, 23
Morgan, E. D., 119, 139
Morton, Marcus, 42-43

Nason, Elias, 233
Natick, Massachusetts: described, 7; shoe industry in, 7, 14-15; abolitionists in, 10; civic and cultural life of, 30; celebrates Wilson's election to Senate, 64; supports Crittenden compromise, 112; honors Wilson's regiment, 119; observes Henry Hamilton Wilson's funeral, 229; celebrates Wilson's vice-presidential nomination, 246; fails to honor Wilson's memory, 258; mentioned, passim
Natick Debating Society: formed, 9; antislavery views of members of, 13, 21, 23; Wilson's role in, 14
New York Evening Post: hopes Wilson will be elected Senator, 61; assesses Wilson's course as Senator, 70-71; critical of Wilson's impeachment vote, 201
New York Herald, 117
New York Independent, 187, 233-34
New York Sun, 247
New York Times, 11, 61

New York Tribune: hopes Wilson will be elected Senator, 61; and coverage of Know-Nothing convention, 73-74; on Wilson's Southern trip, 190
Nye, James W., 185, 186

Otis, Harrison Gray, 41
Owen, Robert Dale, 177

Palfrey, John G.: a Conscience Whig, 24; in Free Soil party, 35; assesses Wilson, 39; opposes coalition, 39-40, 42; Free Soil candidate for governor, 44-45; condemns proposed Massachusetts constitution, 54; mentioned, 28, 50, 54, 66
Parker, Theodore: assesses Wilson's career, 67-68; criticizes Wilson, 71, 95; praises Wilson, 75; mentioned, 79, 81, 90, 142
Phillips, S. C.: Free Soil candidate for governor, 34; wants Senate seat, 42; mentioned, 24, 39, 50, 67
Phillips, Wendell: has disagreements with Wilson, 177, 191, 234; recommends reconstruction policy, 253; compared to Wilson, 262; mentioned, 75, 166n
Pierce, E. L.: defends Wilson, 66, 67, 100; Wilson consults with, 70; mentioned, 241
Pierce, Franklin, 54, 78, 87
Pillsbury, Parker, 235
Polk, James K., 27
Prescott, William H., 231
Purvis, Robert, 266

Quincy, Josiah, 41

Rawlins, John A., 218
Reagan, John H., 182
Redpath, James, 198
Republican party (Massachusetts): formation of, 55-56; early organization collapses, 59-60; revived, 77; Know-Nothings fuse with, 86
Republican party (U. S.): nominates Fremont in 1856, 83-85; hurt by John Brown's raid, 100, 102-3; elects Lincoln president, 106-8;

Republican party (U.S.) (*continued*): nominates Grant in 1868, 199
Republican party (Virginia), 187-88, 192-93
Richmond (Virginia) *Enquirer,* 163, 187
Richmond (Virginia) *Whig,* 193
Riddle, Albert G., 116, 150, 151
Robinson, Charles, 92-93
Robinson, William S.: angry at Wilson, 86; opposes Wilson's reelection to Senate, 220; a Liberal Republican, 242; notes nation's grief at Wilson's death, 256; mentioned, 154, 176, 193
Rockwell, Julius, 77
Russell, William H., 115, 117

Saltonstall, Leverett, 41
Schouler, William: and Wilson, 30; adjutant-general of Massachusetts, 113; estimates Wilson's ability, 202-3; mentioned, 32, 142, 231
Scott, Winfield, 105, 121
Secession crisis, 110-14
Senate Committee on Military Affairs: Wilson chairman of, 121; and conscription act, 130-32; and commutation, 139
Seward, William Henry: applauds Wilson's election to Senate, 68; averts Wilson-Gwin duel, 91; criticizes Wilson's flexibility, 95; loses Republican nomination to Lincoln, 106-7; seeks compromise with South, 111; orders arbitrary arrests, 123; mentioned, 79, 80, 85, 117, 166, 170
Sheridan, Philip H., 200
Sherman, John, 117, 122, 135, 147
Sherman, William T., 155
Sickles, Daniel, 201
Smith, Gerrit, 234, 244
Springfield Republican, 253
Stanton, Edwin M.: refuses to pay bounty to recruits, 128; orders militia draft, 130; opposes commutation, 133; authorizes bounty payments, 135; hesitates to draft slaves, 137; Johnson suspends from office, 200, 201, 202; serves in

Buchanan's cabinet, 233n; mentioned, 139, 140
Stearns, George Luther, 102-3
Stephens, Alexander H., 162, 208
Stevens, Thaddeus: urges emancipation of slaves, 145; opposes first reconstruction act, 184; criticizes Wilson's Southern trip, 190, 191; vindictive toward South, 263, 264
Stewart, William M., 177
Strafford Academy, New Hampshire, 9, 11
Sumner, Charles: becomes Conscience Whig, 24; in Free Soil party, 35; supports coalition, 37; elected to U. S. Senate, 42-43; silent in Senate, 48; assesses Wilson, 59, 66-67, 71, 95; caned by Brooks, 79-81, 236; during secession crisis, 111, 112, 113; reviews military appointments, 126; obtains credits for Massachusetts quota, 139, 140; urges emancipation of slaves, 143, 145; seeks emancipation in West Virginia, 144-45; repeals black codes in Washington, 159; and suffrage issue, 164, 174-76, 183; seeks additional civil rights legislation, 210, 211-12; seeks to amend naturalization laws, 219; opposes Benjamin Butler, 240; opposes Grant, 241; in 1872 campaign, 246; loans Wilson money, 248; death of, 251; mentioned, *passim*

Taylor, Zachary, 31, 32, 33
Texas annexation, 24-25, 26, 27
Thayer, Alexander, 9, 13, 21
Thayer, Eli, 234, 235n
Thirteenth Amendment, 152, 155, 174-75
Thompson, George, 155
Trescot, William H., 182
Trumbull, Lyman, 79, 81, 122-23
Tyler, John, 24

Van Buren, Martin, 16, 34

Wade, Benjamin: criticizes Union generalship, 125; criticizes Wilson's Southern trip, 190-91; seeks vice-presidential nomination in 1868, 198, 199; vindictive toward South, 263, 264; mentioned, 152, 197

Wade-Davis bill, 164-65

Walcott, Edward: befriends Wilson, 8; runs underground railway, 10; an antislavery Whig, 23; mentioned, 231

Walker, Amasa, 37, 41, 75

Webster, Daniel: a leading Whig, 20; Wilson supports in 1848, 32; gives March 7 speech, 40; condemned by Wilson, 43; mentioned, 12, 28, 237

Weed, Thurlow, 255

Welles, Gideon, 172, 190

Whig party (Massachusetts): leaders and program of, 20; opposes Texas annexation, 24-25, 27; criticizes Mexican war, 28

Whitehouse, George L., 4, 13

Whittier, John Greenleaf, 233-34

Wigfall, Louis, 105

Wild, Edward, 169

Wilkinson, James, 128

Wilson, Harriet Howe: marries Henry Wilson, 15; character of, 15, 230; has frequent illnesses, 29, 203, 230; encourages Wilson to join church, 227; cares for Henry Hamilton, 227-28; and Credit Mobilier stock, 247; mentioned, 19, 64, 203

Wilson, Henry:

—Descriptions and characterizations: intense ambition of, 5, 8, 12, 15, 19, 35, 46, 65-66, 260-61; physical description of, 5, 65, 69; class consciousness of, 13-14, 22, 52, 53, 85, 90, 211, 254; speaking manner and delivery of, 17-18, 121; impressionable nature of, 47, 123, 124n, 182; sensitivity to criticism of, 72; forgiving nature of, 94-95

—Personal life: Wilson named Jeremiah Jones Colbath at birth, 1; endures poverty-stricken youth, 3; obtains education, 3-4, 5, 9; apprenticed to farmer, 4-5; takes temperance pledge, 5; changes name to Henry Wilson, 6; leaves New Hampshire, 6-7; enjoys success in shoe business, 7-8, 14-15, 29, 35-36, 55; as member of Natick Debating Society, 9, 10, 14, 23; journeys to Washington, 9, 11, 12-13; marries Harriet Malvina Howe, 15; has a son, 29; joins Massachusetts militia, 30; contributes to Natick's civic life, 30; has financial difficulties, 44, 55, 63, 248-49; experiences religious conversion, 207, 227; fails as a father, 227-30; becomes a widower, 230-31; writes history of Slave Power, 231-32, 233, 234, 251; writes legislative histories, 232-33; takes European trip, 239; suffers paralytic attacks, 249, 255; death and funeral of, 256-57; eulogies and memorials to, 257-58

—in Massachusetts politics: Wilson becomes reformer, 9-10; supports temperance cause, 10, 14, 21, 30; develops antislavery views, 10-11; attacks slavery in the District of Columbia, 11; joins abolition society, 11; seeks political career, 12; opposes Southern political power, 13, 23; loses first political campaign, 14; joins Whig party, 16, 20; lacks interest in economic issues, 16, 21, 261; criticizes Democrats, 16-17; takes pro-labor stance, 17, 21, 39; nicknamed "Natick Cobbler," 17; elected to Massachusetts legislature, 18, 19, 38, 41; comments on racial characteristics of Negroes, 21-22; opposes racial discrimination, 22, 52; seeks to convert Whig party to abolitionism, 23, 27; opposes Texas annexation, 24-27; as Conscience Whig, 24-28, 31-33; cooperates with abolitionists, 25, 26; condemns Slave Power, 26-27; fails to win congressional seat, 31, 49; leaves Whig party, 31-33; helps organize Free Soil party, 33-34, 35-36; edits Boston *Republican,* 36-37, 44; urges Free Soil coalition

Wilson, Henry:
— in Mass. politics (*continued*):
with Democrats, 37-41; elected president of Massachusetts Senate, 41, 45; secures Sumner's election to Senate, 42-44; fails to gain gubernatorial nomination in 1851, 44-45; interested in Louis Kossuth, 46-47; supports Lewis Cass for president, 47; presides over national Free Soil convention, 47; urges Sumner to speak, 48; fails to obtain gubernatorial nomination in 1852, 48-49; active in constitutional convention, 49-52; nominated for governor in 1853, 53; loses election, 54; helps organize Republican party, 55-56; as Republican gubernatorial candidate in 1854, 56, 59; joins Know-Nothings, 58; attitude toward nativism of, 58, 60, 62, 72; Know-Nothings elect to U. S. Senate, 61-63; political ability of, 64; political associates criticize tactics of, 65-66

—as United States Senator: Wilson as freshman senator, 69-71; attitude toward Know-Nothing party of, 69-70, 72; on racial equality of Negroes, 70, 158-59, 171-72; disrupts Know-Nothing convention, 72-75; seeks antislavery fusion movement, 74-77, 86; interest in Kansas affairs of, 78, 85-86, 92-93; faces belligerent Southerners, 79, 81-83, 91; constituents applaud course of, 83, 87; supports Fremont nomination, 84-85; deemphasizes slavery issue, 88-90, 104-5; seeks broader support for Republican party, 88-89, 91-92, 96; and relationship to abolitionists, 89-90, 237, 261-62; replies to Hammond, 90-91; and Amos A. Lawrence, 92, 95; urges support for Douglas, 94-95; and aid to railroads, 96-97; on tariff question, 97-98, 215; reelected to Senate in 1859, 98-99; opposes nativist legislation, 99-100; and John Brown, 100-103; views

Republican presidential candidates, 105-6, and election of 1860, 107-9; and secession crisis, 109-13; urges Union offensive, 115; as chairman of Senate Committee on Military Affairs, 115, 121-24, 126, 128, 130-39, 142; at First Manassas, 115-17; and Rose O'Neal Greenhow, 117-18; serves on McClellan's staff, 118, 120; recruits 22nd Massachusetts Volunteers, 118-20; defends McClellan, 124-25; loses patience with McClellan, 126; aids Andrew in raising troops, 128-29; introduces militia draft bill, 129; writes Conscription Act, 130-31; supports commutation, 132-33, 138-39; criticizes the draft, 134; obtains bounty legislation, 135; obtains recruitment of black troops, 135-36, 137-40; seeks to abolish slavery, 142-43, 144-45, 146-47; and state elections in 1863, 148; attacks Montgomery Blair, 148, 152; praised for abolishing slavery in Washington, 149; withholds support from Chase in 1864, 150-51; and armistice proposal, 151; and campaign of 1864, 152; reelected to Senate in 1865, 152-54; journeys to Charleston, 155; attitude toward Lincoln of, 156; on difficulties posed by reconstruction, 158; seeks federal fund to educate blacks, 159; concern for black troops, 160; and Freedman's Bureau, 160-61; advocates Negro suffrage, 161-62; lacks vindictiveness toward South, 162-63, 171; supports qualified suffrage for blacks, 164, 173-74; and Lincoln's reconstruction plans, 165; praises Andrew Johnson, 165; concerned at abuse of Negroes in South, 166, 169, 170; assesses Johnson's reconstruction program, 166-69; favors universal suffrage and universal amnesty, 167-68, 171; seeks to abolish Black Codes, 170-71; conciliatory toward Johnson, 172; condemns Johnson's vetoes, 173;

opposes Sumner on suffrage issue, 174-77; opposes disfranchising Southern whites, 177, 182, 184, 193; in campaign of 1866, 178-79; renews call for universal suffrage, 180-81; hopes for Republican majorities in South, 181, 185, 192, 202; contacts with Southern moderates, 182; and reconstruction acts, 183-84; wishes to rebuild South, 186; makes political visits to Virginia, 186, 187-88, 192-93; undertakes trip through the South, 187; seeks white votes for Republicans in South, 188-89, 192; assessments of Southern trip of, 189-91; and Fifteenth Amendment, 194-95, 204-6; disappointed by 1867 elections, 194, 196; supports Grant for president, 197-98; seeks vice-presidential nomination in 1868, 198-99; and impeachment of Johnson, 200-202; urges readmission of Southern states, 202; campaigns in 1868, 202-3; seeks cabinet post, 203-4; seeks universal amnesty, 206, 212; predicts end of reconstruction legislation, 206, 212; on Ku Klux Klan, 207, 208-9; hopes for moral regeneration of South, 207-8, 210; urges federal aid to education in South, 208, 210; supports integrated schools, 210-11; supports Sumner's civil rights bill, 212; attacks money power, 214-15; views on banking and currency of, 215-17; advocates eight-hour day, 217-18, 219n; speaks on contract labor importation, 219; reelected to Senate in 1871, 219-21; supports civil service reform, 221-22; advocates temperance reform, 222-23; advocates women's rights, 223-24; loses influence in Republican party, 226
—as Vice President: defines Slave Power, 235-38, 259, 263; seeks vice-presidential nomination in 1872, 239, 240, 242; opposes Butler, 240; attempts to reconcile Sumner and Grant, 241; disturbed by Liberal Republican movement, 242-43; nominated for vice president in 1872, 243-45; campaigns in 1872, 246-48; and Credit Mobilier scandal, 247-48; advises Grant on appointments, 250; and death of Sumner, 251; presides over Senate, 251-52; ambitious for presidency, 252, 255; seeks to conciliate Liberal Republicans, 252, 253, 254; assesses Grant's administration, 252; reviews course of reconstruction, 253; seeks ex-Whig support in South, 254, 255; takes second Southern trip, 254-55; as Radical Republican, 262-65
Wilson, Henry Hamilton: birth of, 29; death of, 227; military career of, 228-29
Winthrop, Robert: leading Massachusetts Whig, 27; replaces Webster in Senate, 40; assesses Wilson, 59, 64; refuses to join antislavery fusion movement, 76; presents Wilson's regiment with flag, 119; a conservative on slavery, 143; Wilson offers office to, 250; mentioned, 28
Wolfeborough Academy, New Hampshire, 9, 11
Wood, Fernando, 132
Wright, Charles, 152-53
Wright, E. M., 63
Wright, Elizur, 176, 242

Yates, Richard, 198